The Philosophy of Law in Historical Perspective

The Philosophy of Law in Historical Perspective

SECOND EDITION

By Carl Joachim Friedrich

THE UNIVERSITY OF CHICAGO PRESS
CHICAGO & LONDON

This book is also available in a clothbound edition from
THE UNIVERSITY OF CHICAGO PRESS

THE UNIVERSITY OF CHICAGO PRESS, CHICAGO 60637
The University of Chicago Press, Ltd., London

 Published 1958
Second Edition 1963. First Phoenix Edition 1963. Fifth Impression 1973. Printed in the United States of America
International Standard Book Number: 0–226–26465–3, (Clothbound)
Library of Congress Catalog Card Number: 57–9546

TO A. N. HOLCOMBE

IN FRIENDSHIP

ERROR MULTIPLEX, VERITAS UNA

Preface to the Second Edition

The present edition contains a few corrections as well as additions, notably on pages 7, 49, 64, 119, 129, 166, 173, 175, 176, 182, and 219, that were suggested by the many helpful reviews that have appeared in learned journals. I would like to add that, in view of my general outlook on law and history, the second part does not pretend to be a rounded philosophy of law, nor is it an outline; it merely seeks to highlight certain problems which seem to me to be in the foreground today, while many others which are also being discussed have received more or less satisfactory treatment in the past. One criticism has often been made, and that is that the contributions of contemporary American jurisprudence, particularly the work of so-called realism, have not been given adequate space. I would plead that a treatment which provides a total of fourteen pages for Plato and Aristotle did rather well by contemporary relativists, formalists, and skeptics in assigning the same amount of space. However, I have added a couple of paragraphs and have included a review article which appeared in the thirties and which contains some of my major doubts about this approach to the philosophy of law. I have also included a paper on "Law and History" which was prepared for a conference on law and the humanities under the auspices of the American Council of Learned Societies in 1960 and which has since appeared in the *Vanderbilt Law Review*, October, 1961.

Some critics stress the fact that I did not go into the political and social realities behind law *in extenso*. Quite apart from the fact that the editorially imposed limitations of space forbade such exploration, it seemed to me that my other writings provided considerable evidence of my views. Since I am publishing a comprehensive political theory this year, I hope I may be forgiven for referring to that work as a companion volume to the present study.

In conclusion, I would like to mention that I do not consider myself a Kantian or a neo-Kantian since I am in basic disagreement with Kant's distinction between noumena and phenomena, of norm and fact, which is such a crucial aspect of most contemporary legal philosophy, including the so-called pure law and realist schools. Rather do I incline toward the view that ultimately norm and fact are aspects of the same reality revealed and known to us only through human experience. This is a point of view which makes me feel akin to Aristotle and Thomas Aquinas, on the one hand, and to the most advanced thinking on the nature of reality in contemporary science, on the other hand.

CAMBRIDGE, MASSACHUSETTS

Preface to the First Edition

This brief volume is an effort to discuss the problems of the philosophy of law, as they present themselves today, within the framework of its history. Such an enterprise presupposes that one is willing to select very carefully among the mass of available materials and viewpoints. Inevitably, one will be influenced in making such a selection by what he considers important to the discussion for our time. Much that is interesting must necessarily remain undiscussed. I have tried to use as a measuring rod and standard of selection the relatively objective one provided by the originality of the different contributions. There is one exception, namely, the natural-law writers of the seventeenth and eighteenth century discussed in chapter xiii; their originality is disputable indeed.

This book is an English version of *Die Philosophie des Rechts in historischer Perspektive,* which appeared as one of the volumes of the "Enzyklopädie der Rechts- und Staatswissenschaft," under the editorship of Professor Wolfgang Kunkel (Munich). I am very grateful for his encouragement and helpful advice. While this English edition in large part follows the German original, there are also significant variations and additions, especially in chapters xi, xx–xxiv, and the notes. The notes make no pretense at completeness, obviously; they merely seek to give some hints as to the sources of some of the more important statements made in the text. The English text was read and criticized in its entirety by Professor A. P. d'Entrèves (Oxford and Turin) and by Professor Samuel Shuman (Wayne University). The comments of both were of very great assistance, as were the observations of a number of European critics and reviewers. Dr. Henry Kissinger (Harvard) had at an earlier date offered valuable comments on the German manuscript.

C. J. F.

Table of Contents

PART ONE

The Historical Development

I. *Introduction*

Every philosophy of law is part of a particular general philosophy, for it offers philosophical reflections upon the general foundation of law. Such reflection can either be derived from an existing philosophical position or may lead to such a position. It is characteristic of the history of the philosophy of law, and very natural too, that philosophers have been inclined toward the first approach, lawyers and jurists toward the second. But not every philosophy leads into a philosophy of law, or has done so. Thus Descartes philosophized little about law. On the other hand, many jurists are satisfied with studying the mass of legal norms in front of them, leaving to others any general philosophical exploration of this world and contenting themselves with the general views that are common to the profession. The common law, which is largely traditional, rests on such a general view of the law. It is unquestionably possible to be a good lawyer or jurist without being clear about one's legal philosophy, as it is certain that one can be a good philosopher without having a philosophy of law. What must be questioned is the thought often expressed by lawyers of the more practical sort that law does not involve any philosophy of law. For the law consists in statements or propositions which are put in words, and such statements, commonly called judgments—and typically being normative judgments in the law—occasion the kind of general, philosophical questions significant for such judgments. If positivists, pragmatists, and formalists at times speak of the law as if it existed in a vacuum, unrelated to values, opinions, or beliefs, this sort of viewpoint implies actually a philosophical position of sorts. Likewise, philosophy cannot declare itself unconcerned with the philosophy of law, and if a particular philosopher does not develop a philosophy of law, this does not prevent others from applying such a philosophy to the law. Thus we have a Cartesian philosophy of law, although Descartes himself did not work it out.

Two viewpoints must therefore be taken into account in considering the philosophy of law, if such a consideration is to be scholarly or "scientific" in the broad sense. The word "science" in such a statement is of course not used in the narrow sense in which science deals only with general regularities, rules, or even "laws," meaning the laws of nature of the natural sciences.[1] We shall, in what follows, always use the term "science" in its more general meaning. According to this meaning, it is the nature of scientific work—in contrast to the opinions of laymen, to religious dogma, to poetry and the like—that such work is related to a *corpus of learning* which, steadily increasing, deals with a particular *body of experience* and which is thus enlarged by men concerned with this particular body of learning, the scholars or scientists, with the aid of *methods* regarding which there exists *agreement*, potential or actual, among the workers in this field of learning.[2] What follows from this general notion of science quite clearly is that there are, as just stated, essentially two viewpoints from which the philosophy of law may be treated, and they will both be presented here. First, a "scientific" philosophy of law must review the development of philosophical doctrines in order to determine which problems have already been clarified significantly so that we can build upon the foundation provided by previous thought. And, second, it is necessary at least to sketch upon which philosophical ground each particular contribution rests, that is to say, from which general philosophy it has emerged. We hope to deal with the first of these viewpoints in the first part of the book, in which a brief history of the philosophy of law is

[1] Such a concept does not even fit the natural sciences in their entirety, for there are very important natural sciences, like anatomy, which do not concentrate upon laws or generalizations but upon structures and configurations. The morphological aspect is important in political science.

[2] This definition is elaborated in "Political Science and Political Philosophy," the author's contribution to a volume entitled *Approaches to Politics* and soon to be published by Northwestern University.

presented. But it may be well to say a few more words concerning the second viewpoint.

All scientific understanding and knowledge rest upon experience. But the sensationalists, at times called empiricists, were in error when they tried to reduce all human experience to the experience of the senses. The intellectual and spiritual life of man is part of his experience. Thinking itself is a kind of experience, as are feeling, willing, and, more especially, creative production. For law, all these kinds of experience are of importance.[3]

It would be much easier to arrive at philosophical clarity if these several kinds of experience could be seen as a logical and coherent unity. This is not in fact possible, and all efforts to date to accomplish this (and they constitute a considerable part of the history of philosophy) have led to the denial of one or another of the realms of experience. This needs further elaboration. The experience of observing a succession of sense impressions leads to the hypothesis of causation. Hume analyzed the hypothetical nature of the law of causation; Kant in turn showed how essential this law is for all orderly thought. Without positing causes, it is impossible to think about the experience of the senses (or about a number of other things—notably about history, which presents itself to the observer in the form of reports about things which allegedly have happened). From this hypothesis of cause and effect one arrives at the philosophical position known as determinism. But the experience of willing, of making a decision in a situation permitting alternatives, leads to the hypothesis of freedom. It is impossible to engage in the act of willing if one does not presuppose that one may act either one way or another. The hypothetical nature of this freedom was formulated most sharply by Hobbes, but here too Kant was able to show that the hypothesis of freedom is necessary for an acting person. It is the meaning of the famous categorical imperative to demonstrate the essential nature of all normative judgments. But the logical consequence of the hypothesis of freedom is a philosophy of indeter-

[3] Cf. Michael Oakeshott, *Experience and Its Modes* (1933); Eduard Husserl, *Erfahrung und Urteil* (1938).

minism. Existing monistic philosophical systems may therefore be divided into two classes, those which rejected the hypothesis of freedom, or at least reduced it in scope, and which therefore are deterministic; and those which, if they did not reject the hypothesis of causation, have greatly restricted its scope, and which are therefore voluntaristic. The latter is true, in a general sense, even when the rejection of the hypothesis of causation is linked to some kind of deity (theological systems). But there is still another possibility, which consists in an attempt to hypostasize two sharply separated worlds, to separate, that is, the world of norms from the world of events in nature, as did Kant (dualistic systems). Yet there always remains a residue of philosophical incoherence; for since the logical component of human behavior is a part of human experience, it follows that we cannot make the whole of experience logically consistent. We have developed this thought with reference to the questions of causation and of freedom, which are related to those of observing and deciding. But similar difficulties appear if one considers the problems of creative experience, and, again, if one turns to feeling, which is still another experience that can be equated with the other kinds of experience only by highly artificial constructions (although this has often been attempted).

A radical philosophy of experience thus appears to be a general view of the world which stresses problems. In this respect, it possesses a certain kinship with pragmatism, but problems are not, as in pragmatism,[4] derived from operational and related notions, but are built into the very fabric of the basic given. They are the first order of being. A philosophy of experience is a philosophy of the problem—the term "problem" taken in the very concrete sense in which the word *problema* originally meant in Greek something which, like a roadblock, is thrown across our path. The ever-recurring problem is how all of human experience may be made fruitful for the progressive understanding of a particular

[4] John Dewey, *The Quest for Certainty: A Study of the Relation of Knowledge and Action* (1929), esp. pp. 99 ff., 122 f., and 223 ff.; see also his important earlier study, *Experience and Nature* (2d ed.; 1924). Cf. Anatol Rapoport, *Operational Philosophy: Integrating Knowledge and Action* (1954).

object of knowledge. Law is such an object, and we are advancing at the outset, in the light of our philosophy of experience, the basic hypothesis that, without a comprehensive grasp of the problems of all experience, law can be presented only in an artificial and contradictory way. Only by taking account of all the different kinds of experience can we give an image of the law adequate to reality and at the same time general. Only thus can a comprehensive philosophy of law be developed.

Consequently, the historical chapters of this book are actually an integral part of the philosophical and systematic approach; for unlike the historicists and positivists, I believe that history, and especially intellectual history, exhibits design and that the successive philosophies of law embody progressive insights, parts of the truth we seek. Therefore, such systematic history will provide the ground for anything we might add. And in turn, the systematic part does not pretend to present a rounded philosophy of law but rather what I conceive to be emerging consensus concerning a number of issues which have remained "open." One's search for the novel is tempered by a realization of "the old truth" which Goethe counseled his romantic contemporaries to grasp.[5] Most of the so-called novelties are old errors in new linguistic garb. But there *are* new perspectives emerging. Mr. Justice Holmes's well-worn phrase that "the life of the law has not been logic, but experience" poignantly overstates a crucial insight—crucial, that is, if experience is seen as broadly and comprehensively human. Therefore, the positions as they emerge from the historical panorama, when implemented by the supplementary systematic observations delineate my philosophy of law. It is not a Kantian or Neo-Kantian position, not a natural law or positivist position, but rather a view of law and justice in which fact and value are seen as intimately related in all human experience in politics.

[5] "Das alte Wahre, fass es an," Goethe wrote. My position is radically at variance with that of H. L. A. Hart (*The Concept of Law*, 1961), who on p. viii explains that "in the text the reader will find very few references to other writers," though at the end of the book "there are extensive notes." Hart adds that he hopes "that this arrangement may discourage the belief that a book on legal theory is primarily a book from which one learns what other books contain. So long as this belief is held by those who write, little progress will be made in the subject. . . ."

II. *Law as the Will of God*

THE HERITAGE OF THE OLD TESTAMENT

Ancient Judaism has played a decisive role in shaping the origins of Western concepts of law.[1] For the one God reveals himself very differently from the Greek gods. Jahweh, the god without name of Israel, was clearly distinguished from surrounding gods of other peoples by his preoccupation with law. The Old Testament is filled with acts of legislation, with the struggle of God to secure the observation and enforcement of these laws, with the reward or punishment of the chosen people consequent upon their behavior toward these laws. Everyone knows that all Christians derive a dual obligation from this heritage. On the one hand, the Ten Commandments; on the other hand, the warning against mere obedience to law, that is to say, against pharisaism and sanctimoniousness. Max Weber has shown in his *Sociology of Religion* how closely the position of the priest in ancient Israel was connected with this god, the legislator. Indeed, the faith itself has drawn nourishment from the position of the priest as interpreter of the law.[2]

It has less frequently been observed how extraordinarily powerful has been the influence of these religious notions upon West-

[1] See Robert Pfeiffer, *Introduction to the Old Testament* (1941), esp. pp. 51 ff. and Part II, chap. vii, pp. 210–70. J. M. P. Smith, *The Origin and History of Hebrew Law* (1931) may be compared with the generalizing approach of H. Spiegelberg for an insight into the categories employed. The most authoritative work on the general historical background is Eduard Meyer, *Geschichte des Altertums* (1881). A brilliant special study related to the problems of legalism is that of Louis Finkelstein, *The Pharisees* (1938), while H. M. Orlinsky, *Ancient Israel* (1954), gives a succinct portrait of the setting of these ideas (esp. pp. 153 ff.).

[2] Max Weber, *Gesammelte Aufsätze zur Religionssoziologie,* Vol. III: *Das Antike Judentum* (1893; 4th printing, 1947); an English edition was published under the title *Ancient Judaism.* Cf. with this the classical account of Julius Wellhausen on Israel in the *Encyclopaedia Britannica* (9th ed.).

ern legal thought and how much they continue to mold it.[3] The connection is most evident in the thought of Calvinism and Puritanism. It was surely no accident that Calvin himself was by profession a lawyer, or rather a jurist. It has rightly been emphasized that Calvin sharpened the doctrine of the Protestants by eliminating both the Lutheran anarchic and the Lutheran patriarchic tendencies; at the same time, he put it into clear but juridical form.[4] The impact of Calvinism in France and the Netherlands, and, more particularly, in England, rests very much upon this return to the Old Testament and its concepts of the deity. And it was surely no accident that the Puritans, fighting for constitutional government, chose as a password of their revolution in 1648, "To Your Tents, O Israel"; indeed, they saw themselves as the lost tribe of Israel. The pronounced emphasis upon law in the political and governmental development of England, and later of America, while antedating these movements, found religious support and reinforcement in these ideas.[5]

For it is always of decisive importance for law that the obligation of its norm is firmly anchored in a conviction concerning the legitimacy of the authority which creates the law, whether it be God or an act of the people. The importance of legal norms in social life will always be deeply influenced by the faith in such legitimacy of the government which is enforcing them and by whom they are created. *Nomos* and *jus* of the Greeks and Romans were enforced as long as the faith in the community of the *polis* endured, for the *polis* was shaped by *nomos* and *jus* because of men's continued faith in the heroic wisdom of a legislator of old times, whether it were a Solon, a Lycurgus, or the Twelve Tables.

[3] Cf. Frederick M. Watkins, *The Political Tradition of the West* (1948).

[4] See the author's Introduction to *Johannes Althusius Politica methodice digesta* (1932) and the references given there; a list of Old Testament citations shows the range of interests in these precedents.

[5] See Perry Miller, *The New England Mind: The Seventeenth Century* (1939), although the Old Testament background is not adequately stressed; the importance of writers like Althusius and Rutherford, not as influences but as patterns of thought, is largely overlooked. See for a more penetrating treatment of the special aspect of political rationality George L. Mosse, *The Holy Pretense* (1957).

But for the Jews of the Old Testament, it was not Moses, let alone the Prophets, but the one God who had spoken to Moses and had called him to communicate His laws to His people (Leviticus 19:1–2). And it was His people who were made a holy community by such communication because the God who had given them the laws was himself holy. Out of this sanctification by giving and obeying the law, there developed, or perhaps it would be better to say from it was derived, as its corollary, the doctrine of the chosen people.[6] It was precisely this doctrine which led, by a transformation, to the doctrine of the invisible church of all the faithful, which finds outward expression only as the visible church of this world and which therein shows that sanctification through law in Old Testament thinking could become an important component of legal thought in the West. This was so in part because Roman legal thinking, usually credited with being the sole basis for the Western outlook, was the outgrowth of a tradition which in some important respects resembled that of ancient Judaism (see chaps. iv and v).

The sanctification of each member of the community who obeys the law of Yahweh implies an equality of all men. The laws of the Old Testament can be obeyed by anyone who is of good will. This markedly egalitarian spiritual attitude toward the law that one finds in ancient Judaism stands out in sharp contrast to the legal thought of the Greeks, at least as expressed in the legal philosophy of Plato and Aristotle, which is markedly that of a spiritual elite. The egalitarian attitude was taken over by Christianity from Judaism in spite of Christianity's sharp objection to the pharisaical legalistic ethics. In this connection, let us recall that the New Testament has Jesus say, "I have not come to destroy the law, but to fulfill it." This fulfilment actually consists in the demand for a pure ethical attitude beyond the reach of men. For it is here again that all men are equal. Such an attitude can readily be combined with an emphasis upon the law which is stripped of the danger of hypocrisy, for it lends to the law a new

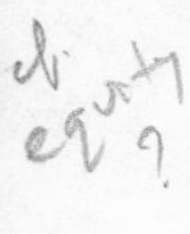

[6] Cf. the challenging study by Eric Voegelin, *Israel and Revelation* (1956), Vol. I of *Order and History,* esp. chap. xi, pp. 356 ff.

spiritual authority. To be sure, no sharper contrast can be imagined than the beatitudes of the Sermon on the Mount and the curses of the Old Testament (Deuteronomy 2:27, 15 ff.). These beatitudes appear to be a pure form of virtue ethics, and yet the thought of the Sermon on the Mount is clearly derived from the basic Jewish attitude toward man and his dignity, and the development of talmudic Judaism shows very clear parallels to the Christian story.

The notion of ancient Judaism which runs through the entire Old Testament like a red thread is that the faithful Jew proves himself to be good by obeying the law and that only in such obedience to firmly established norms can the worth of a man be demonstrated. This basic notion has profoundly influenced Christianity, not in spite but rather because of the Christian notion of the mercy of God and man's faith in it. Catholicism and Protestantism have both remained loyal to this basic attitude for which the retention of the Ten Commandments is a perhaps external, but nonetheless important, expression. For the child who learns from his earliest days that one can insure one's self to be good, insure one's self to be a man, by obeying these commandments has thus already absorbed attitudes which are typical of the Western legal community.

Law and punishment are rooted conceptually in the notion of justice. And, therefore, the God of ancient Judaism is predominantly a god of justice. From this central position of justice in the thinking of ancient Judaism there developed an attitude which finds a terrible expression in the curses of the Old Testament. When confronted with the just judge who is God, man must justify himself by his obedience to the law, and he must atone for his sins by appropriate punishment. Paul eventually stressed this kind of justice through Christ's forgiveness by the subtle doctrine of vicarious atonement. For it is again Christ who, by thus taking the place of disobedient man, manifests the all-important place which obedience toward the one God, His will, His laws, constitutes. In this decisive context, therefore, we see once more the importance of the Jewish tradition of the just God who gives laws, for, if there were no laws, atonement would lose its very meaning. It is well known that this emphasis of Paul's later became of central importance in the theology of Luther and Calvin, thus demonstrating the extraordinary importance of Old Testament thinking upon law for Western notions regarding right and justice.

III. *Law as Participation in the Idea of Ju[illegible]*

PLATO AND ARISTOTLE

The legal philosophy of the Greeks discovered in the age of sophistic enlightenment the problem of law and nature, of *nomos* and *physis*. Originally *nomos* was the sacred custom, that which is enforced and is taken for right in the *polis*. It is the order which embraces all. The poet Pindar gave the comprehensive formula, *nomos basileus panton:* the law of this sacred custom is described as the ruler over all and everything. But the fading of the faith upon which this view had rested led to a gradual deterioration of *nomos*. The doctrine of the Sophists, more particularly that of Protagoras, that man is the measure of all things, brought it about that *nomos* now appeared more in the perspective of habit on the one hand, of statute on the other. One might wonder why *nomos* was not simply interpreted as the set of habits characteristic of each particular and concrete *polis* community. Whatever the explanation, the idea appears that law as the order of the community is a creation of man and a creation according to his nature, that all men are by nature alike, and a *nomos* for all is therefore meaningful. This is one possible approach. The other is to see the nature of man as very unlike. In that case, *nomos* and *physis* are contrasted, and he who is by nature stronger and better is thereby put in the position of discarding the *nomos*.[1]

Thus there were many crosscurrents of ideas when Plato stepped into the discussion. What appeared typical to Plato in all these arguments and what from his point of view was decisive was the general tendency to make relative the very norms which should possess absolute binding force. The sophistic outlook of a Callicles, although much more cynical than that of a Protagoras

[1] Werner Jaeger, *Paideia: The Ideals of Greek Culture* (1939), I, esp. Book I, chap. viii, 134–47, though Jaeger does not give primary attention to *nomos*. Cf. also for the contrast of *dike* Kurt Latte, *Heiliges Recht* (1920).

or even a Gorgias, therefore appears to him as the natural, the logical consequence of the basic position of the Sophists.[2] And although this position is seen by Plato in a rather one-sided, exaggerated way, there is no question that it is the decisive starting point for Plato. We can see here that the *nomos,* to quote a recent scholar, had undergone a basic change: "The original concept of *nomos* as a proud order of universal obligation had become, under the influence of rationalist thinking which spread far and wide by the middle of the fifth century, the prevailing but usually erroneous opinion of the many."[3] *Nomos* as mere habit rather than sacred custom would of course be relative, an emanation of popular opinion in a particular time and place.

For Plato[4] and Aristotle are convinced, and their conviction is quite in keeping with Greek tradition, that law and the laws (*nomos* and *nomoi*) are essential for the structuring of the *polis* —often spoken of in translation as the "state," a modern term which is quite misleading when applied to the Greek political order. In line with their conviction we find that good political orders or constitutions (*politeiai*) are always legal orders, orders according to law.[5] Any sort of legal positivism according to which the arbitrary command of a tyrant could be considered law—a view which has frequently been maintained under modern dic-

[2] Cf. Jaeger, *op. cit.*, pp. 283 ff. For a classic statement of the Sophists' case, see G. Grote, *History of Greece* (1846–56), chap. lxvii, as well as his *Plato and the Other Companions of Socrates* (1865), and H. Gomperz, *Sophistik und Rhetorik* (1912). H. Jackson's article on the Sophists in the *Encyclopaedia Britannica* gives a rather conventional view.

[3] Felix Heinimann, *Nomos und Physis* (1946), p. 89.

[4] Besides the general histories of Greek philosophy, such as those by Benn, Burnet, and Gomperz, not to mention the standard histories of philosophy, the vast literature on Plato (and Socrates) may be sampled for his thoughts on law in Ernest Barker, *Greek Political Theory: Plato and His Predecessors* (1925) and *The Political Thought of Plato and Aristotle* (1906); David Grene, *Man in His Pride* (1950); Werner Jaeger, *op. cit.*, Vol. II; R. L. Nettleship, *Lectures on the Republic of Plato* (1914); Karl Popper, *The Open Society and Its Enemies* (1945), Vol. I; Constantin Ritter, *Platon* (Eng. trans. under the title of *The Essence of Plato's Philosophy,* 1933); A. E. Taylor, *Plato, the Man and His Work* (1927); John Wild, *Plato's Theory of Man* (1946). I also wish to recommend especially the excellent chapter on Plato in Huntington Cairns, *Legal Philosophy from Plato to Hegel* (1949).

[5] For this point, see Plato's *Crito* 50–51.

tatorship—is for them completely excluded. Yet, the other view immediately presents the decisive question: What is the source of law, if it is not to be found in the will of him who possesses the actual power in the state? The answer to this question is central for Platonic legal thought. It is an answer that is greatly complicated and made difficult to comprehend by the Platonic doctrine of ideas. What is more, the greatest differences of opinion exist concerning the meaning of this doctrine. Even the word "idea" has often been considered unsuitable for representing what constitutes the essence of the Socratic-Platonic doctrine of the idea or the *eidos*. Terms such as "form" have been suggested in order to do justice to the fact that these ideas for Plato and Socrates are not something created by the subjective mind of man but rather a transcendental objective reality outside of man.[6] But once one has grasped the fact that the Platonic "ideas" are actually meant to possess such a transcendental and objective reality, indeed that they constitute the true being and reality, it is no longer necessary or even desirable to change the name, especially since a term such as "form" presents new and very considerable difficulties, both linguistic and philosophical.

What is mainly important if one wants to be fair to the Platonic doctrine of ideas is to be very careful not to inject into it later philosophical views such as the idealism of a Berkeley or a Hegel.[7] For, quite apart from the very different cultural setting, one must bear in mind that for Socrates and Plato the problem of the good stood in the very center of philosophical contemplation. It is evident that the idea of the good—the sun of the world of ideas—and the idea of justice and of law which is linked to it have little kinship with a force as active as the world spirit of Hegel. To put it another way, the Platonic philosophy of law is closely linked to ethics, while that of Hegel is related to history. And whereas Hegel could celebrate the rediscovery of Machia-

[6] J. E. Stewart, *Plato's Doctrine of Ideas* (1909); Paul Natorp, *Platon's Ideenlehre* (1903); and A. D. Lindsay's Introduction to his edition of the *Republic* in Everyman's Library, for contrasting viewpoints.

[7] Nor should one accept the Neo-Platonism of Jowett's celebrated translation.

velli by Fichte, there is no doubt that such Machiavellism would have seemed to Socrates and Plato the worst kind of sophism.

Within the context of the Platonic doctrine of ideas, the idea of justice can be most readily demonstrated in relation to the idea of the *polis*, for the contemplation of this idea of the *polis* produces an image in which law and statute play hardly a role at all. The idea of such a *polis* is characterized by the rule of the philosopher-king. And a community in which those seeking the wisdom that results from a grasp of the ideas are the rulers does not need any laws because the wise guardians are capable of realizing justice as each particular situation presents itself. It is customary to speak of this idea of the *polis* as an "ideal state" and thereby to interpret it as a utopia. Such an interpretation does scant justice to the essence of the Platonic doctrine of ideas, for the Platonic idea of the *polis* or state[8] is not a project which, though unrealizable, must be viewed as a program of action. Rather, as we have just said, this idea is the true reality, the true state, and all actually existing states participate in the idea to a greater or lesser extent. The task of the reformer therefore is to try to create a state which "participates" to the fullest possible extent in the idea, for the idea is everlasting and unchangeable. When Plato wrote his celebrated dialogue entitled *Politeia*, or "Constitution" (not "Republic"!), he believed this to be a very difficult but not an insoluble problem. Plato believed the solution to be that either the philosophers become rulers or the rulers philosophers, that is to say, men seeking wisdom through a real understanding of the ideas. He believed that if, by a happy accident, a man who had limitless power in a *polis* should meet with such a seeker after wisdom, the creation of a genuinely good community could be expected. Plato had, as we know, made that effort himself and had acted in line with this belief when he accepted the invitation of his friend Dion to work with Dionysius I and Dionysius II of Syracuse in

[8] Cf. Barker, *Political Thought of Plato and Aristotle, passim.* See also Plato *Republic* 586D–587A (*nomos and taxis*) and 519D–520A (*nomos* and the good life).

the hope of molding the *polis* of Syracuse in this image. But the attempt miscarried.[9]

In consequence, Plato later returned to the traditional Greek doctrine according to which a good order of the *polis* could be secured only by the making of a basic law or *nomos*. But this *nomos* is seen by Plato as a participation in the idea of justice, and through this participation it, in turn, participates in the idea of the good. A *polis* ordered and structured according to the idea of the *polis* is not the idea itself, but it "participates" in the idea. It is evident that the most perplexing aspect of this doctrine is the notion of participation, of taking part in an idea. Plato himself was not able to give this notion a clear, rational form. Instead of that, he took refuge in the myth of the cave. It would lead too far afield to recall this myth here, nor is this necessary, since it can readily be read by anyone interested in the moving poetical description which Plato gives in the *Republic* (vii, at the beginning). But strictly speaking, no part of the swiftly changing phenomenal world of actual sensory beings participates in ideas. The world of ordinary sense experience is merely a reflection of these ideas, as unreal as the image in a mirror.

In this world of ideas, law was especially described in Plato's late dialogue, the *Laws*, and considered real only as an imperfect reproduction of the idea of law and justice. The idea of law cannot of course be in conflict with the idea of justice, and therefore all actually existing conflicts between law and justice must be interpreted as a consequence of the imperfect interpretation of the respective ideas. It follows that positive law is a phenomenon, exposed to becoming and passing away, which participates only incompletely in the timeless world of ideas, a notion very different from that of natural law in modern idealism, where the ideal

[9] Regarding the problem of whether Plato believed his ideas "realizable," cf. Grene, *op. cit.*, esp. chap. xi. Cf. *Republic* 473A, 499B–D, 614B ff. The Seventh Letter, if we take it at all seriously—and one should, it seems to me—shows definitely that Plato at the time of the composition of the *Republic* believed his ideas realizable but, after the experiment in Sicily, became more doubtful that they could be brought about except through education. Taylor, *op. cit.*, overstates this point by claiming that Plato was "an extremely practical thinker." Cf. *Laws* 709 ff., where Plato still maintains a measure of hope.

of justice as the more perfect norm is confronted with the positive law. Law is, like all things in this world, in the vision of Plato, in the last analysis merely a phantom bridge for the wise in their search for eternal verities and values.[10]

But this otherworldliness of the Platonic metaphysics does not mean that Plato lacked the sense for the concrete molding of law. Quite the contrary: the creation of the legal order is seen as the unique act of the legislator who founds the community. Solon and Lycurgus must be understood as the prototypes of such great creators of the law. Their task is not seen as a problem of the will but as a problem of reason. Not the question, What do I want? but What should you do? is the question to which the law created by such a *nomothetes* is supposed to be the answer. Thoughts suggested by this approach lead into ethics. For since it is the task of such a founder of the law to make the community as a whole and its members happy, and since such happiness can be understood only as a participation in the idea of the good, law must in every respect be shaped in such a way that the human beings living under it become better. This means that law has a distinctly educational function. In consequence, we find that, in Plato's laws, a great deal of emphasis is placed upon the preamble of a statute. For these preambles are intended to explain to the citizens what the reasons for the laws are; that is to say, they are to persuade the citizens to obey the laws rather than simply to give them a command. Thus Plato proposes, for example, that a law ordering a man to marry before he is thirty-five should be implemented by a preamble explaining the necessity of procreation for the maintenance of a community. Only through such explanation can the authority of the law be established and maintained (see below, chap. xix).

"Legislation and the establishment of a political order," writes Plato, "are the most perfect means in the world to achieve virtue" (*Laws* 708). For that reason, Plato completely refused to deduce laws from the existing constitution, which is usually an expression of actual relations of rule and subjection. Such class legislation

[10] Taylor, *op. cit.*; Greene, *op. cit.*

Plato does not admit. He insists that he will not recognize as laws, in the sense of being right law, any which have not been given for the general good of the community. Legislation which serves merely the interests of the party he considers a matter of pure expediency, and he would deny it the quality of true law. In these remarks which hint at natural law, Plato finds the ground for asserting that the government is merely the servant of the laws. Only a state in which "law is the ruler over the rulers" (*Laws* 715), that is to say, only a state in which the government is subject to the laws, can be expected to reap all the good which the gods hold ready for genuine communities, namely, the true happiness of the citizens. For the laws are the means to make certain that men do not merely live but live well (*eu zen*) and become as virtuous as is possible. "In my opinion," Plato says in a very significant passage, "only such law can be considered right as aims like a good bowman always at that which has something of the eternally beautiful and which neglects everything, be it wealth or something else of that kind, which is devoid of virtue [*arete*]" (*Laws* 705E–706A). A passage such as this one shows very clearly that Plato is as far removed from positivism as it is possible to be. Law and the laws are an object of free philosophical speculation, and they can be derived only from reason and the idea of good. Even right law is merely an approximation to these eternal verities.

The legal philosophy of Aristotle is in many ways related to that of Plato, more particularly in the practical consequences which it has for law and the state.[11] As in Plato, the educational task of law and of the laws is central, and yet there are, if one looks more closely, very important differences between Aristotle and Plato. These differences are related to that between the Aris-

[11] The bibliography on Aristotle is as extensve as that on Plato. We might mention, besides the work by Barker noted above (n. 4), the following: Barker's Introduction to his translation of the *Politics* (1948); K. von Fritz and E. Kapp's Introduction to their edition of *Aristotle: Constitution of Athens* (1950); Werner Jaeger, *Aristoteles* (1923; also in Eng. trans.); J. A. Stewart, *Notes on the Nicomachean Ethics of Aristotle*, 2 vols. (1892); W. D. Ross, *Aristotle* (1926); A. E. Taylor, *Aristotle* (1919), brief, but excellent; E. Zeller, *Aristotle and the Earlier Peripatetics* (1897).

totelian and the Platonic metaphysics and more particularly to the Aristotelian doctrine of the causes and the notion of the *telos* or final end which is so characteristic of Aristotle. There has been much controversy concerning the meaning of this doctrine. To this day, sharply divergent interpretations are offered concerning it. In my own opinion, the doctrine of the four causes is the key to that of the *telos.* More especially, the *telos* must not be confused with the form or the idea, although such a confusion is very nearly suggested in several places. In fact, it is not entirely correct to call the *telos* the final end, for in all living beings the expression "end," which seems to presuppose a conscious willing of the end, cannot be used without at the same time raising the problem of a conscious divine creator of the world. The doctrine of the final end really means that each existing thing seeks to achieve the perfection which is appropriate to it, that in each object there is alive a propensity to achieve its own perfect configuration. The acorns, the seedling, and the oak tree are united in their propensity to achieve the perfectly shaped oak, and every other thing, in Aristotle's opinion, exhibits the same striving. If one applies this kind of thinking to law, one could say that the various phases observed in the coming into existence of a law are illustrative of this inherent propensity. Thus the original inspiration of how to cope with a given situation, its discussion in offices and in parliament, and its final realization in a statute which is reasonable and just, that is to say, which is appropriate to the situation at hand—all these phases of the creation of a law are to be understood in terms of the final end.

This emphasis upon becoming results in the many-sidedness of Aristotelian legal thought. Aristotle's legal philosophy is not known to us in its entirety, and we have no indication that Aristotle wrote such a general jurisprudence. But in his extant works, notably the *Nicomachean Ethics,* the *Politics,* and the *Rhetoric,* we receive a rich amount of information about the views of Aristotle. More particularly, in the *Nicomachean Ethics,* a whole book is devoted to justice, which, in the light of Aristotle's general philosophy, must be considered the core of his legal philosophy "because law can be determined only in relation to the just."[12]

Central for his point of view is the proposition that the just must be understood in the sense of the equal. But Aristotle draws the decisive distinction between numerical and proportional equality. Numerical equality equates each man as a unit with each other man. It is what we now ordinarily understand by equality and what we mean when we say that all citizens are equal before the law. Proportional equality gives to each man that which he is entitled to in accordance with his ability, his achievements, and so on. Aristotle deduces a great deal of controversy and discussion over justice from this distinction.

Justice he further differentiates into the distributive and the corrective kinds of justice. The first is operative in public law, the second in civil and penal law. But both distributive and corrective justice are subject to the problem of equality and can be comprehended only within its framework. In the sphere of distributive justice, the important point is that equal rewards follow equal accomplishments. In the second, what matters is that inequalities which are caused by, say, the breach of a contract are corrected and eliminated.

To state this a bit more fully, we might let Aristotle speak for himself. Distributive justice "is concerned with the distribution of honor, wealth, and such other goods as may be shared by members of the community." Leaving aside the mathematical "demonstration," it is evident that what Aristotle has in mind is the distribution of property and other such valuable possessions according to the inherent merit of the citizen. A just distribution would be one which corresponded to their virtue, their value to the community.

Corrective justice, on the other hand, is concerned with righting wrongs. If a contract is broken or a tort has been done, then corrective justice seeks to provide adequate compensation to the

[12] All three are in Loeb's Classical Library; I have used the Teubner texts. There are many translations, all possessing certain shortcomings. I have used and altered them, as seemed necessary; the references are given, as in the case of Plato's works, to the traditional pagination of the MSS.

wronged party; if a crime has been committed, then proper punishment is meted out to the wrongdoer. Justice is here, as in the previous case, a mean between two unjust extremes. It has been rightly observed that "the division Aristotle makes between corrective justice into voluntary and involuntary corresponds to the modern classification of contract and tort."[13] In either case, what happened when the injustice was committed was that the established "equality" was disturbed. It is the task of corrective justice to re-establish this equality, or, to use a modern phrase, the equilibrium. "The law looks only to the difference created by the injury and treats the men as previously equal, where the one does and the other suffers injury, or the one has done and the other suffered harm." Evidently, corrective justice is the proper sphere of the judiciary, as distributive justice is the sphere of government.

In developing his argument, Aristotle stresses a thought which we have already encountered in Plato and which leads to natural law.[14] He insists that it is necessary to distinguish between such judgments as derive the just from the nature of the case and are based upon general and ubiquitous human nature, and those others which are derived from the specific views of a particular legal community. This contrast must not be confused with that between positive law fixed in statutes and customary law. For the latter two may, in the sense of Aristotle's distinction, be the source of a judgment which refers only to the particular community, whereas another similar judgment, even though expressed in statutory law, would still be natural law if it could be derived from general human nature. In this connection, Aristotle also mentions the distinction between written and unwritten law, and he notes that the general or natural law is usually unwritten,

13 Cairns, *op. cit.*, p. 123. The passages from Aristotle are from the *Nicomachean Ethics* (trans. D. P. Chase, slightly revised) 1130b, 1131b.

14 An interesting discussion of this problem in Charles H. McIlwain, *The Growth of Political Thought in the West* (1932), p. 69; Leo Strauss, *Natural Right and History* (1953), has rather overstated the same case (cf. my article in *Diogenes*, No. 10 [1955], regarding this issue). See also Glenn R. Morrow, "Plato and the Law of Nature," in *Essays in Political Theory*, ed. Milton R. Konvitz and Arthur E. Murphy (1948).

whereas the positive law is sometimes written and sometimes unwritten.

Quite as important as this basic establishment of the law of nature is Aristotle's clear recognition of the distinction between public and private law, or rather the distinction between constitutional and other law. The constitution or *politeia* is given definitely the pre-eminent position.[15] Other laws must be based upon the constitution, a distinction which Cicero later took over and developed. Through the work of Cicero, this idea has become the common property of Western legal thought. Such a requirement of constitutional derivation did not cause Aristotle, like Plato, to deny to a law its legal quality simply because it was in conflict with the constitution. He meant it as an admonition to the lawgiver rather than as a distinct constitutional norm. The situation is similar in regard to a possible conflict between natural and positive legal norms. According to Aristotle, a conflict between the two cannot be made the basis of declaring the positive norm invalid.

It is in the *Rhetoric* that we find Aristotle's views regarding these and a number of other questions of positive legislation, because the *Rhetoric* is extensively concerned with certain problems of actual living law.[16] The reason is that the *Rhetoric* is occupied with, among other things, the forensic rhetoric, that is to say, with civil and criminal procedure. This forensic rhetoric had been extensively cultivated by the Sophists and played an important role in Greek legal life because of the prevailing practice of having popular courts, particularly in Athens. Aristotle was, like Plato and the general public, very indignant about the skeptical, even cynical, tendency of many Sophists to look upon this forensic situation as a kind of tournament where all that mattered was skill in rhetoric and the capacity to make a bad cause into a good one. In fighting such very general tendencies, both Plato and Aristotle wanted to resuscitate justice and give it

[15] *Politics* 1289a, 1298a, 1292b, 1278b; *Nicomachean Ethics* 1181b.

[16] Erik Wolf, *Die Umformung des Rechtsgedankens durch Historik und Rhetorik* (1956). He argues rightly the importance of the *Rhetoric*, which is often overlooked.

the position they thought it entitled to. But Aristotle recognized much more clearly than Plato the practical problems of carrying out such a task, and he therefore spent a good deal of time in the *Rhetoric* on the question of how a just cause can be led to victory through judicial proceedings.

This is not the place to explore the problem in detail, nor is this necessary in a discussion of legal philosophy. But it is important to realize that Aristotle did not rest content with a single answer to the question of what is the nature of law and that he therefore enters into a discussion of the several tasks of the law. Thus he recognizes, besides the educational function, the function of maintaining peace and of arbitrating controversies. And it is in relation to such differentiated functions that he sees the tasks of the lawyer. This multiplicity of tasks affects the forensic practice.

Aristotle developed a sharp distinction very important for criminal law, namely, acts which although in themselves the same and causing the same damage are distinguished by subjective attitudes accompanying them. For they may be the result of either an accident or negligence or a consciously intended tort. The third category is further subdivided into such torts as have been committed by passion and pathos and such as are the result of free choice (*prohairesis*).[17] The chance of such accidents and such negligence makes it necessary that the existing positive law be modified by equity. But each legal normalization of equity leads to new legal rules concerning how such equity is to be handled. For this reason, the Aristotelian suggestion that such equity results from the general form of laws which does not take care of the individual case can be admitted only within narrow limits. Or perhaps one should rather recognize that it is incorrect or at least imprecise to translate the Aristotelian *epieikeia* as "equity," since basically *epieikeia* refers to the recognition of a possible exception which on the one hand may lead to amnesty or pardon, and on the other hand may justify the discretionary power of decision by the judge, which in turn finds its expression in general formulas, such as modifying circumstances or good

[17] *Nicomachean Ethics* v. 10; *Rhetoric* i. 13.

morals. Aristotle called *epieikeia* a kind of justice. For him it is the corrective for the generality of laws which do not take care of the individual case, a generality which is grounded in law's very nature. Aristotle tries to elucidate this thought by a rather interesting comparison. He says equity is like the Lydian kind of measure which was made of lead and which therefore could be adjusted to the contours of a line that was not straight. But he points out that such a measuring rod is of no use if it is too soft, and likewise *epieikeia* loses all value if it is employed without rhyme, reason, or limitation. In a summary contained in the *Rhetoric,* Aristotle states the matter as follows:

> It is equitable to pardon human weaknesses and to look not to the law but to the legislator, not to the letter of the law but to the intention of the legislator, not to the acts themselves but to the moral purpose, not to the part but to the whole, not to what a man is now but to what he has been always or generally, to remember good rather than ill treatment and benefits received rather than those conferred, to bear injury with patience, to be willing to appeal to the judgment of reason rather than to violence, to prefer arbitration to the law court, for the arbitrator keeps equity in view, whereas the judge looks only to the law. . . . Let this manner of defining equity suffice [*Rhetoric* i. 13. 13].

We can see from this enumeration that in the view of Aristotle the boundaries between equity and justice are fluid and that we are here confronted with an antinomy in Aristotle's legal thought. For his basic conception is, as we have seen, that justice can exist only between men whose relations are regulated by law (*Nicomachean Ethics* v. 6. 1134a). This notion is rooted in the related one of a natural just law which is found within the framework of the constitution which is by nature best (*ibid.* 1135a).

The question of how law is realized Aristotle answers in the sense that "law derives its validity from habit upon which obedience is founded" (*Politics* 1269a). This thought is repeatedly expressed both in the *Ethics* and in the *Politics* and is made the basis of further deductions. More particularly, Aristotle thinks that because it is necessary to habituate the citizens to the law, the greatest caution in altering the laws must be exercised; by such alteration the citizen is made uncertain. And he adds that even the best laws approved by the citizens accomplish little if they are not effectively anchored in the fundamental principles of the constitution (*Politics* 1310a). This strong emphasis upon habit as the basis of the validity of law and the laws does not prevent Aristotle from recognizing the role of force. But such force is always only a necessary additional means which reinforces the coercive power of habit (*Politics* 1286b). The role of habit in the realization of law is only a special case; its role in the realization of any ethical virtue is equally great. The lawgiver makes the citizen good by habituating him by means of law to becoming a good man (*Nicomachean Ethics* 1103b).

From what has been said it can be seen clearly to what an extent Plato and Aristotle laid the foundation for all later philosophy of law. The general law of nature and the particular law of each community, constitutional (public) and other (private) law, statutory law and equity—these and a number of other essential distinctions were abstracted from the concrete law of the Greeks and stated as comprehensive generalizations by these two great philosophers. Besides, Aristotle worked out important applications of these insights to forensic practice. It is therefore justifiable to assert that they established the groundwork for Western legal philosophy. The most important questions had been stated, and valuable answers had been attempted.

IV. *Law as the Expression of the Laws of Human Nature*

THE STOICS AND ROMAN NATURAL LAW

Every jurist knows the formulas of natural law which are preserved in the Justinian Code.[1] Natural law is then discussed in its relation to the law of nations and the civil law, and these three terms, *jus naturale, jus gentium,* and *jus civile,* recur throughout the *Corpus juris civilis.* This discussion opens with a statement by Ulpian that the law of nature is what nature teaches all living beings (*animalia*).[2] Most of the formulations which we encounter are in fact those which had already been set forth by Plato and Aristotle, and yet there is an important difference between the legal conceptions of the Roman jurists and those of Plato and Aristotle. This difference can be fully appreciated only if one takes into account the doctrine of the Stoics which was first announced by Zeno (295–261 B.C., the founder of the school) and later confirmed by Panaetius (around 140 B.C.) and brought to Rome, where finally it was restated by Cicero in a way that made the Stoic law of nature usable within the context of the Roman law and fruitful for its development.

No attempt is made here to present the deep and in many ways obscure doctrine of the Stoics.[3] What is decisive for the philoso-

[1] The edition of the *Corpus juris civilis* used is that by Paul Krueger for the *Institutes* and by Theodor Mommsen for the *Digest* (8th ed., 1899). The statement of Ulpian is found at *Institutes* i. 2 and at *Digest* i. 1. 1. In these quotations, the first numeral designates the book; the second, the chapter; the third, the section.

[2] *Digest* i. 1. 3.

[3] From the extensive literature on the Stoics, the following may be mentioned: Ernest Barker, *From Alexander to Constantine* (1956); Margaret E. Reesor, *The Political Theory of the Old and Middle Stoa* (1951); R. D. Hicks, *Stoic and Epicurean* (1910); Gilbert Murray, *The Stoic Philosophy* (1915); Eduard Zeller, *Stoics, Epicureans, and Sceptics* (1870; this is the English translation of an original German classic); for ready reference to the basic works, see W. J. Oates (ed.), *The Stoics and the Epicurean Philosophers* (1940).

phy of law is above all that the Stoics exploded the framework of the *polis* which had been beyond argument for Plato and Aristotle and proclaimed mankind as an all-embracing community. One god, one state, one law—this well-known formula states the doctrine of the Stoics in a clear and simple way. Man is different from other men not by his belonging to a *polis* but only by being either a wise man who recognizes the doctrine of the Stoics or a fool who does not. The true *polis* for that reason is not any existing *polis* such as Athens but in fact a community of these wise men. All of them are subject to the one God and the one law (*lex*). In the *Digest* (i. 3. 2) the great Chrysippus who shaped the Stoic doctrine into a system is praised as a philosopher of Stoic wisdom and is said to have stated in his work about *nomos:* "The *nomos* [basic law] is the ruler of all divine and human things. . . ."

It is very important to recognize from the outset that at the basis of such a conception of *nomos* or *lex* there is a notion which does not sharply distinguish between what we are wont to look upon as laws of nature and the basic norms of the law. Rather such a conception of the *lex* looks upon both as laws which determine the nature of things. Thus Ulpian remarks in the passage we have already cited that "jus istud non humani generis proprium est, sed omnium animalium, quae in caelo, quae in terra, quae in mari nascuntur" ("law is not peculiar to the human species, but [is the law] of all living beings which are born in the sky, on the earth, or in the sea").[4] He illuminates this statement by referring to the joining of man and woman in the procreation of children and so forth. Evidently we are here face to face with

[4] This and the following translations from the Latin are my own. Some references to classic treatments of Roman law may be indicated here: E. F. Bruck, *Über römisches Recht im Rahmen der Kulturgeschichte* (1954); E. C. Clark, *History of Roman Private Law* (1906–19); P. F. Girard, *Short History of Roman Law* (1906); R. von Ihering, *Der Geist des römischen Rechts* (1866–71); Paul Krueger, *Geschichte der Quellen und Literatur des römischen Rechts* (1888); Theodor Mommsen, *Römisches Staatsrecht* (1871–88); James Muirhead, *Historical Introduction to the Private Law of Rome* (1886); Max Radin, *Handbook of Roman Law* (1927); Fritz Schulz, *History of Roman Legal Science* (1946); R. Sohm, *The Institutions of Roman Law* (1892).

a point of view which is akin to the modern sociological interpretation of law, for such sociological interpretation seeks to explain legal relationships by the natural behavior of men in their social relations. The views of Ulpian, however, are not those of all teachers of natural law in Roman jurisprudence. More particularly we find in Cicero,[5] who, as we said, transmitted the doctrine of the Stoics to the Romans in a rhetorically brilliant form, that the problems are stated somewhat differently. For Cicero treats the law of nature in the way in which it has become familiar in the West as *lex caelestis*. This concept of Cicero is frequently translated in a somewhat deceptive way as "divine" law. Such an interpretation is not entirely wrong, but it hinders one in comprehending that these are laws of nature in the sense of natural science. It is important for the Stoics and Cicero that this law of nature is conceived of as an emanation of *ratio*. Cicero quotes Chrysippus, who, he says, identified Jupiter with the law and explains that "lex ratio summa insita in natura, quae jubet ea, quae facienda sunt, prohibetque contraria" ("Law is highest reason, imbedded in nature, which commands what should be done, and forbids the contrary") (*De legibus* i. 6).

But how are we to understand the relation between such a law, which is the highest reason as found in nature, and the more particular natural law of the human community? There exist several possible interpretations of Cicero, which is natural because Cicero's statements regarding this matter are not unequivocal. Thus it has been asserted that Cicero identified the two;[6] but the exact opposite has also been maintained when it has been

[5] On Cicero, see F. R. Cowell, *Cicero and the Roman Republic* (1948), esp. chaps. ix, x; Mason Hammond, *City State and World State in Greek and Roman Political Theory until Augustus* (1951); Otto Plasberg, *Cicero in seinen Werken und Briefen* (1926); Viktor Pöschl, *Römischer Staat und griechisches Staatsdenken bei Cicero: Untersuchungen zu Ciceros Schrift De re publica* (1936); cf. also the penetrating Introduction by G. H. Sabine and S. B. Smith to their edition of Cicero's *De re publica*. Cicero's works are most readily consulted in Loeb's Classical Library, but I have changed the translations at times.

[6] Cf. A. P. d'Entrèves, *Natural Law: An Introduction to Legal Philosophy* (1951), esp. chap. i, pp. 20 f.; C. H. McIlwain, *The Growth of Political Thought in the West* (1932), chap. iv, pp. 106 ff.

claimed that Cicero separated the two very definitely and clearly.[7] It seems more correct to interpret the natural law of human society as a part or realm of those laws which dominate all nature. This interpretation seems particularly clearly suggested in a passage of *De re publica* (iii. 22, according to Lactantius) in which it is said that the true law is the reason of nature, the *logos* of nature, as it was called by the older Stoics. This *ratio* is constant, eternal, and "distributed among all."

What is crucial is that man, contrasted to other living beings, participates consciously in this *ratio* because he himself possesses reason and therefore can understand the laws of nature. But this does not mean that the laws of nature are a product of human reason (*lex non hominum ingeniis excogitata*) nor that law is an order instituted by some peoples or states, but rather that it is "something eternal which rules the entire world by the wisdom of what it commands and what it forbids" (*De legibus* ii. 4). The law is therefore right reasoning (*recta ratio*), and we must assume that God and men have it in common. For Cicero expressly states that the knowledge of law (*juris disciplina*) cannot be derived from the decisions of the praetors or from the Twelve Tables but only from philosophy. To put this another and modern way, one could say that the *juris disciplina* is a rationalization of the existing legal order. When conflicts occur between this *recta ratio* and the positive law, Cicero has no doubt that the positive norm is not necessarily law in the true sense. What follows from the assertion that "the whole world is a community of gods and men" (*De legibus* i. 7), that man is "akin to God," and that man, like God, possesses virtue (*virtus*), which is nothing but a more perfect nature—I say what follows from all this is that "we are born for justice, and law is not based upon opinion but upon the very nature of man" (*De legibus* i. 28). In the same context Cicero explains that all men form one great community, that all men are equal, and that, however man may be defined, such definition must fit all men, and therefore all men share with one another the same basic law.

[7] G. H. Sabine, *A History of Political Theory* (rev. ed.; 1951), chap. ix.

It has been asserted that this doctrine represents the great turning point, that this juristic formulation of the basic Stoic doctrine is the point at which occidental legal thought turns away from the legal and political philosophy of Plato and Aristotle which is rooted in the *polis.* It has even been said that Chrysippus and Cicero are closer to Kant than to Aristotle.[8] Certainly it is true that this Stoical doctrine of the universal validity of law is of very great importance. But we have seen that it plays a certain role in Plato and Aristotle as well. It is an error to confuse this question of universal validity with that of its realization. Neither Plato nor Aristotle wrote for Athens or for any other particular *polis,* as might be done by a modern nationalist. Their essential limitation lay in the fact that they did not believe the realization of a universally valid law possible except within the framework of a *polis.* And in this respect Cicero is entirely of the same opinion; it was Cicero's own weakness that he could not transcend the framework of the *polis,* of the *civitas,* and think of the empire as a state in the modern sense.[9] In Cicero's *De re publica,* Scipio describes the Roman Republic very much in the tradition of Aristotle, which Polybius had applied to Roman conditions. The best *civitas* is one with a mixed constitution in which monarchical, aristocratic, and democratic elements are equilibrated and brought into harmony. Cicero was hostile to the dictatorial and monarchical solution of the problem of the empire and finally had to pay for his convictions with his life—a martyr to the old Roman *civitas* as Socrates had been to the Greek *polis.*

If we are not justified in treating the contrast between Plato and Cicero as a radical one, it is at the same time erroneous to interpret Cicero and the Roman natural law as merely a copy of Platonic and Aristotelian legal thought. The touch of genius in Cicero's thought must be found in the fact that he undertook

[8] A. J. Carlyle, *A History of Medieval Political Theory in the West,* I (1903), 8, provided the background for Sabine's statement that "Chrysippus and Cicero are closer to Kant than they are to Aristotle," *op. cit.*, p. 165.

[9] Hammond, *op. cit., passim* and more esp. pp. 139–40; cf. also Pöschl, *op. cit., passim.*

to systematize the viewpoints imbedded in Roman jurisprudence and that he placed them within the framework of Platonic, Aristotelian, and Stoic philosophical ideas. In this respect Cicero resembles Locke, who similarly rationalized views immanent in English legal and constitutional development in terms of the prevailing philosophical notions of natural law as they had developed on the Continent. In Cicero's work, we find a skilful use of the system of rhetoric as an art of persuasion, as it had been systematized by Aristotle.[10] Cicero's doctrine of interpretation is a great juristic achievement in its systematic clarity and elaboration.

But I want in conclusion to sketch another very important and very controversial matter, the definition of *jus naturale, jus gentium,* and *jus civile* in their relation to one another. It has often been asserted that Cicero identified the *jus naturale* and the *jus gentium.* This point of view cannot be maintained in the light of a number of statements in Cicero. Cicero, like Ulpian and others, considered the *jus gentium,* in contrast to the *jus naturale,* as a law by institution even though this institution was very general. An institution such as slavery does not become just simply because it is found everywhere. Other legal norms of the *jus gentium* which the Roman law had developed could, according to Cicero, be considered *jus naturale* only if they could be shown to have a philosophical foundation. The most that can be admitted is that there is a presumption in favor of the contention that a legal institution found in diverse *civitates* is part of the law of nature.

For a definitive clarification of the relation between *jus naturale* and other legal norms it is necessary to ask what the content of this law of nature or *jus naturale* is. Neither Cicero nor Roman law gives a perfectly clear and unequivocal answer to this question. The most famous and best known is the formula of the *Digest: honeste vivere, neminem laedere, suum cuique tribuere.*

[10] Though whether Cicero knew Aristotle's work has not been established, it seems likely, in view of his extended studies of Greek philosophy and his explicit preference for Plato (*De officiis* ii. 8), that he knew, but did not accept it.

But general and largely ethical propositions such as that one should live decently, should hurt no one, and should give to everyone what is his own, are so imprecise that they can be used for the evaluation of the legal norms of a developed system only in the sense of the Aristotelian *epieikeia,* that is to say, some kind of equity.[11] However, we find in Cicero a passage which gives more detailed information concerning what is to be understood by *jus naturale.* We are told that the natural law consists in reverence for the gods; duty toward the fatherland, parents, and relatives; gratitude and readiness to forgive; and respect for all those who are superior to us in age, wisdom, or status, and finally he adds that *jus naturale* also consists in truthfulness.[12] Such an enumeration of a variety of ethically desirable kinds of behavior may be implemented by a longish passage (*De legibus* i. 31–32) where the equality of men is demonstrated by the fact that irritations, pleasures, desires, and anxieties (*molestiae, laetitiae, cupiditates, timores*) are the same for all men. In order further to strengthen his point, Cicero asks: "Which people does not like courtesy, kindness, and gratitude, and hates the arrogant, the mean, the cruel, and the ungrateful?" All this seems to him to prove the reasonableness of a decent life (*ratio recte vivendi*), which is the concrete content of natural law upon which every true legal order must be based. Cicero himself acted in accordance with such convictions; when he became proconsul in Cilicia, he administered the province with probity and gentleness, and he acted similarly in Sicily.

I think one can say in summary that the Stoic-Ciceronian legal philosophy is rooted in a rational ethic to which there is ascribed a universal validity as a law of human nature. This law, like all laws of nature, is the reason inherent in all nature, perhaps one could say even more correctly, its meaning. And therefore one can derive and one must derive law from these laws (*a lege ducendum est juris exordium*), for this law, the law of nature, is the

[11] Nonetheless, this statement has echoed down the ages. Even Kant's *Rechtslehre* is built upon it; see below, chap. xiv.

[12] Cited by Krueger, *op. cit.*, p. 40.

power of nature (*naturae vis*), and for this reason it is the norm for right and wrong. The realization of this natural law is a task imposed upon the several states (*civitates*), which express the true law in the norms of the *jus gentium* common to them all. But each community has its own *jus civile,* valid only for its citizens, as it takes account of the special conditions, both spiritual and material, which are peculiar to this particular community. But neither the *jus gentium* nor the *jus civile* ought to be in conflict with the *jus naturale.* If they do conflict, such norms are not true law but arbitrary commands.

The basic views of Cicero have dominated legal thought for a thousand years. Again and again one encounters them in the course of the centuries. They were argued in a novel and philosophically original way by Kant. When the fathers of the American constitutions proclaimed that their constitutions were establishing governments of laws and not of men, they merely restated what Cicero had already formulated admirably well when he said: "We are servants of the law in order to be able to be free" (*Pro Cluentio* 53. 146).

V. *Law as Order and Peace of the Community of Love*

ST. AUGUSTINE

Even though there is a real kinship between the legal philosophy of the Stoics and that of the Christians, the Christian political and legal doctrines are animated by so different a spirit that the legal concepts imbedded in it must be differently understood. But in doing so, one must not make the opposite mistake and interpret the legal philosophy of the patristic writers in the sense of the later Middle Ages. For these patristic doctrines have a meaning of their own which can only be understood in terms of late antiquity.[1] St. Augustine "is in truth the fulfilment and perfection of Christian antiquity, its last and its greatest thinker, its spiritual practitioner and tribune. He must be understood in this perspective."[2] But even though the thinkers in the Germanic tradition of the Middle Ages misunderstood him, he nonetheless remains the dominant influence down to Thomas Aquinas. He is "the father of medieval Catholicism."[3]

We have seen that in the legal philosophy of pagan antiquity,

[1] Ernst Troeltsch, *Die Soziallehren der christlichen Kirchen* (1923), pp. 156 ff.; see also the same, "Das stoisch-christliche und das moderne profane Naturrecht," *Historische Zeitschrift,* CVI (1911), 247 ff. Cf. also the same author's lecture on "The Ideas of Natural Law and Humanity in World Politics" as translated by Ernest Barker and included as an Appendix in his English version of portions of Gierke's *Genossenschaftsrecht,* under the title *Natural Law and the Theory of Society, 1500–1800* (1934). Troeltsch acknowledges his indebtedness to R. W. and A. J. Carlyle, *A History of Medieval Political Theory in the West* (1903), Vol. I.

[2] Ernst Troeltsch, "Augustin, die christliche Antike und das Mittelalter," *Historische Bibliothek,* Vol. XXXVI (1915); cf. also his more general remarks in *Die Soziallehren der christlichen Kirchen,* esp. pp. 148 ff.

[3] For St. Augustine cf., besides the works cited in the Bibliography, H.-I. Marrou, *Saint Augustin et la fin de la culture antique* (1949), and the interesting discussion in C. H. McIlwain, *The Growth of Political Thought in the West* (1932), chap. v, pp. 154–60. For the background see also Edgar Salin, *Civitas Dei* (1926).

the image and the experience of the *polis* was dominant, that *polis* in which political and religious life, governmental and ecclesiastical rulership, were realized in an undifferentiated closed order of the community. In patristic teaching, and more particularly in the work of Augustine, the church as a higher community stands above the *polis,* above the *civitas,* indeed represents something of an antithesis to the pagan polity. It is this fact which gives essential meaning to the docrine of the *civitas Dei,* which is in many respects so difficult and obscure. To be sure, the true *civitas Dei* exists only in heaven and not on earth, but it is represented on earth by the community of the faithful. This community must not simply be identified with the church. But even in Augustine we find a firm inclination to treat the visible church as the representative of the community of the faithful. In any case, this church is imbedded in the *civitas terrena,* the secular community of mankind, which in turn is organized into the different political bodies, the *res publicae,* the *gentes,* the *regna,* and the *imperia.* Augustine's thought has been interpreted in many different ways, and more particularly the use of the term "state" has created much confusion with reference to his ideas on the political and secular order. But it is clear that Augustine makes a fairly definite distinction between *res publica* and *regnum;* for one thing, he defines a republic in transforming Cicero and the Roman tradition, while the *regnum,* the state in the more narrow sense of rule, he declares essentially a great band of robbers, *since* it is devoid of justice or at any rate *when* it is devoid of justice. The republic on the other hand is the rational community determined by the values which all those belonging to the community have in common.[4] In a literal sense, these values are the things which the members of a community cherish or love (*diligere*). It is possible to question how far this expression

[4] The *res publica* is *res populi* and *populus est coetus multitudinis rationalis rerum quas diligit concordi communione sociatus* ("a people is the gathering of a rational multitude which is associated by the sharing in concord of the things it loves") (*Civitas Dei* xix. 24). For contrary views see the works cited in the Bibliography, esp. Barker; for interesting support, see Herbert A. Deane, *The Political and Social Ideas of St. Augustine* (1963).

diligere is identical with the Christian concept of love or charity. But in view of the term *dilectio proximi*, or "love of neighbor," it seems probable that Augustine intended to transform or reinerpret in a Christian sense the pagan concept of the legal community as found in Cicero. For it is precisely this term *diligere*, this notion of things which are cherished by the community members in concord, which in Augustine takes the place of Cicero's notion of an agreement on law and a mutuality of interests; furthermore, Augustine explicitly quotes Cicero. To put it another way, Augustine replaces the community of law by the community of charity or love. And such a community of love is essential to a republic.[5] It is self-evident that among the values cherished by such a community we find justice, although this has often been overlooked. In turn, the concept of justice is reinterpreted in a very decisive way. For the Stoics and the Romans it had, as we saw, the meaning of decent living, of not hurting anyone, and of giving everyone his own. Augustine makes the giving everyone his own more predominant, and he puts foremost among those to whom one must give his own God himself, who thus made the center of the whole argument. Thus justice becomes a quality which comprehends piety. To believe in God, to venerate and adore him, to give to his church its proper place in the community, all this is now included in the concept of justice.[6]

But in spite of or perhaps precisely because of this conception of justice, which resembles that of Plato, we do not find in Augustine a specific legal philosophy. Yet he shows a particularly striking tendency which is part of legal philosophy, namely, the tendency to see the political order as dominated by the purpose of peace. The reason is that the political order has now been reduced to the negative function of maintaining peace, for it merely serves the purpose of enabling the faithful to occupy themselves with the more lasting task of eternal salvation. This new outlook

[5] See Hannah Arendt, *Der Liebesbegriff bei Augustin* (1929), *passim.*

[6] To be sure, the concept of law of the ancient Romans had had a strongly religious root, as I pointed out earlier. Cf. E. F. Bruck, *Über römisches Recht im Rahmen der Kulturgeschichte* (1954), esp. pp. 1–10.

thus manifests itself not only in Augustine's famous doctrine of the just war between empires and republics but in his emphasis upon internal order.[7] It would seem that this was a natural and indeed necessary result of the shift in emphasis as far as the community's purpose is concerned. Since the *civitas Dei,* and more particularly its representative on earth, the church, is charged with the realization of the higher values, there remains only the ordering and the maintaining of peace as the purpose of the secular political community, of the *civitas terrena* and its subdivisions. This is by no means an indifferent task, and the hard phrase which describes the *regnum* as a band of robbers must not be misinterpreted to mean that Augustine completely rejected the state. But he subjects it entirely, in this respect like Plato and the Stoics, to the measuring rod of justice. This measuring rod is no longer represented by some wise men who proudly point to their reason as a justification for their rulership. Instead it is represented by the church, which rests upon divine revelation and which therefore as the higher community is in a position to decide whether a particular ruler or government is acting justly or not.

Thus the decisive turn had come. The community was split. Centuries later this was to lead to the separation of church and state, but for the time being it merely caused an interdependence of state and church within which the unity of Christendom was realized. As far as law was concerned, it was obviously greatly reduced in importance. When Emperor Justinian sometime later (A.D. 530) undertook to have the legal notions of the Romans codified, he simply placed these notions within the Christian framework. No real effort was made to renew the philosophical foundations of this legal system from a Christian standpoint, since it was considered quite unnecessary.[8] Emperor Justinian's enter-

[7] Cf. my *Inevitable Peace* (1948), *passim.*

[8] See Otto von Gierke, *Das deutsche Genossenschaftsrecht,* Vol. III (1881): *Die Staats- und Korporationslehre des Altertums und des Mittelalters und ihre Aufnahme in Deutschland,* p. 128 f. A different view is expressed by A. P. d'Entrèves, *Natural Law: An Introduction to Legal Philosophy,* chap. i.

prise was quite in keeping with the ideas of Augustine, who accepted the empire although he would probably have preferred a federation of free republics in Cicero's sense. But at the same time he wished to subject the emperor to the divine gift of love, for, if that were done, ruling and obeying could happen as a consequence of love and public life could be conducted as if the state were one great family. For the virtues of a Christian man would then determine the political order. "This would be a status of genuine humility which expected of the state merely protection of the peace, maintenance of welfare, and a moral order, and for the rest did not ask much under what kind of secular government we prepare ourselves for eternal life and heaven."[9]

It is not necessary to be as sharply critical of this outlook as Gierke was, to insist that these theological views had no influence whatever upon the existing legal order and that they did not affect the thought of jurists in any way.[10] For these ideas did reinforce all efforts which sought to make the Roman legal order more humane, as the Stoics had tried to do. This is true even though the patristic writers on the whole tended to accept the existing conditions in state and law. At the same time, one basic problem in legal philosophy is answered by all the church fathers uniformly in the sense of classical philosophy: the question whether positive law must be considered true law. Augustine formulated the negative answer to this question particularly clearly when he wrote: "Mihi lex esse von videtur, quae justa non fuerit" ("It seems to me that that which would not be just is not law"). This thought recurs in a variety of forms in Augustine and is developed by him. What is more, Augustine applies this idea not only to the individual statute but also to the law as a whole and declares in this connection that law can be understood only as an emanation of justice (*Civitas Dei* xix. 21).

But in contrast to Ambrose and Lactantius, Augustine further

[9] Cf. Troeltsch, *Die Soziallehren der christlichen Kirchen*, pp. 148–78.

[10] See the discussion in Bks. ii and xix of the *Civitas Dei;* note the link to Cicero and Stoic natural law in this respect.

believed that there must be a clear distinction between law and morals or ethics. The positive law (*lex temporalis*) does not punish sin but merely the violation of the order of peace within a particular rule, whether such rule be *imperium, regnum,* or *res publica.* The coercive power of positive law therefore was interpreted by Augustine definitely in the sense of the Roman legal tradition with the obvious limitation that it is restricted to the relatively unimportant realm of this world, whereas the truly important realm is that of eternal life which is subject to the eternal law (*lex aeterna*). Thus ordinary positive law is restrictive and merely prevents evil but does not make men good. Even so, it would be a mistake to think that there was no connection between morals and law, beween the *lex aeterna* and the *lex temporalis.* On the contrary, the eternal law of God places limits upon all positive law which the latter may not transgress without losing its quality of law. But this positive law permits much that the law of God forbids and punishes. This contrast is powerfully stated by Augustine: "Quod fieri per leges licebat, quia id nec divina prohibuit et nondum prohibuerat lex humana" ("What by laws is permitted to happen, because divine law does not forbid it, and human law not yet") (*Civitas Dei* xv. 16). The distinction was considered by Augustine to be related to the highest matters.

The doctrines of Augustine represent the most important jurisprudence of the patristic school of writers, but it would be a mistake to believe that these docrines exhaust their thought. Tertullian, Origen, and Cyprian, to mention only three important thinkers, had very original ideas about law and the legal community.[11] Tertullian, the jurist, worked out the legal aspects of the Christian teachings and of their precedents in the Old Testament, while Origen, the Alexandrian, the Greek, sought to fit the Greek *polis* community into the edifice of Christian faith. But the "fathers of the church" did not, on the whole, contribute much to the development of the philosophy of law as such, nor did the

[11] For these patristic writers, cf. Salin, *op. cit., passim.*

Gnostics and their archenemy, Plotinus.[12] Only the Christian Middle Ages, confronted as they were by the task of comprehending the law of the church and the law of the empire, and along with them the local laws and customs as a new unity, made a novel and decisive step forward in this field.

[12] On the Gnostics see the magistral treatment by Hans Jonas, *Gnosis und spätantiker Geist,* Vol. I (1934); Vol. II, Part I (1954). On Plotinus see F. Altheim, *Aus Spätantike und Christentum* (1951).

VI. *Law as the Mirror and Part of the Divine World Order*

THOMAS AQUINAS AND THE SCHOLASTICS

In spite of a great richness of detailed formulations, the legal philosophy of the Middle Ages is of an extraordinary uniformity in essentials. It culminates in the legal philosophy of Thomas Aquinas, who devoted a long section of the *Summa theologica* to law.[1] Basically, this legal philosophy is being taught to this day by those Catholic thinkers who see in the system of Thomas Aquinas the perfect expression of the *philosophia perennis*. For, at least in the field of legal philosophy, the transition from Augustine and the Platonic elements contained in his thought to Thomas Aquinas and his Aristotelian point of view shows a great deal of continuity, the more so since Thomas Aquinas in the field of law frequently maintains medieval notions and rejects Aristotle. We find something similar in the field of political thought; for here Thomas Aquinas, in contrast to Aristotle, leans toward monarchy, although this monarchical inclination is modified by a recognition of the importance of constitutional limitations to implement the restraints imposed by the church on behalf of Christian justice,

[1] Besides the works cited in the Bibliography, the following studies concerning Thomas Aquinas deserve the attention of the student of his legal philosophy: M. Grabmann, *Die Werke des hl. Thomas von Aquin*, in *Beiträge zur Geschichte der Philosophie und Theologie des Mittelalters*, Vol. XXII, Parts I–II (1931); P. Mandonnet, *Des ecrits authentiques de Saint Thomas d'Aquin* (2d ed., 1910)—see also the same author's (with J. Destrez) *Bibliographie Thomiste* (1921); Jacques Zeller, *L'idée de l'état dans Saint Thomas d'Aquin* (1910). For the works of Thomas Aquinas in English, one would consult for the *Summa theologica* the standard edition published by Benziger, of which a handy extract of the main questions concerning law was published by Regnery, while for the *De regimine principum* the translation by Dr. B. P. Phelan (with introduction) published for the Institute of Medieval Studies is best. For the Latin text, two good editions of both works, as well as the commentaries on Aristotle and others exist; one is that published by Marietti (Rome); another is that of the Biblioteca de Autores Cristianos (Madrid). Most of the quotations in the text are my own translations; the orderly systematic arrangement of Thomas Aquinas' work makes specific reference rather unnecessary. "*ST*" refers to the *Summa theologica*, of course. Mention should be made of A. P. d'Entrèves' admirable *Aquinas—Selected Political Writings* (1948).

more especially in the spiritual realm.[2] The role of the church in its relation to government persuaded Thomas Aquinas, as it did most thinkers of the Middle Ages, that natural law is of decisive importance, for only with such a more general norm above the positive law was there any hope of bringing about some measure of Christian justice. However, within this general framework, Thomas Aquinas, in contrast to Augustine and following Aristotle, interpreted the political order as a natural emanation of human sociability and reason. It will be recalled that Augustine saw all government, no matter how organized, as a consequence of sin, primarily justified by the spiritual task of assisting the church in its struggle against this sinfulness of man by commanding and punishing. Aquinas stressed the positive, constructive, and creative role of the political order. I say political order rather than state because I regret the long-established habit of speaking of medieval government as a state when nothing justifies this sort of anachronism. For medieval thought there were princes, lords, rule, and government (*principes, domini, dominium, regimen*). These were the subjects of political thought. Characteristically, the political study of Thomas Aquinas is called *De regimine principum*. Like many others of its kind, it deals under this title with the government of princes.[3] The difference is of considerable importance for legal philosophy because in the concept of the modern state unrestricted legislative power is central. Yet it was precisely such unrestricted legislative power which medieval natural law denied to the prince, and, within the narrow limits it set for recognizing any legislative authority, it tied the prince to co-operation of the estates. Really crucial was the notion that all law was basically legal custom and that legislation had only the function of clarifying and elucidating such customary law. And since the executive in the sense of modern administration

[2] When writing the earlier German edition of this book, I was still of the opinion, as are most writers in the field (cf. Phelan, *op. cit.*, Introd.), that Thomas Aquinas favored monarchy as a form of government, regardless of constitutional limitations. This view I no longer consider tenable, and I shall hope to show this at some length before long. See the interesting article by Katherine Archibald, "The Concept of Social Hierarchy in the Writings of St. Thomas Aquinas," in *Historian*, XII (1949), 28–54.

[3] See Phelan, *op. cit.*

did not play an important role either—a central bureaucracy such as that characteristic of the modern state was only faintly beginning in the thirteenth century—the main task of the prince, aside from war and foreign relations, was the effecting of justice through his being the highest judge and meting out the punishments connected with the enforcement of the law. It is only within this framework of a primarily judicial government that the legal philosophy of medieval and natural law can be comprehended.

If one asks what the specific content of the legal philosophy of Thomas Aquinas and the Scholastics was, one may note first that it can be comprehended only within the general framework of Scholastic cosmology and ontology. Since we cannot deal here with this vast and complicated subject, it is desirable to indicate the general frame within which the law of man finds its place and achieves its meaning. This general frame is, of course, that of Scholastic rational theology, which provides a wide range of speculation for natural reason, provided the limits set by supernatural revelation are respected.[4]

Human law in its different forms implements the divine law, natural law, and eternal law, by dealing with the specific problems of a concrete community. This human positive law is divided into the Roman law, the canon law, the local law of the king, and the customary law. Clearly, Thomas Aquinas had a distinct notion of legislation in contrast to adjudication; it is evident in all his discussion. This must be stated in contrast to the tendency to consider all medieval law as given, but it ought to be equally clear that Thomas Aquinas subjects all political order, that is to say, all government, to the law, or, to put it another way, law is the primary datum within the framework of which all Christian government must move. It is in keeping with this general outlook that he subjects secular authority in the last analysis to spiritual authority. For although Thomas Aquinas was not radically ecclesiastical in his outlook, his views on how to judge the action and

[4] When I speak here of a "rational" theology, I do not, of course, mean what came to be known in the age of rationalism and enlightenment as "rational religion." Rather I have in mind the kind of highly rationalized dogma which employs "reasoning" on an extended scale for supporting the propositions which revelation presents.

behavior of princes were so decidedly moral that, in his opinion, this task must be attributed to the church.

In keeping with this general conception of law, Thomas Aquinas considers four major questions in an effort to define law.[5] First, he asks whether law and the laws (*lex*) are something rational or reasonable. He answers that since law is a rule and a measure of human action it must necessarily be related to reason. As is customary with him, Thomas Aquinas mentions three counter-arguments: one from Holy Scripture, since the Apostle has spoken of the law of the members of the body, and evidently this has no relation to reason. The second argument is derived from the Scholastic doctrine of essence and says in effect that law is neither the power of reason nor a mode of reason nor yet the realization of reason. The third argument rests upon the reflection that law is a command and therefore a matter of will, not of reason. Thomas Aquinas answers all three arguments in a subtle way which cannot be set forth here. It is significant that he observes, on the one hand, that reason must receive its moving force from the will but that reason describes the means which are necessary for realizing the purpose which the will has determined, and, on the other hand, that precisely because the will is "legislating" the will must be subject to law. In view of this consideration, Thomas Aquinas notes that the legal rule *voluntas principis legis habet vigorem* must be understood as being subject to a higher reason, for he says that otherwise the will of the prince would not be law but injustice.

The second main question which Thomas Aquinas treats is whether law is directed toward the general good. His answer is positive. Since law is a rule for human behavior and since the purpose of all such behavior is happiness, it follows that law must necessarily be directed towards the common good. The objections considered by Aquinas are mostly related to the fact that all laws are concerned with particular good purposes and actions and therefore are seemingly not related to the general good but to the well-being of individuals or of a particular group. In his

[5] *ST* ii. 1. 90. 1, reply to objection 3. Question 90 contains the whole discussion here summarized.

answer he insists that all these special goods and purposes are, as purposes, related to the final purpose and end, which for the community is its entire end. In this connection he quotes Aristotle, who called the polis a perfect community and the laws just only when they serve the well-being of the polis. Only the community of the common final end produces a legal order out of the special ends and purposes.

The third main question revolves around the issue of whether everyone's reason is suited to make a law. Thomas Aquinas denies this in view of his answer to the second question, for since a law is directed toward the general good and well-being it can be created only by the reason of all or of the prince acting on their behalf. The rather artificial objections, which seem almost dragged in by the hair, Thomas Aquinas answers in the sense of his previous reply. The general good, which possesses objective existence, can be ascertained only by the community or its representatives. It is perhaps significant that no specific reasons are given for this proposition. The assertion is simply repeated and repeated again, both in regard to the legislative capacity of the multitude and in regard to the representative quality of the prince.

Without going into details, the fourth main question to be mentioned inquires into whether publication is of the essence of law. Aquinas answers very explicitly that this is the case. His argument is that, since law contains the rule which applies to those who are subject to it, such rule must be brought to their knowledge if it is to have any obligatory force. This rule is derived from canon law, which Thomas Aquinas cites in this connection.

On the basis of this fourfold analysis, Thomas Aquinas establishes his definition of law. A law is an ordering of reason for the common good, made public by him who has to take care of the community: *quaedam rationis ordinatio ad bonum commune, ab eo qui cura communitatis habet promulgata.*[6] The rationalism of

[6] *Ibid.*, Art. 4, Answer. The next quotation is from *De regimine principum* i. 18. The entire discussion is crucial. Note also *ST* ii. 2. 60. 6.

the great Scholastic is clearly apparent in this definition. The element of will is completely subordinated to the reasonable basis of all law. Such a viewpoint leaves open the question of what the situation is in connection with rules which are evidently contrary to reason. At this point, the church as the guardian of spiritual and related values has an important function to fulfil. "Kings must be subject to priests," Aquinas wrote. It is the task of the church to make sure that the princes, as I have already said, act in accordance with Christian views and the Christian order of life. Should they fail to obey the admonitions of the church, they must be disobeyed. In that case, their commands cease to be laws.

Are the subjects, then, called upon to resist? Yes, in case of excommunication. "Therefore, as soon as a ruler falls under sentence of excommunication, for apostasy from the faith, his subjects are *ipso facto* absolved from his rule, and from the oath of fealty which bound them to him" (*ST* ii. 2. 12. 2). But that is not all. Obedience, to be sure, is a precept of both the divine and the natural law (*ST* ii. 2. 104. 1), and therefore a religious duty. It is the old argument that there would be no order possible, if there were no obedience. "Man is bound to obey secular rulers to the extent that the order of justice requires" (*ibid.* Art. 6). But there is an important limitation. "If such rulers have no just title to power, but have usurped it, or if they command things to be done which are unjust, their subjects are not obliged to obey them; except, perhaps, in certain special cases, when it is a matter of avoiding scandal or some particular danger" (*ibid.*). It is a view we find restated in various forms again and again; it is the logical consequence of any doctrine which maintains that law is antecedent to government and limits it.[7]

The dangerous consequences of such a doctrine for the legal order, which were strikingly illustrated in the generation follow-

[7] See for a significant discussion of this, Carlyle and Carlyle, *A History of Medieval Political Theory in the West,* Vol. III, chap. v, and John Dickinson, Introduction to his edition of *The Statesman's Book of John of Salisbury, Being the Fourth, Fifth, and Sixth Books, and Selections from the Seventh and Eighth Books, of the Policraticus* (1927), esp. pp. lxvi ff.

ing Thomas Aquinas both in the Babylonian captivity of the pope and in the conflict with Emperor Louis of Bavaria, soon led to a sharply opposed doctrine. Its metaphysical side found expression in the great struggle over nominalism and realism. William of Occam (1280–1349) was the most acute representative of the view that the universals, the general concepts, are not real (*realia*) but merely names (*nominalia*).[8] Sense impression and other human experiences are actually given, and names are derived from them, but reality is separate and apart and independent of these names. This viewpoint, which destroys the foundation of a rational theology (the problem turns up again in the Reformation in a more acerbated form), has great importance for legal philosophy. For practical reason becomes, in such a context, an expression of pure will, and the connection between pure reason and acts of the will is destroyed. The will of God is the last and final ground of all law and all laws. Even a great sin cannot be understood by means of pure reason. Such a doctrine frees God of all rationalizing objections; the matters of faith are mysterious. Furthermore, what applies to God and his unfathomable will is believed to be true by analogy for human society. The legal order and its laws are here and are valid because those who are in authority have willed it so. In this perspective, the authority of the emperor cannot be contested as long as he is emperor by right and legitimacy. The thoughts of Occam are linked here with those of Marsilius of Padua (1275–1343?).[9] Marsilius builds his

[8] For Occam, see Georges de Lagarde, *La naissance de l'esprit laïque au declin du moyen âge*, Vols. IV–VI (1946), dealing with Occam's "individualism"; Max A. Shepard, "William of Occam and the Higher Law," *American Political Science Review*, Vol. XXVI (1932), 1005 ff., and XXVII (1933), 24 ff., and the literature cited there. Cf. also Henry O. Taylor, *The Medieval Mind* (1919), II, 548 ff., and the thoughtful comments by Ewart Lewis in her *Medieval Political Ideas* (1954), a skilful set of selections. See also Carlyle and Carlyle, *op. cit.*, Vol. VI, Part I, and Alois Dempf, *Sacrum imperium* (1929), Part III, chap. iv.

[9] For this, see Alan Gewirth, *A Defender of Peace: Marsilius of Padua* (1951); C. W. Previté-Orton's Introduction to his edition of the *Defensor pacis;* Alberto Checchini and Noberto Bobbio, *Marsilio da Padova: studi raccolti* (1941); De Lagarde, *op. cit.*, Vol. II (1942), dealing with Marsilio; A. P. d'Entrèves, *The Medieval Contribution to Political Thought;* and L. Stieglitz, *Die Staatstheorie des Marsilius von Padua—ein Beitrag . . .* (1914).

argument upon a naturalist interpretation of Aristotle in the sense of Averroës, that is to say, not colored by Scholastic thinking. Law and the laws owe their validity in the last analysis to the will of the people, which decides either directly or by elected representatives what shall be law. The validity of law is derived from the person who participates in its creation. However, the people are seen rather more aristocratically than democratically, as is suggested by his well-known qualification concerning the *valentior pars* (i.e., the *sanior et melior pars* of the medieval tradition). In this connection, Marsilius emphasizes the procedural aspects of law, which are not similarly stressed by Aristotle or in the Aristotelian tradition. This is an aspect which was to assume major significance in later political and legal thought, being to some considerable extent rooted in institutional peculiarities of the feudal period as epitomized in Magna Carta (see below, chap. ix). It is striking that immediately and at this early period the danger of positivism rears its head: law is essentially coercive command.[10] Such coercive command constitutes the essential "form" of a law, regardless of its content. When such a command is joined to adequate sanctions—punishment, in Marsilius' terms—then we have law, whether affirmative, prohibitive, or permissive. The underlying distinction between formal and material aspects, and the related dichotomy of peace and order as contrasted with justice, was to have far-reaching consequences, as will appear in the sequel.

The stress upon the command aspect of law in the formal sense is of course closely linked to Marsilius' emphasis upon "popular" participation. It made him a major influence in the development of conciliar theory, which basically attempted to apply thought on law and legislation to the law of the church. Limitations of space forbid our more detailed exploration of this significant practical

[10] Gewirth, *op. cit.* 1, 134; on p. 135 Gewirth rightly observes that "Marsilius' positivism thus consists not in a denial that there are objective norms of justice but rather in an insistence upon not confusing those norms with the precepts which effectively function as laws in the state." This interpretation has recently been challenged by Mrs. Ewart Lewis, "The 'Positivism' of Marsiglio of Padua," *Speculum,* XXXVIII (1963), 541–88. On the problem of the *valentior pars,* cf. C. H. McIlwain, *The Growth of Political Thought in the West* (1932), pp. 302 ff.

consequence.[11] But let it be added that Marsilius specifically insists that a law is useless when it is not obeyed and that a law has the greatest chance of being obeyed when it has been adopted by a majority of the people. Marsilius cites Aristotle as the man who explains that that law is the best which is the result of the common consultation of the citizens: the son of an Italian city-state recognizes in the thought of the Athenian the legal reality of his own political home.

Unfortunately we cannot explore here the interesting problems presented by the question of how the jurists, more especially the postglossators, developed and transformed this metaphysical argument. Nor can we trace the connection with the doctrine of Azo (around 1200) concerning the *imperium merum* as the exercise of local power. It is an interesting doctrine from the viewpoint of legal philosophy because it points in the direction of the problem of sovereignty which later, in the thought of Bodin and others, was to play such a great role.[12]

To sum up, we might say that the Scholastics, regardless of whether they considered law and the laws as an expression of will or of reason, attributed not only to the prince but to the people a decisive role. All strict absolutism is alien to the Middle Ages. Law is believed to be above the political, that is to say, the governmental, order. The prince is primarily the highest judge as far as the inner order of the legal community is concerned, and the exercise of his office as judge depends upon his recognition of law as an eternal order of being. This order of being (*ordo*) is the true meaning of Christian natural law.

[11] See Paul E. Sigmund, Jr., "The Influence of Marsilius of Padua on XVth-Century Conciliarism," *Journal of the History of Ideas,* XXIII (1962), 392–402, esp. p. 398. The key passages of Marsilius on these issues are found in his *Defensor Pacis,* Dictio I, chap. xii, esp. para. 3: "legislatorem seu causam legis effectivam primam et propriam esse populum seu civium universitatem aut eius valenciorem partem . . . valenciorem inquam partem considerata quantitate personarum et qualitate in communitate illa super quam lex fertur. . . ."

[12] Compare for these matters the classic discussion in Friedrich Carl von Savigny, *Geschichte des römischen Rechts im Mittelalter* (6 vols., 1851–81). Further interesting material is contained in Otto von Gierke, *Das Deutsche Genossenschaftsrecht,* Vol. III. See also Myron Gilmore, *Argument from Roman Law in Political Thought, 1200–1600* (1941), and below, chap. vii.

VII. *Law as a Historical Fact*

THE HUMANISTS

The natural law which medieval theology and philosophy had evolved, which Thomas Aquinas had most profoundly formulated, which the later medieval jurists had used as the fixed and established basis for their general thoughts on law, this Christian natural law received its first serious challenge from the historical-minded Humanists of the sixteenth century. Their enthusiasm for classical antiquity made them search out in various authors, notably Cicero, what might be the precise meaning of the well-known juristic passages in the *Corpus juris civilis*. Such a search led them, inescapably, into Stoic natural law. But besides this rediscovery, or should we say re-emphasis, of Stoic views of the law of nature, there emerged at the same time a clearer insight into the processes of creating the law and more particularly of legislation, for these two aspects of law depend upon a historical understanding of the growth of law.

Actually, there had already occurred, a century before the great juristic Humanists, a turning toward a more historical view of the law in the jurisprudence of Sir John Fortescue (1400–1476). For he, reflecting upon the political situation in England, as contrasted with that of France, had turned for an explanation to the specific historical conditions of English legal development. More particularly, in his work *De laudibus legum Angliae*, Fortescue, who as a high judge was familiar with the practical enforcement of the law, had clearly stated that the better statute laws of England were the result of a better method of creating law. He emphasized that what brought this about was the work of a parliament representing the people in conjunction with the practice of the Inns of Court conscious of the legal traditions of the land. For such a parliament both interpreted and amended the law. This government according to law, in which the laws and hence the law come into existence only with the consent of the people's representatives, he designated a *regimen politicum et regale* and he contrasted it with the *regimen tantum regale* as it in his opinion existed in France. That such a contrast between England and France did not rest upon a very clear understanding of the actual political institutions of France at the time is less interesting than that it reflected a reaction toward certain tendencies which were manifesting themselves there and which were eventually to culminate in France's royal absolutism. It therefore suggests a sense of historical development.[1]

Thus, even before 1500, the antithesis between English and Continental legal thought was clearly defined; it was to exert a continuing influence upon the evolution of European juristic thought. I expect to return to this contrast in two later chapters (ix and x). As far as the Humanistic jurists of the sixteenth century are concerned, this problem of the historical uniqueness of particular systems of law takes a more general turn. The belief that every legal system is the creation of a particular political community, as had been presumed in classical antiquity, is intertwined with the cosmopolitan tendencies of the Stoics in a manner which does not seem very consistent at first. But the enthusiasm for a purer Latin is in part the reflection of an enthusiasm for one's own vernacular, which in turn is related to an interest in the legal institutions of one's own nation. For it was the interest in reinforcing the royal power and authority in France which lent a certain impetus to the rediscovery of political ideas that had flourished in the heyday of Roman antiquity. The situation was somewhat different in the case of those German and Italian Humanists who emphasized the autonomy of the city republics in ancient Greece.[2]

[1] Fortescue explicitly refers to Thomas Aquinas' terminology to reinforce this distinction, however, and his links to established medieval patterns of thought must not be neglected. See *The Governance of England, Otherwise Called the Difference between Absolute and Limited Monarchy,* edited with Introduction, Notes, and Appendixes by Charles Plummer (1885, 1926).

[2] Cf. especially Ulrich Zasius (1461–1535) of Freiburg. For him see Erik Wolf, *Grosse Rechtsdenker der deutschen Geistesgeschichte* (2d ed., 1944), I, 55 ff.

In the center of this contrast, we find the doctrine of the *merum imperium,* which is of crucial importance for the legal views of the Humanistic jurists. This doctrine already had, as we have noted (chap. vi), played a great role among the glossators and postglossators. But now it came into its own. Men like Guillaume Budé (1468–1540) and Andrea Alciati (1492–1550) based their legal philosophy upon the rediscovery of the later Roman concept of *imperium* which was to become of greatest importance for the purely secular authority of a national ruler. Alciati particularly developed these notions.[3] He resumed the old controversy between Azo and Lotharius and demonstrated on the basis of his study of the sources, and hence of a purified text, that Lotharius, contrary to the prevailing opinion, had interpreted the right of *imperium* as belonging to the *princeps* or ruler and that he had merely intrusted the *merum imperium* to his subordinate magistrate. These views, which are shown in a long and very learned discourse by Alciati to have been the correct ones, depend basically upon the fact that the concept of property (*dominium*) was at this time once again approaching the one that had been prevalent in the days of the Roman Empire. This kind of property concept is in sharp contrast to the medieval and feudal tendency to confound property and rulership.[4]

But such details, even though politically speaking they stand in the center of the jurisprudence of these historical-minded Humanists, must not prevent us from seeing the real essence of this whole movement in two other characteristics. For there is, on the one hand, the return to original sources and, on the other, the understanding which the study of the sources yielded, namely, the understanding of the historical development of law. In very much the same spirit in which Erasmus undertook to uncover the true text of the New Testament in order to derive therefrom the true Christianity, Alciati was seeking to free the well-known text

[3] See his *Paradoxa* (1518), Bk. VI, chaps. vi–viii. See also Myron Gilmore, *Argument from Roman Law in Political Thought, 1200–1600* (1941), pp. 85 ff.

[4] For the concept of property, see Walton Hamilton's imaginative discussion in the *Encyclopedia of the Social Sciences;* cf. also C. F. von Savigny, *Das Recht des Besitzes* (4th ed., 1822), for a classic treatment.

of the *Corpus juris* of all the embellishments of an interpretative gloss and to interpret it anew with the aid of historical, philosophical, and literary sources of classical antiquity. For our own historical sense, stressing as it does the uniqueness of the past, there is involved here a denial of genuine historical interpretation. The glossators and postglossators were in a very modern way much more nearly right when they interpreted the Roman legal material in the sense of the institutions and customs of their times. On the other hand, one must not forget that the Humanists too were in the service of their time insofar as they were concerned with rediscovering the law of a more rational and bureaucratic society such as imperial Rome had been and Europe was now becoming. For such a law was much more suited to the requirements of early capitalism than were the legal institutions of the disintegrating feudal system.[5] It is therefore justifiable to say that behind this learned façade there was taking place a struggle for the "right" law in the sense of a law which would be appropriate to the conditions of the times. The place of Scholastic and theological reason was being taken by historical reason, which in turn opened the road to the basic philosophical questions of modern natural law.

If one reviews the work of three leading scholars who were typical of Humanist jurisprudence, namely, Alciati, Zasius (Ulrich Zäsi, 1461–1535) and Cujacius (Jacques Cujas, 1522–90), one finds that the Italian, the German, and the Frenchman are quite different in style and attitude but that they share a common philosophy of law. For the Humanists continued to be deeply attached to the thought that there is one law which is valid for all men. This idea, indeed, is anchored in the very foundation of Humanism. (Christian Humanism, it might be added, rarely went as far as the Greek Sophists in asserting that man is the measure of all things, as Protagoras had done. But man and his life on earth were put into the foreground of attention. How could this

[5] See for this Otto von Gierke, *Das Deutsche Genossenschaftsrecht,* Vol. IV, and the famous discussion in Werner Sombart, *Der moderne Kapitalismus* (5th ed., 1922), I, Part I, 334 ff.

be otherwise if the "delight to be alive"[6] was to become reality and often did become reality?) In order to make concrete the idea of one universal law, these Humanists declared Roman law to be the basic source of such an all-human law. Again and again, Zasius returned to this central idea, as indeed did Alciati and others. And since the *Corpus juris civilis* appeared to be resting unequivocally upon a natural-law basis, these Humanists did not have to develop a philosophical doctrine of natural law of their own.

But what the Humanist legal scholars did was to advance the "reception" of Roman law very much indeed. They were often later reproached for this, especially in the period of the Romantics, for from the latter's point of view it appeared as if the creative spirit of the people, the "folk spirit," had been falsified or corrupted.[7] Understandably, a view which interprets the law essentially in national and cultural terms finds it hard to accept or indeed to condone the Humanists' cosmopolitanism. What is more important, the Romantics' outlook cannot "comprehend" the Humanists' because people who take this national view forget that Germans, Englishmen, and Frenchmen are, after all, men, and that, in spite of all variations of a national or regional kind, there still remains the question whether there might not be legal conceptions and legal institutions common and suitable for all men.

It is a curious but undeniable fact that these historicizing Humanists tended, as theorists of law, to be very dogmatic, even when they clearly recognized the historical development of Roman law, as was certainly true of Alciati and his school. The most important among the historicizing Humanists, Cujacius was characteristically unworldly in his preoccupation with scholarly problems. When, in the great controversies of his day, he was occasionally asked what was his point of view on Protestantism, he had the habit of replying: "Nihil hoc ad edictum praetoris."

[6] For Ulrich von Hutten and the background of his celebrated expression, see Hajo Holborn, *Ulrich von Hutten* (1929).

[7] But see the modern work on Savigny, cited below, chap. xv, n. 5.

Basing his thought upon an extraordinary knowledge of Roman history and literature, he directed his whole effort toward clarifying the development of this law and interpreting the several texts within its general context. His work[8] is in some ways the most remarkable that historical legal scholarship has ever achieved. But this great treatise at the same time reduced the practical influence of the *Corpus juris civilis.* For now its position was made quite relative to its time and place. In this respect there is a very strong contrast between Cujacius and the other Humanists, such as Zasius, for whom, as I have said, Roman law had a very general human importance.[9] The fact that the positive Roman law was thus made relative robbed it of its philosophical quality and deprived its general sentences of universality. Perhaps one could even say that the development of law and legal philosophy parallels that of general philosophy, for just as general philosophy more and more was taking the place of theology, so here we find a gradual turning from the legal dogmatism of Roman law to a more general legal philosophy. What this means is that the older Christian natural law was about to be replaced by a secular and philosophical natural law. At the same time, we must recognize that in the sixteenth century the importance of man-made positive law became fully visible, as contrasted with all natural law. Thus we can see that the historicizing Humanists by their scholarly labors cleared the field, so to speak, for the doctrine of sovereignty in which insight into the legislative aspects of law became fully realized.

[8] See *Observationum et emendationum libri XXVIII* (1536 and later).

[9] For this general development, see Wilhelm Dilthey, *Einleitung in die Geisteswissenschaften,* in *Gesammelte Schriften,* Vol. I (1922), Bk. II.

VIII. *Statutory Law against Natural Law*

THE DOCTRINE OF SOVEREIGNTY IN BODIN, ALTHUSIUS, AND GROTIUS

The philosophical detachment of law from its religious foundation was carried through in its most decided form by Jean Bodin (1530–96). In recent years several writers have attempted, on the basis of careful textual studies, to describe Bodin as a representative of a largely medieval political theory which built essentially upon the traditional basis of natural law and constitutional customs. This view cannot be accepted. In spite of all contradictions and the extraordinary confusion of his work—Bodin is one of the most unclear writers in the history of the philosophy of law—Bodin always maintains his central position clearly. This position is effectively expressed in his famous definition of sovereignty. "Sovereignty is the absolute and perpetual power of a republic," he wrote, and a republic is "a government based on the laws of nature" and is one of several households of that which they share in common. The sovereign power (*puissance souveraine*) which Bodin makes the center of his theory is further defined as the legislative power, and where there is no legislative power, he says, there is no *respublica,* there is no genuine polity, there is no "state," as later writers got into the habit of saying.[1]

The decisive thing in these definitions is that Bodin, though basing his views upon the medieval Christian doctrine of the rule of law which must be above all legal order and government, nonetheless gives the untrammeled making of laws most of his

[1] In the Latin edition of Bodin's main work, *De republica libri sex* (1576), the emphasis is somewhat different. *Respublica* is here defined as *familiarum rerumque inter ipsas communium summa potestate ac ratione moderata multitudo,* that is to say, the multitude of families and of their common property which is moderated by the highest power and by reason. Accordingly, *majestas* (sovereignty) is later on defined as *summa in cives ac subditos legibusque soluta potestas,* that is, as the highest power over the citizens and subjects not bound by laws. I believe personally that one should take the Latin and the French definitions together in order to get the whole position of Bodin, which is confirmed when one reads the text as a whole. For other views, cf. the works cited in the Bibliography, esp. Mesnard.

attention. That there was such a thing as complete innovation in the law had always been recognized, as we have noted, but there is a marked change in emphasis here. With statutory law in the center, the sovereign who is intrusted with making such laws becomes all-important for the order of the polity or commonwealth. This means that, from a philosophical standpoint, law thus posited is much more readily understood as the product of the will, that is to say, the will not only decides but in many respects replaces reason. This certainly was not yet the case in Bodin, for Bodin readily recognized that freeing the sovereign from the laws did not mean freeing him from natural law or the laws of nature. The sovereign was quite definitely subject to these, as indeed he was to the eternal law of God. But the decision as to what was to be considered such higher law—and this is, after all, the crucial decision—Bodin attributed to the sovereign; therefore a really tangible limitation such as medieval times attributed to the ecclesiastical authority no longer existed. The situation is similar regarding the so-called *leges imperii,* the rules of law which determine how the highest power is to be exercised and more particularly what shall be the law of succession. It has lately been popular to speak of these *leges imperii,* these "laws of rule," in analogy to later developments, as constitutional law, and it has then been argued that Bodin therefore subjected the sovereign to the constitution because he subjected him to these *leges imperii.* This is only partially true. His school was, on the whole, very definitely of the opinion that a subjection of the sovereign to any kind of basic law would destroy the essential meaning of sovereignty.[2] For sovereignty ceases to be sovereignty if it is tied to conditions: "summum imperium conditione aliqua vel lege datum summum non est."[3] In this vigorous way, Bodin himself rejected any such interpretation. On the other hand, it is the very essence of modern constitutional law that it defines such conditions. By contrast, Bodin considered sovereignty to confer the right to be able to do anything at all times, to be responsible only to God and nature for any transgres-

[2] Otto von Gierke, *Johannes Althusius und die Entwicklung der naturrechtlichen Staatstheorien* (1880; 4th ed., 1929), chap. iii.

[3] Bodin, *op. cit.*, Bk. I, chap. viii.

sions of divine or natural law. He who is sovereign has the last word. And therefore Bodin defined law very consistently as the command of the sovereign, which as a general rule applied to the subjects and to general matters. Bodin emphasized again and again that the giving of such laws is the very essence of sovereignty, and he offered many illustrations. A senate which truly participates in legislation is a partner in sovereignty. Such an arrangement, in Bodin's view, would undermine the essence of sovereignty, for it must be indivisible. This does not mean that it could not be placed in the hands of a number of persons or even of the people, but it could not be divided, could not be distributed, among several independent organs without ceasing to be sovereignty and therefore being destroyed. No separation-of-powers doctrine can find a place within the context of the Bodinian legal and political philosophy.[4]

All customs and customary law become valid only by the command of the sovereign who confirms them. Thus Bodin clearly states what I have already emphasized, that laws and customs depend upon the arbitrary will of him who possesses the highest power.[5] It has often been remarked, as I have just mentioned, that Bodin does provide for a limitation by *leges imperii* and that Bodin expressly refers to the *lex Salica* in this connection. But the

[4] See for this, *ibid.*: "Hoc igitur primum sit ac praecipuum caput majestatis: legem universis ac singulis civibus dare posse. Neque tamen id satis est, sed id fiat oportet sine superiorum, aut aequalium, aut inferiorum necessario consensu . . . "; similarly: "ut verissime dici possit, summum Reipublicae imperium una re comprehensum; scilicet universis ac singulis civibus leges dare, a civibus accipere numquam . . ." (chap. x); and again: "Diximus jura majestatis eum habere, qui post Deum immortalem subditus sit nemini: quod si cuiquam servire, aut imperanti parere cogatur, seu sponte, seu invitus id faciat, majestatis nomen amittit" (chap. ix). Numerous similar quotations could be given; Bodin returns again and again to this problem. And it follows that no legal limitation can be admitted: "Sic quoque, summum imperium conditione aliqua vel lege datum summum non est, nec legibus solutum; nisi lex aut conditio majestatis dicta divinis aut naturae legibus sit comprehensa . . ." (chap. viii). The power of divine and natural law is maintained only by God himself: "Sed legibus divinis ac naturalibus principes omnes ac populi aeque obligantur, quas qui perrumpere aut infirmare tentabunt, divinae majestatis judicia non effugient" (*ibid.*). It is interesting to trace how Bodin misinterprets the English constitution to make it fit his theory. For this compare chap. xi and what is said below concerning Althusius.

[5] *Ibid.*, chap. x: "Leges ac mores ab eorum, qui summam in Republica potestatem habent, arbitrio ac voluntate pendere."

situation is basically the same as it is in the case of natural law. A strictly legal protection against the violation of the "laws of rule" is not recognized by Bodin, who simply mentions that if such a change of the *leges imperii* takes place, the courts usually manage to restore the law.[6] But what happens when the courts do not manage to accomplish this Bodin does not say, for he does not wish to question the omnipotence of the sovereign, which is based upon his omnipotence in the field of legislation. And therefore Bodin denies that the true sovereign can be restricted by any oaths or can restrict himself by such oaths. The only obligations he accepts are in the nature of private law touching possession and property. The sovereign not only must not but does not violate private property, Bodin thinks, and if he owes something to anyone he pays for it.[7] This argument is somewhat inconsistent, for Bodin maintains that the sovereign is bound to the observation of treaties by natural law, since to everybody must be given what is his own. But I believe that even here Bodin is really stating moral demands addressed to the sovereign, who in his own interest must seek to maintain good faith. A strictly legal protection is lacking, since the sovereign is above all laws. But is he truly above all laws? Bodin makes an important concession: the sovereign is above the law only insofar as law can be changed without someone being thereby cheated: "Principem legibus civilibus derogare posse, dum tamen id fiat sine fraude cujusdam," Bodin says, citing the High Court of Paris.

At the basis of Bodin's legal thought we find a clearly expressed antithesis between laws and the law, between *lex* and *jus*. He does not always stick to this distinction, but there is no doubt that he recognized it. He explains that the laws are quite different and removed from the law. The law (*jus*) is good and equitable without command, but the laws (*leges*) result from the exercise of

[6] *Ibid.*, chap. viii: "Quantum vero ad imperii leges attinet, cum sint ipsa majestate conjunctae, principes nec eas abrogare, nec eis derogare possunt . . . quod si legibus imperii derogatum sit, hoc sarciri solet a magistratibus mortuo principe. . . ." In this connection, Bodin explicitly rejects the constitutional doctrine regarding England: "quod satis est argumenti, concilia ejusmodi nullam habere imperandi prohibendive potestatem."

[7] *Ibid.*, pp. 162–63 (1591).

the sovereignty of him who commands. For the laws are nothing but the commands of the highest power.[8] Therefore the decisive point is this: law as positive statutory law must be clearly distinguished from any kind of law derived from morals and equity. This tearing apart of the two sides of law, which until then had always been considered intimately related and together constituting a unity, parallels in its historical impact the analogous separation of power politics and morals by Machiavelli. And although Bodin sharply rejects Machiavelli, it is undeniable that his precise argument in support of statutory law as the command of the sovereign is just as important a step in the direction of the doctrine of the modern state as that of Machiavelli.

Bodin's basic conception of law and the laws becomes very clear in a less frequently read, but from a philosophical standpoint very interesting, small treatise published in 1578, that is to say, shortly after his main work.[9] It was written much earlier, however, and probably even before his study on the method of historical knowledge.[10] It was his idea in this little treatise to distil from Roman law a kind of universal common law. In contrast to his main work, this brief essay is remarkably systematic and shows the material in clear organization. After a general introduction, Bodin defines jurisprudence as the art of giving to everyone his own and doing it in such a way that human community is maintained. Its form, which constitutes its essence and substance, is nothing but the law. Law is described as the light of divine goodness and reason (*prudentia*). Bodin divides this law into natural law and human law. The first is implanted in everyone since the beginning of mankind and is always equitable and just. Human law is that which men have established according to considerations of utility. The latter is further subdivided into civil law and the law which is common to all nations (*jus gentium*), in both of

[8] "Sed plurimum distat lex a jure: jus enim sine jussu ad id, quod aequum, bonum est: lex autem ad imperantis majestatem pertinet. Est enim lex nihil aliud, quam summae potestatis jussum" (*ibid.*).

[9] See Bodin, as edited by Pierre Mesnard for *Corpus général des philosophes français,* Vol. V, Part III (1951). Kenneth D. McRae will soon publish a new edition of the Knolles translation of 1606, with a learned Introduction.

[10] Bodin, "La méthode de l'histoire," in Mesnard, *op. cit.*

which Bodin distinguishes a *jus antecedens* and a *jus consequens.* The *jus antecedens* is substantive law which may be public or private. The *jus consequens* is procedural law, broadly speaking, and is either provided with a sanction or not. The sanction is the statutory law (*lex*), whereas the *jus sine sanctione* is equity and custom. All this is said of the *jus gentium.* By way of contrast, Bodin says that the *jus civile* is the law which is peculiar to a particular state and for that reason, believe it or not, he would not include it in the art of how to handle law in the sense of *jus* (right)! Thus he states clearly what he showed to be his view in the *Republic* also, where it was covered over by many other considerations: that a clear distinction must be made between the statutory law of a particular state and the law which is common to all people and which is properly *jus.*

For Bodin another concept was of very great importance, namely, *legis actio.* This *legis actio,* or realization of the law, he considered to have two forms, that outside the courts and that within the courts. He brought together a large variety of law-generating acts, such as sacred customs, legislation, institution of courts, and even the several kinds of actions of legal counsel, whereas he considered the judicial *legis actio* to be the application of the law by the judge.

This brings us to the last essential aspect of Bodin's legal philosophy. He attributes to the judge as the custodian of true law a very great role. The exceptions to the competence of the sovereign, such as his obligations under private law, are tied to actions of judges and courts. In such judges and courts there is embodied the Bodinian conception of a sphere of law which is to a degree autonomous vis-à-vis the state. There is no question that we have here distinctly medieval thought elements. But whereas in the Middle Ages the law of the government as the enforcer of the law was seen as separate and unalterable, we now find that this presumably unalterable law has taken refuge with the judges, while the ruler has become the legislator.

In the period after Bodin, the development bifurcates. On the one hand, the absolutists made ever more emphatic the liberation of the sovereign from all laws; on the other hand, the constitutionalists re-emphasized the fact that every ruler is bound by the limitations of natural law and international law as law common to all people.

Despite any limitations which Bodin was willing to admit, the doctrine of the omnipotence of a unitary and indivisible legislative power as the essential characteristic of a well-ordered state meant the end of any genuine participation of estates in the creation of law. That which might be called a "government with estates" (*Ständestaat*) was finished once such a doctrine was accepted. It is therefore not surprising that along with a rejection of the new doctrine, as we frequently find it, particularly in Germany and England, we encounter also the attempt to transform the new doctrine of sovereignty in such a way that the power of the estates is put upon a new basis. Even Bodin had not excluded this possibility but had treated it as a marginal case. To attribute sovereignty to the estates as the rule rather than as the exception was another matter, for thereby the great achievement of clearly recognizing the role of legislation as the essential source of law was retained without adopting the strongly monarchical and absolutist implications which Bodin had derived from this doctrine. It is the great merit of Althusius that he undertook such a presentation of the matter.[11] Of course he recognized the importance of natural law for the legal order, but he attributed only to the people as a whole the power to make the basic laws, to exercise what later was called the power to make and amend a constitution. Only the people therefore could exercise an unlimited legislative power which was truly sovereign (*majestas*). But we must recognize that this power had become something different from the sovereignty of Bodin. It was not, strictly speaking, unlimited by the laws but was directed toward organizing the legal community. The people themselves are, in this connection, not seen as a multitude of individuals but as an organic whole ordered in accordance with medieval tradition, in terms of corporations com-

[11] See my Introduction to *Politica methodice digesta of Johannes Althusius* (*Althaus*) (1932), and Erik Wolf, *Grosse Rechtsdenker der deutschen Geistesgeschichte* (1944), I, 167 ff.

posed of families, guilds, towns, counties, and so forth. It is, however, true that this constitutional legislator is seen as bound only through his conscience by the divine and natural law. There is no higher appeal against his decisions.

This Althusian theory served to provide a generalized framework for the doctrine of resistance to "tyrants," which, though medieval in origin, had taken on new vigor and been given new formulations within the context of the religious wars following upon the Reformation. More especially, Jesuits and Calvinists developed the doctrine into an instrument with which to combat monarchical rulers not belonging to the "true" faith. The entire group were labeled "monarchomachs," obviously a disparaging misnomer for advocates of tyrannicide.[12] As a matter of fact, the actual murder of a tyrant, although the most dramatic, was by no means the most important part of the doctrine. This lay rather in its arguments concerning the limits of law and its attempts to define these limits as well as to develop legally tenable views about possible sanctions. Here we discern the beginnings of a doctrine of limitation and separation of powers in terms not only of the estates but also of the subordinate officials. There are glimmerings of a distinct constitutional order provided with magistral (judicial) safeguards. And it is the defense of such an order, rather than merely the concern with the prescriptions of natural law, which the right, indeed the duty, of resistance implies for Althusius and his precursors.[13]

Many objections were raised against such a popular interpretation, or rather transformation, of the doctrine of Bodin—of the

[12] John D. Lewis and Oscar Jaszi, in *Against the Tyrant: The Tradition and Theory of Tyrannicide* (1957), give the most magistral treatment, though the comprehensive theory of Althusius is hardly mentioned. Besides my own and Gierke's studies, one might add Kurt Wolzendorff, *Staatsrecht und Naturrecht in der Lehre vom Widerstandsrecht des Volkes gegen rechtswidrige Ausuebung der Staatsgewalt* (1916), in which the seminal importance of the doctrine for constitutionalism is stressed.

[13] The text of much of Althusius' major work is being made available in English in an edition prepared by Frederick Carney, which is expected to be published in 1963. Note especially chap. xxxviii. For the broader problems of resistance to the political order and law, cf. chap. xxxiv of my political theory as developed in *Man and His Government* (1963).

law as necessarily in its basic relations established by the people. The most important of these objections were those formulated by Hugo Grotius (1583–1645). We find in Grotius two basic thoughts which are closely related to each other. On the one hand, Grotius, in contrast to Althusius, Bodin, and other representatives of the doctrine of sovereignty, recognized more clearly the role of natural law. On the other hand, he was inclined, as were a number of lesser German constitutional theorists, to divide the sovereign power which Bodin had insisted must be one and indivisible. Grotius developed the concept of a general right to rule in contrast to the particular right to rule (*imperium generale* and *imperium proprium*). He did so in building upon the doctrine found in a number of other writers which is known as the doctrine of dual sovereignty (*majestas realis* and *majestas personalis*). The general right to rule (*imperium generale*) and the real sovereignty (*majestas realis*) Grotius declared to be the property of the *civitas* or politically organized community (state), whereas personal sovereignty (*majestas personalis* and *imperium proprium*) usually belonged to a monarchy but at times to an aristocracy or even to the people.[14]

In the light of this construction, Grotius expounded the theory of a purely secular natural law based upon Stoic doctrine and freed from all ecclesiastical authority. It has at times been asserted in recent years, but I believe incorrectly, that the doctrine of Grotius is hardly different from that of the Spanish Neo-Scholastics of the sixteenth century. The decisive achievement of Grotius was to separate natural law from its Christian and theological basis as it had been understood in the Middle Ages (see chap. vi). Only this freeing of natural law from its religious bonds made it possible for him to place the law outside the bitter opposition which the conflict in matters of religion had created since the Reformation and Counter-Reformation. What Grotius really did was to return to the common and rational basis of all law, which we have already seen to be generally recognized by the Human-

[14] Cf. Gierke, *op. cit.*, chap. iii. See also James Brown Scott, *The Spanish Origin of International Law* (1934), Part I, chaps. i, vi, for what follows.

ists as they rediscovered the Stoics. It is upon this general view that Grotius based his treatment of international law as a law binding all sovereigns by reason. He developed this, his most celebrated body of ideas, in his famous book on the law of war and peace. While thus exploring the problem of sovereignty regarding the relations between states, Grotius rounded out in a very important way the reflections of Bodin and Althusius, who had been preoccupied with the internal order and structure of states.[15]

In contrast to Catholic natural-law doctrine and even in contrast to the most radically rationalist representatives, who always and naturally retained the idea of a spiritual role of the church, Grotius developed a rationalistic eclecticism which he set forth in a work, celebrated in his time, dealing with the truth of the question of religion.[16] "He recommended tolerance in all dogmatic controversies and had respect for all positive religions as long as they recognized one God and his immortal soul."[17] This work was an expression of his passionate desire for peace, which he considered a task of religious significance. That these Grotian views were different from the Neo-Thomism of a Suárez[18] his own time understood very well and hence recognized the consequences for legal philosophy.

But, to sum up briefly, such a natural law, derived from pure human reason, binds the sovereign only through his conscience; no institutional guaranty can be derived from it. If thus the sovereign becomes independent of any spiritual legitimation, such a natural law provides no protection against the omnipotence of the state and its ruler. Justice is subordinated to order and thus to the will of him who possesses the authority to make the laws.

[15] *De Jure Belli ac Pacis* (1625). The refinement of international law and the principles of legal philosophy connected therewith as we find them in Pufendorf, Burlamaqui, Vattel, and others must unfortunately be neglected here. Regarding Pufendorf's views of natural law, see below, chap. xiii, where a few additional points are made concerning Grotius.

[16] *De vertitate religionis Christianae* (1627).

[17] See Erik Wolf, *op. cit.*, p. 238, translation my own.

[18] Francisco Suárez, *Tractatus de lege ac Deo legislatore* (1612).

IX. *The English Constitutional Tradition*

SIR THOMAS SMITH AND RICHARD HOOKER

In one of the few references to other writers found in his famous discourse on civil government, Locke speaks with high respect of Richard Hooker (1553–1600), whom he calls the judicious Hooker. Although primarily a theologian, Richard Hooker is among the most important legal philosophers of the English-speaking world. Like Sir Thomas Smith (1514?–77), Hooker belonged to the age of Queen Elizabeth I. He reinterpreted the political and legal theories of Thomas Aquinas to fit them into Anglican Protestantism.[1] In doing so, he created the foundation for a modern constitutionalism resting upon tradition. The concrete form of this constitutionalism was established by Sir Thomas Smith in his *De republica Anglorum*, in which he authoritatively interpreted the political and governmental systems of the Elizabethan Age.[2]

Sir Thomas Smith, in his concise little book, develops the basic notions which Sir John Fortescue had established when, in the fifteenth century, he praised English political and legal practice because the English constitutional order rested upon the participating co-determination of the people. To recall, Fortescue con-

[1] The treatise by Richard Hooker, *The Laws of Ecclesiastical Polity*, is actually incomplete. We have the first five books; of the remaining three, there have been attempts at reconstruction, and it is generally believed that the eighth is largely available to us in the form which Hooker would have given it. Compare the standard edition of the *Works* by John Keble, which was reissued in a revised edition by R. W. Church and Francis Paget (7th ed., 1888); cf. also *Hooker's Ecclesiastical Polity: Book VIII*, ed. R. A. Houk (1931). The Introductions to these editions are important. See also A. P. d'Entrèves, *Riccardo Hooker: Contributo alla teoria e alla storia del diritto naturale* (1932).

[2] Sir Thomas Smith, *De republica Anglorum* (1583); a critical modern edition, with important Introduction by L. Alston, was published in 1906. Cf. the discussion of Smith in J. W. Allen, *A History of Political Thought in the Sixteenth Century* (1928), pp. 262–68, where he is placed within the context of "theories of the constitution" (Part II, chap. x). Cf. also the discussion in George L. Mosse, *The Struggle for Sovereignty in England* (1950), pp. 21 ff.

trasted this kind of system with what he believed to be the royal absolutism of the French. Though historically quite inaccurate, this sharp contrast with France was an important part of the thought of English constitutionalists. Sir Thomas Smith, like Sir John Fortescue, was keen about it and spoke with some knowledge of the facts, since he had come to know the French situation in the course of a legation to the court at Paris.

Behind the customary pride of Englishmen who cherished their English freedom, we find in Sir Thomas Smith a clearly developed doctrine of the omnipotence of "the king in parliament" or even simply of the parliament. Of this we must speak at some greater length. Smith attributes to the parliament a quite unequivocal capacity to represent the people at large. He declares every Englishman is present in this parliament either in person or by a delegate. And when he says everyone, he means everyone from the prince on down to the lowest person. For this reason, consent of the parliament may be taken as the consent of everyone.[3] He rounds out this general proposition by a longish description of the procedure of the English parliament. It is noteworthy that he stresses the fact that "no slanderous or offensive words may be used; otherwise the whole house protests and declares that such speech is contrary to the order of the house."

The clear delineation of the position of the parliament must not, however, be misunderstood as implying modern parliamentarism and the sovereignty of parliament. For one thing, he is talking about the king *in* parliament; together the king, lords, and commons possess the highest power in legislation, finance, and adjudication. But the crown possesses two further powers, namely, that of appointing officials and that over war and peace. Obviously there is here indicated a conscious recognition of a separation of powers which in fact is being rationalized in the tradition of the theory of the mixed form of government. For legal philosophy, the judicial and the legislative powers are naturally of the greatest interest. There has been a good deal of argument on whether parliament was considered by Smith primarily a

[3] Smith, *op. cit.*, Bk. II, chap. ii.

legislative or a judicial body. If one studies the text carefully, one sees clearly that Smith attributes to the king in parliament both these powers and that he subjects the complicated medieval relationships to a very detailed examination. But what is more important is that he clearly recognizes the separate role of legislation as the making of law and that he clearly distinguishes it from adjudication. In addition, Smith asserts a complete sovereignty toward other sovereigns which is quite in keeping with earlier law and the statutes adopted under Henry VIII and Elizabeth I. No English king ever received the crown from an emperor or pope, so the argument runs, and therefore the king does not recognize any prince or potentate of this earth as his overlord. The secular constitutional state as the one and only creator and guarantor of the legal order is clearly apparent here. But the further problem of who, in the case of a conflict between crown and parliament, should have the last word remains unresolved in the treatise by Sir Thomas Smith. This problem in fact did not present itself as long as there was agreement on basic questions. But in the case of religion there was no such agreement; indeed, there was sharp disagreement. Yet under Elizabeth I there was still hope that these antagonisms might be overcome.[4]

The most important intellectual labor in this general area was done by Richard Hooker. His work is very notable for its almost Scholastic explorations of the theological foundations of legal philosophy. Richard Hooker was, like any good Englishman, preoccupied with the expressly practical and governmental problem, and more especially with the question of church government. Indeed, it is perhaps one of the most interesting aspects of the

[4] Charles H. McIlwain, *The High Court of Parliament and Its Supremacy* (1910), pp. 124 ff., following Alston, *op. cit.*, has learnedly argued that Smith "failed to grasp the meaning of the growing legislative activity of parliament" (p. 127) and that "Sir Thomas Smith was too near the events that were leading to legislative sovereignty to perceive their trend." He does so in opposition to James Bryce, *Studies in History and Jurisprudence* (1901), p. 553; Frederick Maitland, *Constitutional History of England* (1908), pp. 254 ff.; and Frederick Pollock, *First Book of Juprisprudence* (1929), pp. 247 ff., all of whom claimed that Smith had recognized the legislative supremacy of parliament. The truth lies, as so often, in the middle, as stated in the text.

Reformation in England that it emphasized so much more than the reformers had done on the Continent the concrete problem of church government and authority. In keeping with this emphasis, Richard Hooker was much concerned to prove to the Puritans that they were wrong on specific points in their criticism of the ecclesiastical settlement of Elizabeth as well as in general. He tried to show that a rational proof could not be established for their refusal to obey the ecclesiastical law. We cannot explore these questions in detail. What is decisive is that the practical problem led Hooker to explore the general philosophical question of a legitimate exercise of power. It was by facing this question that he became an important theorist of constitutional lawmaking.[5] In order to give a firm basis to his argumentation, Hooker had to try to deal with the nature of law and of legislation. His way of approaching the problem is both complicated and facilitated by the fact that the English word "law" covers not only what the Continental lawyer meant when he spoke of *lex* or *loi* but also what was designated by the term *jus* or *droit*. However, even in Hooker, right is recognized alongside law, but of course right carries non-legal, ethical, and moral implications. This dual nature of law explains much in the argumentation of Richard Hooker. He could not derive the obligation of the law only from the right to rule of him who is responsible for positive legislation. Nor could he explain it by the reference to truth and reason which natural law contains. It was Hooker's genius to try to combine these two elements and to infuse all with a profoundly reasonable spirit of moderation.

Hooker sees the law, the norm of human community, within the broad cosmological framework of a world which is universally ordered by law and hence reasonable. We see here clearly the Thomistic foundations of Hooker's thinking. It is very important for the development of jurisprudence in the West that Hooker

[5] Cf. Mosse, *op. cit.*, pp. 17 ff. Francis D. Wormuth, in his able *The Origins of Modern Constitutionalism* (1949), neglects Hooker's contribution, but it is fully set forth in F. J. Shirley, *Richard Hooker and the Contemporary Political Ideas* (1949); cf. also Peter Munz, *The Place of Hooker in the History of Thought* (1952).

thus brought about a combination of the scholastic and rational conception of law with the traditional conception characteristic for the common law (see next chapter); for originally the latter was not very readily compatible with the former. What Hooker really attempted was to eliminate Thomas Aquinas' stress on papal authority in connection with his legal and rational conception of the world and man. He wished to supplant it with a political or governmental authority which rests upon the consent of the people, the citizens of the state. Thus the traditional king in parliament takes the place of the ecclesiastical power in interpreting the law of nature, since the prince, according to Lutheran and Anglican views, is the head of the church. This consent of the king in parliament is, as we shall see in a moment, believed by Hooker to be of a very general nature. It can be tacit consent, and it need not rest upon an explicit decision of the people or their representatives. Yet even though somewhat indistinct, the secular predominance and indeed omnipotence of a united people, as the final authority, comes into view. It was grounded, as we said, in the general philosophical insistence upon the importance of law, an idea which places legal norms in clear parallel to natural laws and sees both of them as willed norms of right conduct. At the end of the first book of the *Laws of Ecclesiastical Polity,* which is primarily devoted to these questions, Hooker sings a veritable paean of praise for the law: "Of law there can be no less knowledged, than that her seat is the bosom of God and her voice the harmony of the world: all things in heaven and earth do her homage, the very least as feeling her care, and the greatest as not exempted from her power: both angels and men and creatures of what condition so ever, though each different in thought and manner, yet all in uniform consent, admiring her as the mother of their peace and joy."

Hooker, like the Scholastics and like his contemporaries, the Spanish Neo-Thomists such as Suárez, looked upon law as a coherent system of the world as a whole. This system is composed of several constituent parts: (1) God's eternal law, (2) the natural laws, (3) the laws of the angels, and (4) the laws of men. This last category, the laws of men, is further subdivided into the law of reason, statutory law, customary law, and international law. All these laws are held together by reason, which is the basis of them all. Their obligatory quality is related to reason, but whereas God's eternal law and the laws of nature are unalterable and inexorable, the laws of angels and men not only are subject to changes but can also be violated and transgressed. The reason is that man with a part of his being belongs to the natural order of the animal kingdom, but with the other part he belongs to the kingdom of God. Hooker, as a pronounced believer in freedom of the will, reinforces these views much in the spirit of the Scholastics and the Humanists. He rejects the radical dogma of the Reformation. The binding power of statutory law, customary law, and international law he bases upon a rational law of nature, the law of reason which Hooker clearly distinguishes from the other law of nature which creatures follow without reference to reason. It is only the former, the rational law of nature or law of reason, with which we will be further concerned. Man's readiness to accept this law of reason Hooker explains as the Stoics had done by the fact that human reason guides man and does so more particularly because of man's desire to become like God. This thought, both hopeful and rationalist, leads Hooker to assert that whatever is, is good. The effort to achieve perfection is an effort at improvement and therefore good. Everything seeks improvement and is therefore good.[6]

That "the laws of well-doing are the dictates of right reason" (I, vii, 4) is the central thought around which Hooker groups his whole argument. Man cannot want what he considers false and bad. Wrongdoing is the consequence of a lack of insight. That

[6] "And for this cause there is in all things an appetite or desire, whereby they incline to something which they may be; and when they are it, they shall be perfecter than now they are. All which perfections are contained under the general name of goodness. And because there is not in the world any thing whereby another may not some way be made perfecter, therefore all things that are are good" (*The Laws of Ecclesiastical Polity,* Bk. I, chap. v, par. 1). References to this work hereafter include only figures, referring to book, chapter, and paragraph, respectively.

does not mean that correct insight necessarily leads to right action, for a prejudice derived from sense experience may interfere (I, vii, 4–6). If it is asked how one can know what is good and right, Hooker answers that such knowledge is derived either from an understanding of the grounds and reasons of the action or from signs and tokens: "The most certain token of evident goodness is if the general persuasion of all men do so account it," writes Hooker, and again, "the general and perpetual voice of men is as the assent of God Himself. For that which all men have at all times learned nature herself must needs have taught" (I, viii, 3). These facts, Hooker thinks, explain why it is so difficult for a common error to be eliminated; only when we are able to penetrate causes, having formerly been guided by signs and tokens, does that take place.[7]

Having made these general philosophical observations, Hooker is now in a position to define the law as "a directive rule onto goodness of operation." Rational laws are ordinances of reason, and Hooker is very insistent that such rational laws can be known and understood by reason without any aid from revelation. This law of reason contains all that men know on the basis of their natural understanding, and it guides them in their actions. "Wherefore the natural measure whereby to judge our doings is the sentence of reason, determining and setting down what is good to be done" (I, viii, 8). This law of reason is something which Hooker is convinced no man can reject once he has comprehended it, nor is it easy to find men who have not at least some inkling of it. "Law rational therefore which men commonly use to call the law of nature meaning thereby the law which human nature knows itself in reason universally bound unto, which also for that cause may be termed most fitly the law of reason; this law, I say, comprehendeth all those things which men by the light

[7] It is not without interest that Hooker at this point cites a great mystic, the medieval philosopher Nicholas of Cusa, who, he says, declared that the common sense of all men is universally recognized. The work of Nicholas of Cusa to which he refers is the *Directio veritatis,* which is found in the *Opera* (Basel, 1565).

of their natural understanding evidently know, or at leastwise may know, to beseeming or unbeseeming, virtuous or vicious, good or evil for them to do" (I, viii, 9).

Upon this foundation, which shows that nature gives laws which are suitable to live by, Hooker erects his theory of the legal community. Such a community does not necessarily rest upon a contract, but besides being founded upon the sociable instincts of man, it rests upon an order which, whether explicitly or tacitly agreed to, determines the nature of the association and of the living together. This order, says Hooker, we call the law of a commonweal; it is the true soul of a political body. It is evident that such a formulation, which almost word by word corresponds to that of Bodin or Althusius (cf. chap. viii), makes the constitution the basis of the legal community. Such a constitution as the basic legal order may be customary or statutory, but in any case its validity rests upon the rational insight of men into the nature of human "living together." And because this is so, the individual cannot resist this order in a legally justifiable way. His reason tells him that his co-operation is reasonable. For all human laws are either rational and then binding because of that, or they are binding because they possess the legitimation of a constitutional basic law which rests upon consent. Hooker is thus led to advocate an absolute duty of obedience to the laws, as Erasmus had done before him and Kant was to do later. Thus, in spite of his insistence upon the necessity of the consent of the people or its representatives, Hooker sees no legal possibility of escaping the duty of obedience. Even when this consent or recognition has completely disappeared, there is no right of resistance possible. "I see not how the body [politic] should be able by any just means to help itself."[8] We are confronted here with a dilemma which re-

[8] See *op. cit.*, VIII, ii, 10. It is perhaps not without interest to consider the passages immediately preceding this statement: "May then a body politic withdraw in whole or in part that influence of dominion which passeth from it, if inconvenience doth grow thereby? It must be presumed, that supreme governors will not, in such case, oppose themselves, and be still in detaining that, the use whereof is with public detriment: but surely without their consent. . . ." I shall add another statement that reinforces the "medieval" line of

currently troubles those legal philosophers who are oriented toward the law. It is not of much practical consequence that Hooker repeatedly insists that those rules are not laws at all which no public consent has made into such (e.g., I, v, 8). And yet this insistence upon consent is important, for it is upon this need for consent that Hooker builds his demand for the participation of parliament, of councils as the representatives of the whole people, which is of course in keeping with the traditional English order. Such councils or parliaments sanction new legal norms which are from time to time necessary to implement or alter customary law. Such assent may be tacit or it may be explicit, but it is in one form or another necessary, for otherwise the rule lacks an essential feature of a true legal norm. To quote two or three key passages: "The lawful power of making laws to command whole politic societies of men belongs properly onto the same entire societies," and again, "laws they are not therefore which public probation hath not made so," and finally, "laws therefore human of what kind so ever are available by consent" (I, x, 8). Much of what Hooker writes sounds like the voice of a later time, the voice indeed of the eighteenth century. But it is equally important to recognize that it is an echo of much older thought, the echo of the voice of Cicero. And what is particularly important is that, just as in Roman constitutional law, consent can only be fully operative when the constitutional order makes certain by the establishment of representative bodies that such consent possesses an institutional guaranty.[9]

To sum up, I might say that Hooker and Sir Thomas Smith formulated the juristic and philosophical implications of the par-

---

reasoning: "Happier that people whose law is their king in the greatest things, than that whose king is himself their law. Where the king doth guide the state, and the law the king, that commonwealth is like an harp or melodious instrument, the strings whereof are tuned and handled all by one, following as laws the rules and canons of musical science" (VIII, ii, 12).

9 We must pass over the interesting comments of Hooker concerning international law which, anticipating Grotius, remind one of the great Spanish rationalists of the sixteenth century. See for this Scott, *The Spanish Origin of International Law* (1934), *passim,* and my comments upon it (chap. viii, n. 12, above).

ticular English political development. Law is seen as the basic constitutional order, resting on popular consent; from it all other laws derive their obligatory quality. However, what these constitutionalists have to say on this score is still untouched by the great controversy as to who has the last word, the king or the parliament. But in what they say we can discern the essence of the conflict which later on produced the revolution.

X. *Common Law against Natural Law*

JAMES I, EDWARD COKE, AND FRANCIS BACON

The conflict over the respective spheres of king and parliament developed soon into the complex struggle of James I with his estates and courts, in which Sir Edward Coke (1552–1634) played a decisive role. The antithesis of English legal development found a very distinct expression here. The peculiar dialectics of the issues sketched in the previous chapter thereby are fully unfolded. In this struggle, Sir Francis Bacon (1561–1626) took a strong and open position in favor of the views of the king. By his arguments, the basic political and legal conflict was philosophically sharpened and deepened. James I's attempt to prove that the absolute ruler by divine right is reasonable—an attempt with which he cast aside the skilful compromises of the Elizabethan reign as they had been expressed by Sir Thomas Smith and Richard Hooker—was unable to gain the upper hand against the legal views of Sir Edward Coke, who was sure of his hold on English tradition and who founded his arguments upon concrete law. Part of the reason for the failure of the king must, however, be seen in the very practical power of the English legal guild, which stood behind Coke and later expressed its views effectively in parliament. The peculiar English conflicts resulted from the fact that the parliament can be imagined only as an institution of positive law which includes the king. Coke himself is quite explicit about it, and he states it in much the same way as did Sir Thomas Smith. In the first chapter of the fourth book of his *Institutes of the Laws of England,* which deals with parliament as the highest court, Coke opens the discussion with the statement that "this court consists of the King's majesty . . . and the three estates of the realm, that is of the Lords Spiritual . . . the Lords Temporal. . . . The third estate is the Commons of the Realm. . . ." It is very interesting to note how strongly Coke emphasized the judicial function of parliament and how much he treated it together with the legislative one as lawmaking or establishing law. For if one were to consider lawmaking as merely legislating, one would hardly be fair to Coke's view. Coke generally believed that "of the power and jurisdiction of the parliament for making of laws and proceeding by bill it is so transcendent and absolute, as it cannot be confined either for causes or persons within any bounds."[1] We can see here, if we for the moment disregard the judicial aspect, how in England the legislative power as the decisive power in the state is not intrusted to one authority but is quite consciously divided among several authorities which together are seen as representing the people as a whole.

Even the power of parliament as the source of all law is, according to Coke's view, subject to a very decisive limitation, namely the limitation by the common law. In Bonham's case (1610), Coke formulated this position with particular sharpness: "It appears in our books [of law] that in many cases the common law will control the Acts of Parliament and sometimes adjudge them to be utterly void; for when an Act of Parliament is against the common right or repugnant or impossible to be performed, the common law will control it and adjudge such act to be void."[2] And since this common law can become valid only through a decision of the courts, one can see here the clear basis for judicial review of legislative acts as it later became reality under the written constitution of the United States.

Behind this general view we find a philosophical position which must not be confused with the law of nature. For the law of

[1] *Institutes,* Part IV, chap. i, p. 36. Coke is, of course, dealt with in all the classical treatments of English legal and constitutional history, such as Holdsworth (1903), Maitland (1908), and Stubbs (1880). Dean Roscoe Pound emphasized his role in *The Spirit of the Common Law* (1921) as well as in his recent *The Development of Constitutional Guarantees of Liberty* (1957). C. D. Bowen has given a brilliant portrait of Coke, *The Lion and the Throne* (1956–57), with remarkably full documentation and extensive bibliography.

[2] *Reports,* Vol. VIII. See also T. F. T. Plucknett, "Bonham's Case and Judicial Review," *Harvard Law Review* (1926), and S. E. Thorne, "Dr. Bonham's Case," *Law Quarterly Review* (1938).

nature as it was developed in the seventeenth century in continental Europe was something very different and was, in fact, advocated by James I and Bacon. In a famous controversy between James I and Coke, which occurred in 1616 when Coke was Lord Chief Justice, this problem of the role of the law of nature was the central point at issue. Coke had once told the King that the common law protects the king, whereupon the King shouted angrily at him, "That is a traitorous speech. The King protecteth the law, and not the law the King. The King maketh judges and bishops." Indeed the King got so angry, shaking his fists at Coke, that the Lord Chief Justice "fell flat on all fower" before the King and asked his pardon. That was in 1608.[3] When, in 1616, Coke argued similarly—and again it was a question of the jurisdiction of secular and ecclesiastical courts—James told Coke that "although we have never studied the common law of England, yet we are not ignorant of any points which belong to a King to know." We have here, in the King's view, the notion that natural or common-sense human reason suffices for the interpretation of the law. Coke had already rejected this view. In the 1608 conflict with the High Commission he had argued that cases involving the "Life, or Inheritance, or Goods, or Fortunes of his [the king's] Subjects are not to be decided by natural Reason, but by the artificial Reason and Judgment of Law, which requires long study and experience . . ." (*Reports,* XII, 64–65). And in the introductory essay to the fourth book of his *Institutes*, where Coke discussed the nature of English government and warned against any rash change in the law, he pointed out that such change was "most dangerous"; for, said he, "that which has been refined and perfected by all the wisest men in former succession of ages, and proved and approved by continual experience cannot but with great hazard and danger be altered and changed."[4] This doctrine of the artificial reason of the law is, as can clearly be seen from

[3] Bowen, *op. cit.*, pp. 302 ff.

[4] For a further discussion of the doctrine of the artificial reason of the law, see Roscoe Pound, *An Introduction to the Philosophy of Law* (1922), and my *Constitutional Government and Democracy* (3d ed., 1950), chap. vi, esp. pp. 103–5.

Coke's statements, based upon an empirical approach to the law which is firmly founded in tradition, such as one might expect from a judge.

The natural-law viewpoint of the King, which is also represented by Bacon, is clearly opposed to Coke's view. Bacon in his *Advancement of Learning* had suggested that all who have written about laws and the law had always been either jurists or philosophers, never statesmen. The philosophers had, so he said, dreamed up imaginary states, while the jurists were always talking about the institutions which they found in the existing law, "what is law and not what ought to be law." Bacon added very pointedly that the wisdom of a lawmaker is something very different from the wisdom of a jurist. And while he was quite willing to recognize the judge as a lion, he maintained that there should be "lions under the throne." By contrast, it is the task of the statesman to shape law by reason and to develop it in this sense. Bacon was quite ready to admit that the common law is above the statutory law; but superior to and above both, he said, is reason.[5] Clearly there is here a similarity of thought to that which we find in Continental philosophy of law and natural law. The sentences in Bacon could have been written by Grotius or Pufendorf, even by Rousseau or Kant. They were grounded upon the new conception of sovereignty. Bacon and King James wished to prevent the judiciary, including the parliament, from limiting sovereignty. It was precisely this limitation which Coke and the English lawyers had in mind. At some point, Coke declared that sovereignty and the common law were not good bedfellows. This is a matter which calls for further exploration.

In English law and in the sharp conflict between James I and Coke we find alongside the expression "sovereignty" that of the "prerogative," a term which occurs frequently in the Latin literature of the times. This right of prerogative has been maintained in English constitutional law to the present day, although it now occupies a very marginal position indeed. Locke defines preroga-

[5] Francis Bacon, *Works* (Philadelphia, 1842), II, 169 (in "The Case of the Post-Nati of Scotland").

tive as "the power to act according to discretion for the public good without the prescription of the law and sometimes even against it."[6] Such a prerogative is even today the right of the crown, but of course it is restricted to a very narrow scope indeed. Still it is not unimportant that this last trace of an emergency power remains.[7] King James, as well as his councilors, wanted to bring this power of the prerogative continually into play in all situations in which, according to his opinion, public welfare made it necessary. A radical representative of royal omnipotence, Crowell, declared in his *Interpreter* (1607) that the prerogative was a special power and a privilege of the king, for the king had a right to his crown, a right above all other persons and above the common law. And although the king might, out of political prudence, avoid the exercise of this ultimate power, there could be no doubt that the king of England was an absolute king. All learned students of the science of politics counted the power to establish law and to give laws among the signs of "the highest, the most absolute" power. True, King James recognized upon request of parliament in 1610 that he did not possess any legislative power by himself, but he nonetheless declared in the Star Chamber, meeting secretly in 1616, that he, the king, possessed this power, that the king, as far as his prerogative was concerned, was above the law, and that the judges did not possess the right to occupy themselves with such questions as touched the prerogative. In this connection he declared significantly that the prerogative concerned "the mystery of state," and he added that the exercise of this power resulting from the mysteries of state was strictly reserved to the king. James I developed this idea further in his *True Law of Free Monarchies.* Here too he conceded that the king might avoid the exercise of this power but that this would be merely an act of grace and not a matter of law. In law, the king's power was by divine right, and it rested upon

[6] See *Of Civil Government,* Book II, "An Essay concerning the true original, extent and end . . . ," chap. clx. See also Francis D. Wormuth, *The Royal Prerogative: 1603–1649* (1939), esp chap. v, and my article on prerogative in *the Encyclopaedia of the Social Sciences.*

[7] See W. Ivor Jennings, *Cabinet Government* (1936), chap. xii.

divine law. It could not be questioned any more than the omnipotence of God. Hence the king could suspend all positive law by royal prerogative.[8]

This viewpoint encountered the sharpest objection of Coke and the lawyers. Coke completely rejected the doctrine of the royal prerogative. Prerogative, he said, was valid only within the framework of the law. The matter became a primary issue in the debate concerning the Petition of Rights at the time when parliament was engaged in a struggle with James's son, Charles I, in 1628. The House of Lords had tried to arrive at a compromise concerning the abuses of the Crown, more particularly, arbitrary taxation, arbitrary imprisonment, arbitrary searches and seizures, etc. What the parliament meant by "arbitrary" was, of course, without any authority in law through act of parliament. As a compromise, the lords tried to construct a concept of "intrinsical prerogative." If, then, the king considered it necessary, for reasons of national security, to arrest persons and to perform other acts contrary to the law, one ought to petition him to give such persons a quick trial as a matter of grace. To this Coke replied with great anger, "Admit this intrinsical prerogative and all our laws are out," and further, "What is intrinsical prerogative? It is a word we find not much in the law." He added, "this intrinsical prerogative is entrusted to the king by God. It is *jure divino*. No law can take it away. King John strove in vain for this power." Coke would not deny that the king possesses the prerogative. He was much too good a lawyer for that. But he stated that "the king has only the prerogative which the law of the land grants him."[9] It is clear from this that, in Coke's opinion, prerogative is not, like sovereignty in monarchical continental Europe, a very general power to do whatever is necessary but a power carefully circumscribed by law and the constitution and limited thereby. The prerogative can be employed only on distinct and definitely defined occasions. It is

[8] Cf. for this Charles H. McIlwain's Introduction to *The Political Works of James I* (1918), where the work of James I cited in the text is also found.

[9] See *Reports,* XII, 76. How extensive this was can be seen from what is said in the case *Non obstante,* as quoted by Wormuth, *op. cit.*, pp. 56–58.

obvious that Coke was struggling to grasp clearly the concept of a basic law or constitution, but he again and again got lost in medieval notions which were then still very much alive in English law. It is perhaps particularly striking in this connection that when Charles tried to get out of the difficulty precipitated by the unlawful acts which the Petition of Rights was seeking to remedy by reconfirming Magna Carta and six other statutes, the House of Commons in reply resolved: "We sit now in Parliament and therefore must take His Majesty's word no otherwise than in a parliamentary way; that is, of a matter agreed on by both Houses, His Majesty sitting on his throne in his robe with his crown on his head, scepter in his hand, and in full Parliament. . . ."[10] This was medieval doctrine, and it tried to resolve the conflicts over who had the last word, the king or the parliament, by reasserting the idea that the king and parliament must act together. But suppose they did not. This was the question which only the revolution succeeded in settling. What is clear—and it may serve as a summary—is that neither the common law nor the natural law were found adequate to cope with the legal issues presented by the conflict between the king and parliament. The issue of sovereignty would not be gainsaid.

[10] See for all this the several documents quoted in S. R. Gardiner, *The Constitutional Documents of the Puritan Revolution, 1625–1660* (3d ed., 1906), esp. pp. 66 ff.

XI. *Law as Command*

HOBBES AND THE UTILITARIANS

The political and legal philosophy of Thomas Hobbes is different indeed from that of Sir Edward Coke, whose views were deeply rooted in the traditional judicial and parliamentary ways. Hobbes possessed only very limited knowledge of English law, which is probably one of the reasons that he has never been a major direct influence among Anglo-American jurists, though his indirect impact is great, owing to the Utilitarians. Curiously enough, and in spite of this lack of relationship to his legal and political environment, Hobbes's legal philosophy is markedly positivist. The only source of law he recognizes is the will of the sovereign. This will is presumably directed toward the carrying-out of prudential rules which are natural in Hobbes's view, but these rules are merely guides for reasonable conduct—rules of prudence, as he calls them. They owe their legal validity to the will of the sovereign alone. For "the laws of nature (as justice, equity, modesty, mercy and in sum doing to others as we would be done to), of themselves, without the terror of some power to cause them to be observed are contrary to our natural passions that carry us to partiality, pride, revenge and the like." Therefore, he believes that "if there be no power erected or not great enough for our security, every man will and may rely on his own strength."[1] In other

[1] This statement is found in *Leviathan,* chap. xvii. The Roman numerals in the text citations refer to this work. The edition by Michael Oakeshott has been used. His Introduction is recommended, though the interpretation is rather daring. In addition to the works cited in the Bibliography, attention should be drawn to a recent French work of exceptional quality, Raymond Polin, *Politique et philosophie chez Thomas Hobbes* (1953). John Bowle has skilfully set Hobbes's thought within the context of the English constitutionalist tradition by his study *Hobbes and His Critics* (1952), while the published first volume of J. W. Allen's *English Political Thought, 1603–1660,* which extends to 1644, unfortunately does not deal with Hobbes, even though his seminal work *De cive* was published in 1642. Allen justifies his omission by saying that Hobbes was "extremely isolated" (p. 49). Allen's treatise is very valuable, though, for the setting of Hobbes's thought.

words, as he puts it elsewhere, there must be "some coercive power to compel men equally to the performance of their covenants by the terror of some punishment greater than the benefit they expect by the breach of their covenant." Hobbes insists in this context that such rules are improperly called laws, for, to speak precisely, "law properly is the word of him that by right hath command over others" (chap. xv). In other words, all laws achieve validity only when a government with the power to command declares them to be valid. In the state of nature, neither law nor justice has any meaning: "Where there is no common power, there is no law: where no law, no injustice" (chap. xiii).

We must explore somewhat more fully the state of nature in Hobbes, for his political and legal conceptions are logically derived from it. This state of nature is a war of all against all. Man is continually worried by the fear of his fellow man. He is full of mistrust and meanness. His only purpose in life is to maintain life, and from this passionate will to live, this haunting anxiety not to suffer a violent death, there results a never-ending struggle for power. Power Hobbes defines as "the present means to obtain some future apparent good" (chap. x). There is no true highest good or *summum bonum* as the philosophers called it, for the happiness of man consists in a continuous progress from one desire to the next, so that each purpose becomes a means to the next one. Therefore, Hobbes declares in a celebrated sentence, "I put it for a general inclination of all mankind, a perpetual and restless desire of power after power that ceaseth only in death" (chap. xi). For all other goods such as wealth and friendship can be reduced to power and upon closer inspection appear to be forms of power. This applies not only to the state of nature but to the life of man in general. In the state of nature, this desire for power leads to the complete isolation of man; when a war is not a hot one, then it is apt to be a cold one. Peace could occur only if the danger of war were eliminated. Hence this state of nature is detestable. For not only are all the advantages of civilization and culture lacking, but there exist at all times a continuous anxiety and a danger of violent death.[2] And Hobbes concludes his description of the state of nature by the famous phrase, "and the life of man is solitary, poor, nasty, brutish and short" (chap. xiii). In reply to the objection that such a state probably never existed, Hobbes is willing to concede that perhaps it never did exist between individual human beings, but it does exist between sovereigns, for they are independent and face each other in the "posture of gladiators." In other words, the state of nature is a construct; it enables us to comprehend how man came to organize a state and to establish law.

In order to escape from this detestable state of nature, the isolated human beings enter into a strange relationship. They make a covenant among themselves according to which they all subject themselves to one sovereign, and they do so almost without condition. The sovereign may be an individual or he may be a group. In any case, the sovereign, once established, acts completely arbitrarily. He makes laws, administers the government, conducts foreign policy and international relations, and decides concerning war and peace. He organizes adjudication, and all of this according to his arbitrary will and preference, while the subjects are passive and obliged to be satisfied. For even the most arbitrary condition of this kind, the most lawless order, is preferable to the state of nature. There is only one condition stated by Hobbes which is very characteristic of his outlook: if the sovereign threatens the life of a subject, then such a subject is entitled to resist, for, in that case, the subject has returned to the state of nature. How far this applies to criminals is not clear in Hobbes; the criminal is evidently, as an enemy of society, in the state of nature; yet Hobbes seems to hesitate to draw the logically necessary consequences. On the other hand, the refusal to serve when conscripted for military service appears to a considerable extent to be within the framework of man's right to self-defense.

[2] This aspect of Hobbes's thought, though generally familiar, has been given particular emphasis by Leo Strauss, *The Political Philosophy of Thomas Hobbes* (1936), esp. pp. 111 ff. Cf. also my review article, "Thomas Hobbes—Myth Builder of the Modern World," *Journal of Social Philosophy*, Vol. III (1938). Cf. also my *Inevitable Peace* (1948), pp. 126 ff.

It is evident that Hobbes's legal philosophy is almost entirely seen as based upon the principle of utility. Only because men have come to recognize peace and order as useful are they ready to accept law and to obey the laws.[3] We have already observed that Hobbes in the *Leviathan* recognizes laws of nature as rules of prudence, and indeed he develops these in considerable detail. They must be understood as insights which the mind, oriented toward self-interest, has derived from the nature of things. Nonetheless, they serve to moderate, if not to modify, the Hobbesian doctrine of sovereignty. For although one might at first think that one could derive from his philosophy a justification for fascist tyranny, this is not, in fact, the case. The policy of a Hitler or a Mussolini would have been condemned outright by Hobbes, for the simple reason that these totalitarian dictators neglected in a senseless fashion the prudential rules, that is, the "laws of human nature." The catastrophe which both brought upon their people as well as themselves Hobbes would have considered quite inescapable and would have described as grounded in the nature of things. The intuitional romantic emphasis upon the will of these political leaders would have appalled him, but probably he would have reacted by mocking them.

Hobbes sees in all social goings-on a very pronounced lawfulness, but the laws involved in this lawfulness are laws of nature in the sense of the law of gravitation. This lawfulness is grounded in the utility which men themselves recognize. It is this situation which Hobbes's definition of power tries to suggest. Therefore the law which the sovereign institutes is essentially a legal order related to consideration of the utility of peace and public security. We have seen that all these laws are considered decisions of the will and that the sovereign has complete power concerning them. Here we find one of the paradoxes of Hobbes's construction. Since the subjects make the covenant only with each other and not with the sovereign, there can never be any question of a breach of

[3] Plamenatz, *The English Utilitarians* (1949), pp. 10 ff. This utilitarian stress on happiness (in material terms) as the basis of utility is the main butt of Kant's argument against Hobbes in his *Theory and Practice*, Bk. II, which may be consulted in my *The Philosophy of Kant* (1949), pp. 412 ff.

covenant such as was suggested by the writers who maintained the right of resistance. For since all subjects have subjected *themselves* to the sovereign, all must be considered as participating in his decision. Theirs is a most comprehensive case of "generic consent." Why should they accept one big terror for many small fears?

Civil law specifically is seen by Hobbes as the law of property, of the *meum* and *tuum*. The civil law consists of rules of what is proper in relation to these. In other words, the sense of the words "good" and "bad" must be sought in positive law. In a long chapter concerning civil laws, Hobbes nonetheless declares that we must exclude from this civil law all that is valid only in a particular legal order, and that we should put under civil law only that which is valid in every political order. "For the knowledge of particular laws belongs to them that protest the study of the laws of their several countries; but the knowledge of civil law in general to any man" (chap. xxvi). He accordingly defines civil law as "the laws that men are bound to observe because they are members not of this or that commonwealth in particular but of a commonwealth." Civil law is that law which contains for every subject "those rules which the commonwealth has commanded him by word, writing or other sufficient sign of the will to make use of for the distinction of right and wrong, that is to say of what is contrary and what is not contrary to the rule." This definition does not really correspond to the distinction between general and particular civil law and therefore presents one of the contradictions in Hobbes's legal philosophy. In this context too Hobbes stresses that laws are a pure decision of the will and that therefore the legislator is not bound by them. He can change them whenever it suits him, or disregard them. Customary law is, in Hobbes's view, law merely by the tacit consent of the sovereign legislator and in no sense hallowed by time or the consent of those who are subject to it. We have already seen that natural law becomes law only by the recognition of political power. Prudential rules are seen nonetheless to contain some kind of validity for all men. And yet, for Hobbes, civil law and the law of nature do, as a result, to some extent coincide. "The law of nature," he writes, "is a part of the civil law in all commonwealths of the world. Reciprocally also the civil law is a part of the dictates of nature." Hence one can say that the law of nature and the civil law contain each other. The law of nature is effectuated by the civil law, and the civil law makes manifest the rules that are contained in the law of nature. Thus the fulfilment of a contract is such a prudential rule, but it is at the same time the basis of the civil law of contracts. Likewise, obedience toward the civil law is a rule of the law of nature. It is therefore not surprising that Hobbes maintains that civil law and natural law are not two different kinds of law but different parts of the same law. At one point he even tries to interpret the difference between them as that between written and unwritten law.

Hobbes attempts to embody traditional English legal thought in his system by subordinating the common law, understood as civil law in his sense, to the king in parliament as the true sovereign. He rejects the opinion of those, however, who would make the parliament without the king sovereign. In short, in the practical application of his ideas he returns to traditional English notions. Nonetheless, he rejects the views of men like Sir Edward Coke concerning the artificial reason of the law. Hobbes thinks that one can study a long time and still be wrong. And if the foundation is wrong, the conclusions drawn will be in error. Therefore, it is not jurisprudence or the wisdom of judges which is truly creative of law but the reason of this artificial being, the commonwealth, which finds representative expression in the commands of the sovereign. The judges have only to ask what is the will of this sovereign. If they fail to do so, they are bad judges and decide unjustly. This passage shows particularly clearly how much Hobbes fits into the continental European and not into the English and American tradition, although we must admit that as far as England is concerned this statement holds true only down to Blackstone and Bentham.

What is more, Hobbes seems immediately to retract what he has just said. For he assigns to the judges the task of interpreting the law of nature. To be sure, the judge has this power only as the representative of the sovereign, but realistically considered, this means that Hobbes assigns to the judges a rather extensive role in the creation of law after all. Nonetheless, Hobbes would unquestionably have sided with James against Coke, for in Hobbes's view, the judge, like any other subject, is never in the position of maintaining his interests against the will of the sovereign. What is more, every judge faces anew the task of re-examining precedents, more particularly in regard to their natural-law ground. For the fact that a judge has made his decision in a legally valid way does not mean that he is necessarily right. The truth of a rule of the law of nature is entirely independent of the authority of a judge. Repeatedly, Hobbes insists that the rules of the law of nature as such possess eternal verity but that this truth is strictly cognitive. In a state only that which has the authority of the judge behind it is valid, and his authority is in turn based upon the will of the sovereign. Once again Hobbes states flatly, "law is a command." In a very real sense, judge and subject are alike in their relation to the law of nature. There is a striking passage illustrating this: "For whatsoever men are to take knowledge of for law not upon other men's words, but everyone from his own reason, must be such as is agreeable to the reason of all men; which no Law can be but the Law of Nature." This is true, Hobbes maintains, although strictly speaking "law is a command," as he insists again and again.

Why, we may ask, is Hobbes assigning to the judge along with the legislator such authority regarding the law of nature? The reason is that natural law is unwritten; it is the one and only legally relevant set of rules the validity of which does not depend upon publication. For since the law of nature addresses itself in its rules directly to the reasonable insight and understanding of every man, it does not require proclamation. All other legal rules are fully validated only by publication, either by word of mouth or writing or some other sign. As soon as it can be verified as the will of the authorities, the duty of obedience is implicit.

Hobbes would link the validity of the legal rule to a clear indication of the intention of the maker of such a rule, for only then can an unequivocal interpretation be secured. But it remains unclear how this can be done. Hobbes is very much aware of the fact that words may have different meanings and that therefore laws are always exposed to the danger of misinterpretation. Yet he would assign to the legislator only the determination of the purpose and, it would seem, the interpretation of this purpose. The judge, Hobbes says explicitly, has only the task of ascertaining the text of the law along with the determination of the facts in the case at hand. It is not surprising, therefore, that Hobbes would claim laymen to be capable of being judges. He refers to the parliament as the highest judge, as well as to juries, and observes that finding the law and the decision concerning it does not depend upon a knowledge of the entire law such as is possessed by jurists. The qualities of a good judge, he thinks, are four: right understanding of the law of nature as equity, contempt for riches, objectivity, and patience.[4] Patience is the capacity to listen and to have a good memory so as to retain, digest, and apply what one has heard. This emphasis upon common sense as the source of good law is clearly related to what Bacon and James I had considered essential. It is obviously opposed to the professional convictions and prejudices of English lawyers (and not only English ones).

If Hobbes retained the verbiage of natural law while draining it of its substance, David Hume (1711–76) is generally credited with its destruction.[5] This is something of an exaggeration, since

[4] It might be interesting to give Hobbes's view concerning the qualities of a good judge *in extenso*. He describes him as follows: "First, he must possess right understanding of the law of nature as equity; secondly, he must possess contempt of unnecessary riches; thirdly, he must be able in judgment to divest himself of all fear, anger, hatred, love and compassion; and fourthly, he must possess the patience to hear, must be diligent in hearing, and must possess the memory to retain, digest and apply what he has heard" (xxvi).

[5] David Hume's works are essentially three, *A Treatise of Human Nature* (1739–40), *An Enquiry concerning the Principles of Morals* (1777), and *Essays, Moral, Political, and Literary* (1777). The references to the first are given by "T," followed by numerals indicating book, part, and section; the references to the second and third, by "E," followed by the page in the edition of 1779 (entitled *Essays and Treatises,* in 2 vols.) in Arabic numerals. Frederick M. Watkins has published a very useful selection under the title,

Hume very clearly recognized three fundamental laws of human nature and generally insisted upon the fact that man had certain traits in common in all times and places. "The stability of possession, its transference by consent, and the performance of promises" are decisive rules: "on the strict observance of those three laws entirely depend the peace and security of human society" (T, III, I, 6). What really distinguishes Hume's juristic outlook is the fact that he rejects the idea that these laws are grounded in reason and insists that "those laws" are "entirely artificial and of human invention" (*ibid.*). Reason, to be sure, recognizes their utility, but "passions" provide them with compelling force. If justice consists in acting in accordance with these laws, then "self-interest is the original motive to the establishment of justice, but a sympathy with public interest is the source of the moral approbation which attends that virtue" (T, VI, I, 2. Italics omitted). Hume was much concerned to show that men are not entirely motivated by self-interest and that what he called benevolence is a primary emotion of man (E, 223 ff. and 261 ff.). It is always present, and the notion of a state of nature which consisted in a war of all against all is a "philosophical fiction" (E, 237). But these emotions are not sufficiently strong, and hence reasoning based upon them does not suffice to provide security. "Had every man sufficient sagacity to perceive, at all times, that strong interest, which binds him to the observance of justice and equity, and the strength of mind sufficient to persevere in a steady adherence to a general and distant interest . . . there had never, in that case, been any such thing as government or political society . . ." (E, 253). But since this is not the case, men need law. Hume notes the parallel between laws and the rules of games: "In societies for play, there are laws required for the conduct of the game . . ."; wherever men have any intercourse with each other, rules are necessary

---

Hume: Theory of Politics (1951), with a good Introduction; the chapter in Huntington Cairns, *Legal Philosophy from Plato to Hegel* (1949), is the most succinct treatment of Hume's legal philosophy that I know of. A discussion relating Hume to the other Utilitarians is found in Plamenatz, *op. cit.*, chaps. ii, iii.

(E, 258). These rules, that is to say, the laws, derive a good part of their obligation from their utility, but this utility is not merely something rationally perceived, as Hobbes and others following him had thought;[6] it has, as already remarked, a firm emotional basis: "it follows, that everything, which contributes to the happiness of society, recommends itself directly to our approbation and good-will" (E, 263). "Utility pleases," in the view of Hume, and to the question of why it does, which Hume puts explicitly, he answers: "It appears to be matter of fact, that the circumstance of *utility*, in all subjects, is a source of praise and approbation: That it is constantly appealed to in all moral decisions concerning the merit and demerit of actions: That it is the *sole* source of that high regard paid to justice, fidelity, honour, allegiance and chastity: That it is inseparable from all the other social virtues, humanity, generosity, charity, affability, lenity, mercy and moderation: And, in a word, that it is a foundation of the chief part of morals, which has a reference to mankind and to our fellow-creatures" (E, 279). The public good, peace, harmony, and order in society, in short, all that a legal order seeks to achieve when it undertakes to realize justice, rest upon our benevolence. The principles of humanity and sympathy are the mainstay, in other words, of the legal order.

Although Hume did not try to formulate an explicit philosophy of law in the strict sense, the foregoing general principles provide something of a foundation. It was Bentham who eventually built on this basis a comprehensive theory of law, as we shall presently see. It remains to say a few words about the general philosophical foundation of these principles. That they rest upon the principle of utility does not suffice; utility can be fitted into a variety of philosophical positions. In the case of Hume, the broader framework was provided by a thoroughgoing skepticism, based upon a radical criticism of reason. We cannot here go into his famous critique of the "law of causation" in the course of which he under-

[6] Hume specifically excuses the overemphasis on self-love (E, 267 ff.) and happiness which is found in many philosophers, but he rejects it, in spite of its "extensive energy."

took to show that all causal relations are inferences from observed sequences of events. What matters to us is that the argument is built upon a radical separation of fact and value and an insistence that reason deals only with the "facts" given by observation, i.e., sense impressions, and by the "passions" of man in action. "It seems evident, that reason, in a strict sense, as meaning the judgment of truth and falsehood, can never, of itself, be any motive to the will, and can have no influence but so far as it touches some passion or affection."[7] The kind of reason, often called "higher reason" which is involved in value judgments Hume proposed to call "nothing but a general and calm passion." Hence the outlook called "strength of mind" implies the prevalence of the calm passions above the violent. Having thus assimilated value judgments and other emotional givens, Hume argues that any system of ethics ought to be built upon "fact and observation" (E, 221). Hume thought that such observation disclosed that the "facts" underlying value judgments are "conventions," and he spent much effort showing the presence of such conventions in the fields with which social science, including jurisprudence, deals. These conventions are variable in the scope of their application, but their validity rests upon "habit." Such habits, in turn, can be traced to their utility. It has been rightly observed that "if the premises of Hume's argument be granted, it can hardly be denied that he made a clean sweep of the whole rational philosophy of natural right, of self-evident truths, and of the laws of eternal and immutable morality. . . ."[8] Yet Hume is not a radical antirationalist; he grants reason wide scope in the determination of human affairs. But his is a "critical rationalism" which trims the limitless pretensions of the "age of reason."[9] This critical rationalism was taken over and developed by Kant (see below, chap. xiv). But its implications for jurisprudence were unfolded by Bentham.

[7] In *A Dissertation on the Passions;* the passions meaning, of course, what are nowadays referred to more usually as emotions or sentiments.

[8] George H. Sabine, *A History of Political Theory* (rev. ed., 1954), p. 604.

[9] Cf. Ernst Cassirer, *Die Philosophie der Aufklärung* (1932), Vol. III, and Preserved Smith, *A History of Modern Culture: The Enlightenment, 1687–1776* (1934).

Many of Hume's positions have remained the working basis of the social sciences to this day.[10]

Jeremy Bentham (1748–1842) has himself told of the great sense of discovery that inspired him when he first read Hume and through him learned of the principle of utility.[11] Bentham was in revolt against the pat, conservative William Blackstone (1723–80), who as his tutor at Oxford had irritated him by his bland, conventional views. Of his celebrated *Commentaries on the Laws of England* (1765–69) it has justly been said that Blackstone "adopted the method of *exposition,* and taught law as it was." By contrast, it could be said of Bentham that he used "the method of *censure,* teaching law 'as it should be.' "[12] The latter, of course, is not jurisprudence in the accepted sense, but Bentham thought of it as the new legal science. In the beginning of his major work, he stated: "Nature has placed mankind under the governance of two sovereign masters, *pain* and *pleasure.* It is for them alone to point out what we ought to do, as well as to determine what we shall do. . . . They govern us in all we do, in all we say, in all we think" (chap. i). This is the radical credo built upon Hume's belief that all action is related to the "passions," and like Hume, Bentham believed that he was an empiricist and that he was building a jurisprudence on the experimental method. Bentham made as little distinction as possible between morals and legislation, basing both on utility. Reason for him, as for Hobbes and Hume, was essentially "reckoning," both in theory and in practice. What he was striving for in the latter realm was a "logic of the will."

[10] Cairns, *op. cit.*, pp. 365, 389; Watkins, *op. cit.*, p. xxv.

[11] Jeremy Bentham, *Fragment on Government* (1776), Introduction; see also *Introduction to the Principles of Morals and Legislation* (1789). References in the text are to this work unless otherwise noted. The classic, though uneven, edition of Bentham's works is by John Bowring (11 vols.), but there are numerous reprints. Besides Plamenatz, *op. cit.*, chap. iv, Elie Halévy, *La formation du radicalisme philosophique* (3 vols., 1901–4; Eng. trans. by M. Morris, 1928), and Leslie Stephen, *The English Utilitarians* (3 vols., 1900), are basic. See also G. De Ruggiero, *The History of European Liberalism* (trans. Collingwood, 1927), Part I, chap. i.

[12] Halévy, *op. cit.*, p. 35; the observations concerning the best method are well worth pondering.

The science of law he believed to be the "most considerable branch" of this new "logic of the will" (Preface).

What Bentham hoped for was an objective science of human behavior. The fact that he did not achieve it is as patent as the fact that in the pursuit of it he developed the most comprehensive critique of an established legal order that was ever composed by any one man. His scorn for the common law was limitless. He called it judiciary law and said that it was "that fictitious composition which has no known person for its author, no known assemblage of words for its substance" (Preface). What he thought followed from its phantomlike quality was that he who wants a complete body of law "must begin with making one" (Preface). It follows readily enough that "the art of politics consists in governing individuals through their own interests, in creating artifices of such a kind that in spite of their avarice and ambition they shall cooperate for the public good." We see here a massive restatement of Hobbes's pessimistic view of human nature; Bentham discarded Hume's emphasis on benevolence and humanity in favor of a radically unitary view of man as motivated by what Hume called self-love; that is to say, each man is preoccupied with his own pleasure and pain, his self-interest.

Any emphasis on self-interest raises the problem of how effective co-operation might be achieved so that human society might become possible. For Bentham, the solution was an "identification of interests," made possible by the legislative activity of government, more especially in the criminal-law field. The criminal law was, characteristically, one of Bentham's preoccupations, and he labored long and arduously over a rational code of criminal law. There are two other solutions possible, Adam Smith's (and Mandeville's)[13] belief in a natural identity of interests and Hume's

[13] Adam Smith, *Theory of Moral Sentiments* (1759), who stressed sympathy as a human motive; Book V of *The Wealth of Nations* (1776) develops his thoughts on government; Bernard de Mandeville, *The Fable of the Bees: or Private Vices, Public Benefits* (1714–29), stresses self-love but argues that it benefits the community. See for this group of writers the study by Simon N. Patten, *The Development of English Thought: A Study in the Economic Interpretation of History* (1910).

fusion of interests by way of the sympathetic emotions.[14] It was, of course, the Benthamite notion of an artificially invented "identification" that maximizes the role of law and government. Passionate reformer that he was, Bentham spent a lifetime inventing detailed legal devices for the improvement of society. Considering the deep conservatism of English society in his time, there was a very real social need for this kind of doctrine. The triumph of Bentham's long struggle was the great reforms which transformed English politics and society before and after 1832.

In the center of such legal activism, an all-powerful sovereign had to function whose commands would be law. It is no accident that Bentham shifted from the benevolent despotism of his youth to the espousal of parliamentary absolutism (aristocracy) and finally to popular mass party action (democracy) in his search for the "sovereign" who would put through his reforms. In a way, there is a curious parallel here to Plato—in spite of the vast gulf which separates the two men philosophically, temperamentally, and environmentally. Plato moved only from the benevolent monarch to the spiritual elite, an aristocracy. Nor did he want to "progress"; rather, he wished to restore. But in the passion for reform and in the belief that men can be made to act right and become good through proper legislation, Bentham and the Plato of the *Laws* are very much alike.

The persuasive vagueness of Bentham's formulations does not withstand any kind of searching criticism. Such questions as, What does the sovereign mastery of pleasure and pain mean? find no answer in Bentham's writings. The celebrated principle of "the greatest happiness of the greatest number" evaporates into thin air, when so simple a question as, What is to be understood by happiness? is asked.[15] It has been rather sharply but nonetheless justly said by a recent critic that "the truth is that it is not

14 Cf. the discussion in Halévy, *op. cit.*, pp. 13 ff.

15 The primitivism of the psychology involved in the reasoning of the Utilitarians, and more especially of Bentham, is so removed from our own thought, shaped by the development of modern psychology and psychoanalysis, as well as by the writings of men like Nietzsche and Dostoevski, that it is difficult for us to appreciate the very real significance of this body of thought.

possible to make sense of what Bentham is saying."[16] The truth is that Bentham is not so much a philosopher as a man of action. Hence his tendency to break into oratorical flourishes. Indeed, the entire utilitarian school, and more especially Bentham, has been characterized by its ablest exponent as "not so much great inventors, as great arrangers of ideas." If the term "inventions" is here taken to mean the discovery of deep philosophical insight, that is very just. But as we have pointed out above, in the invention of specific legal ideas Bentham was more fertile than any other major figure of Western intellectual history.[17]

It remained for a great jurist, John Austin (1790–1859), to spell out the juristic, if not the philosophical foundations of Utilitarianism. He correctly fastened upon the problem of sovereignty and undertook to develop a strictly imperative theory of law—law as the command of the sovereign. In his two major works Austin separates jurisprudence from morals so radically that Hobbes's doctrine of the absorption of natural law by civil law is denied and transcended (as well as Hume's and Bentham's views on this score).[18]

Austin was the founder of the so-called analytical school of jurisprudence. Having based his general theory upon the proposition that law is the command of the sovereign, he limited jurisprudence to an analysis of the more general concepts which occur in any given system of positive law, its rules and principles. In short, like Blackstone he followed the "method of exposition," and in that sense is sharply at variance with Bentham, but Austin rested his exposition upon general utilitarian views. It was the

[16] Plamenatz, *op. cit.*, p. 71.

[17] Halévy, *op. cit.*, p. 33.

[18] See his *Lectures on Jurisprudence* (1869) as well as his *The Province of Jurisprudence Defined* (1832). Besides the many discussions in general reference works, see Ernest Roguin, *La science juridique pure*, Vol. I (1923). See also the discussion by John Stuart Mill, *Dissertations and Discussions*, Vol. III (1875), No. 7. Surely we are not justified in saying that "in fact, Austin did little more than bring together systematically ideas that were scattered through Bentham's voluminous and not always very readable works," as does Sabine (*op. cit.*, p. 684). On the other hand, I would agee with him that "in political theory the chief effect of Austin's work was to attach an exaggerated importance to the theory of sovereignty . . ." (*ibid.*).

first time that anyone in England had undertaken "to deal systematically and critically with the fundamental ideas and forms involved in any developed legal system."[19] Rights and duties, actions of various kinds, and the legal transactions corresponding to them are the subjects of his analysis, greatly refined later by such followers as Sir Thomas E. Holland in England, Wesley N. Hohfeld in America, and Felix Somló in Germany. Austin is necessarily concerned only with the existing institutions of the particular legal system under review (he himself concentrated on the common law and the Roman law); he seeks to distil the essential by classifying the legal data which are given, and he relates them to a hypostatized "nature of the thing." This analytical jurisprudence has held extensive sway in both England and America, and as such has given the development of legal philosophy in these countries a very special slant, until recently. Analytical jurisprudence has always refused to consider law as such and its meta-juristic foundations. It has preferred to deal with specific institutions and has achieved great results in critical analysis of them.[20]

Analytical jurisprudence bears a close relation to what is known on the Continent, and more particularly in Germany, as the "general theory of law." The latter, like analytical jurisprudence, saw as its task the analysis of general legal concepts found in the various bodies of law of a particular legal system.[21] A German

19 Morris Cohen in his article on Austin in the *Encyclopaedia of the Social Sciences.*

20 Leading representatives of the analytical school of jursprudence were: T. E. Holland, *Elements of Jurisprudence* (13th ed., 1925); J. W. Salmond, *Jurisprudence* (1891); J. C. Gray, *The Nature and Sources of Law* (1909); K. Binding, *Die Normen und ihre Übertretung* (4 vols., 1872–1920); Levy-Ullmann, *Éléments d'introduction générale à l'étude des sciences juridiques* (2 vols., 1917–28). See also Hans Kelsen, below, chap. xviii and literature there.

21 Hans Kelsen himself has recognized this kinship to analytical jurisprudence. He is really a philosophical representative of this general point of view. See his *General Theory of Law and State* (1945), p. xv: "The orientation of the pure theory of law is in principle the same as that of so-called analytical jurisprudence. Like John Austin in his famous lectures on jurisprudence, pure theory of law seeks to attain its results exclusively by an analysis

legal philosopher has commented very appropriately: "The legal dogmatist of the nineteenth century saw the center of his work in the establishment and discovery of ever new legal concepts and in the exploration of supposed juristic facts and the legal consequences following from them, as well as the intellectual states corresponding to them, such as *the* state, *the* property, *the* procedure."[22] But in spite of this sharp denial of the broader "philosophical" problems, a philosophic set of issues is implied in the general theory of law. For concepts such as legal subject, legal relationship, and others are, to speak with Kant, cognitional conditions of any kind of legal understanding so that, even if they are empirically derived by comparative methods, they nonetheless demand an answer to the question of their logical value. At this point, Ihering and Stammler and their citicism become crucial.[23]

---

of positive law." Kelsen says, however, that there was a difference, and this difference he believed to be due to the fact that the pure theory of law tries to carry on the methods of analytical jurisprudence more consistently than Austin and his followers had done.

[22] See Fritz von Hippel, "Rechtsphilosophie," in *Einführung in die Rechtswissenschaft* (1949), edited by Rudolf Reinhardt. Compare also the sharp criticism of "Rechtstatsache" as a basic concept in Von Hippel's *Zur Gesetzmässigkeit juristischer Systembildung* (1930).

[23] For the general theory of law, compare more particularly Karl Bergbohm, *Jurisprudenz und Rechtsphilosophie* (1892). The relation to analytical jurisprudence is often neglected. See also below, chap. xvi.

XII. *Law as the Basic Law of the Constitution*

LOCKE AND MONTESQUIEU

Locke's legal philosophy, like Hobbes's, is shaped by the idea of a positive legislation which results from decisions of the will. But this legislation is imbedded in a constitutional law which is given a positive legal interpretation by making it flow from the will of the people. The place of sovereignty is taken by a constituent power as the legitimizing force upon which the constitutional order is based.

John Locke (1632–1704) has given us in his two *Treatises on Civil Government* (1690) only a very general sketch of his basic philosophical thoughts concerning law.[1] He recognized natural law and made it the starting point of his considerations. According to him, its main purpose is to explain the foundation and the maintenance of a legal order. It also proves that the right of the people to establish such a legal order is primary, original, and inalienable. The decisive passage reads: "For no man or society of men having a power to deliver up their preservation, or consequently the means of it, to the absolute will and arbitrary dominion of another, whenever anyone shall go about to bring them into

[1] Besides the *Of Civil Government*, and more especially the second treatise on "An Essay concerning the true original, extent and end of civil government," we now have, as the result of W. von Leyden's devoted editorial labors, John Locke's *Essays on the Law of Nature* (1954). Von Leyden's learned Introduction of more than ninety pages serves as a most important commentary on Locke's philosophy of law. Besides this work, mention ought to be made of J. W. Gough, *Locke's Political Philosophy* (1950). Peter Laslett's studies will, we hope, soon give us a modern critical edition of *Of Civil Government*. See also the excellent chapter in Huntington Cairns, *Legal Philosophy from Plato to Hegel* (1949), chap. x. Otherwise, and for a more extended treatment, A. R. Fox Bourne's magistral biography, *Life of John Locke* (2 vols., 1876), and R. I. Aaron, *Locke* (1936 and 1955), should be consulted. For Laslett's views, see "The English Revolution and Locke's 'Two Treatises on Government,'" *Cambridge Historical Journal*, XII (1956), 40–55. Laslett has also given us a new edition of Sir Robert Filmer's *Patriarcha* (1949), with an illuminating Introduction.

such a slavish condition they will always have a right to preserve what they have not a power to part with and to rid themselves of those who invade this fundamental, sacred and unalterable law of self-preservation for which they entered into society. And thus the community may be said in this respect to be always the supreme power but not as considered under any form of government because this power of the people can never take place 'till the government be dissolved."[2] Supporting all political and legal order, we find as the genuine authority the natural right of man to preserve himself—in a sense this was also Hobbes's idea—and to participate in the founding and molding of a political and legal order which satisfies him—this clearly contrary to Hobbes. Thus the right of resistance has become the right of revolution. But this right is a natural right, is part of natural law, and appears only when the existing order is dissolving. In this connection, it is important that Locke considers the tyrannical transformation of an existing legal order as the beginning of such a process of dissolution. A natural right of dominion which would be based upon conquest he would not admit at all.

Within the framework of such a constitution founded upon natural law, Locke places the legislative power in the center of everything. It is the highest power, the decisive power, the exercise of which determines all important matters. In contrast to the older English tradition, this legislative power is clearly and unequivocally placed above all judicial power, above all customary law, subject only to the laws of nature and reason. The legislative power, therefore, is restricted only by this reasonable natural law. And why? Because this natural law is the legal ground for the creation of the positive legal order. Men, when they accept the political order and leave the state of nature, have brought along their previous natural state of legal autonomy. "But though men when they enter into society give up the equality, liberty and

[2] Chap. cxlix; all references in parentheses in the text are to the second essay, unless otherwise noted. As far as this particular statement is concerned, I undertook a modern reformulation of its generalization in *Constitutional Government and Democracy* (3d ed., 1950), p. 130.

executive power they had in the state of nature into the hands of the society, to be so far disposed of by the legislative as the good of society shall require, yet it being only with an intention in everyone the better to preserve himself, his liberty and property, the power of the society or legislative constituted by them can never be supposed to extend farther than the common good" (§ 131). Because this is so, he who exercises the legislative power must govern according to existing laws and not according to temporary ordinances. Laws must be published and must be known to the people. Neutral and honest judges must decide all controversies according to these laws. The force of the community must be employed only for the execution of these laws at home and for the defense of the community against external enemies. Locke explicitly states that all public power should be used only for peace, security, and the public welfare of the people, and for no other purpose. The first and most fundamental positive law of all political commonwealths is the establishing of the legislative power, exactly as the first and fundamental natural law is the preservation of society and, as far as is compatible therewith, the preservation of each member belonging to it (§ 134). This natural law binds even the legislative power, but apart from that the legislative power is described by Locke explicitly as sacred and unalterable. It is the very core of the entire constitutional order. Law can be created only by this power and by nothing else.[3]

This does not, however, mean that the legislative power, regardless of who exercises it, could arbitrarily dispose of the life and property of the people. On the contrary, no one possesses, according to the absolutely valid law of nature, the power to transfer to somebody else what he does not possess himself. No one possesses absolute power over himself or anyone else, since everyone is limited by the law of nature which forbids him to

[3] This emphasis upon the legislative activity in the time of Locke, and indeed ever since Bodin, stands in striking contrast to our own time's stress upon "policy," the slogan of the absolutists and "Machiavellians" then. Cf. for this my *Constitutional Reason of State* (1957), *passim*.

destroy his own life or to take the life or property of another. The power of the legislator is thus limited, as we said, to the public welfare of the society. And this means for Locke that the law of nature is and remains an everlasting rule for all men whether legislators or others.[4] Yet it remains uncertain how Locke believed this limitation could be made secure. Locke does not envisage a legal sanction apart from the right of revolution. It is the same with regard to property, although Locke explicitly states that no one's property can be taken without his consent. It appears to be merely a rule of the law of nature according to which one of the purposes of society is the protection of property. But there is no institutional sanction; rather, the customary power of the purse is pragmatically expected to take care of the situation. Locke emphasizes one other point: the legislative power cannot be transferred to another, for the people, as the constitution-making power, have decided who should exercise this highest power under the constitution (§§ 132–42).

All in all, one might say that law is largely positive legislation which is made by a legislature for the public good, that this legislative power as the highest power in the commonwealth receives its legitimation from the decision of the people as fixed in the constitution, while this constitution in turn is rooted in the natural right of man to self-preservation. James Harrington had already constructed law in his utopia, *Oceana* (1656), in this fashion—as a positive order of decision-making within the context of a separation of powers.[5] Such a doctrine of the separation of powers was afterward fully developed by Montesquieu in the eighteenth century. We must now turn to his constitutional theory as the basis of his philosophy of law.

The Spirit of the Laws (1748) of Charles-Louis Secondat, Baron

[4] See Huntington Cairns, *op. cit.*, pp. 351 ff.

[5] See the author's *Constitutional Reason of State* (1957), chap. iii. For Harrington, see the standard edition by John Toland (1700). For his biography see H. F. Russell Smith, *Harrington and His Oceana* (1914), the standard treatment, and Charles Blitzer's "The Political Thought of James Harrington" (Ph.D. dissertation, Yale University, 1954), soon to be published by the Yale University Press.

de la Brède et de Montesquieu (1689–1755) is an extraordinarily brilliant work of many facets.[6] Legal philosophy as such is imbedded in and to some extent buried by political, sociological, and historical details. But the basic ideas of Montesquieu are clear and very important. For Montesquieu, too, law is oriented toward the idea of justice and must be judged by it. But it would, in his opinion, not be wise to expect that the positive law as expressed in the laws realizes justice; only an approximation is possible. Therefore, the question presents itself upon what basis such an approximation can be envisaged. In answering this question, Montesquieu turns away from the tradition of natural law, which attempted to give a general answer to this question, and declares that every community must solve this task in response to its own particular spirit; the historical, sociological, political, and economic conditions will shape the solution and must be allowed for by the legislator.[7] We find something of this kind of approach in Pufendorf, but Pufendorf remained within the framework of natural law even though his historical studies tended to push him in a different direction. Montesquieu, on the contrary, clearly has the intention of explaining law and the laws within the context of a particular cultural system.

Behind this modern and relativistic approach, Montesquieu maintains a consistent principle which has general scope. This is the distinction among the three forms of government; the republic, the monarchy, and despotism, and these three are further

[6] This work is now conveniently available in English in the Nugent translation, with an interesting Introduction by Franz Neumann. The original is readily accessible in many editions. I have used *Œuvres complètes de Montesquieu avec des notes de Dupin, Crevier, Voltaire, Mably, Servan, La Harpe, etc.* (1835). References in the text are to *The Spirit of the Laws* by book and chapter. For the general literature on Montesquieu, see the Bibliography. See also Enrico Vidal, *Saggio sul Montesquieu: con particulare riguardo alla sua concezione dell'uomo, del diritto e della politica* (1950).

[7] This prismatic effect of Montesquieu is well reflected in *Montesquieu: sa pensée politique et constitutionelle,* edited by Boris Mirkine-Guetzévitch and Henry Puget in 1948, on the bicentenary of the *Esprit des lois'* publication. See also the special number of the *Revue internationale de philosophie* (1955) dedicated to Montesquieu, and more especially the papers by J.-J. Chevallier, Charles W. Hendel, Robert Derathé, and Sergio Cotta.

grouped according to whether they have a basis in law or not. For republic and monarchy are seen as resting upon law, whereas despotism is not. Obviously despotism or tyranny is, in Montesquieu's view, no legal order at all; dominated by fear, it is altogether condemned by him. It does not possess any laws but only customs (XIX, xii). What this means is that law, and more particularly constitutional law, has a very general, indeed absolute, significance. The famous doctrine of the separation of powers, associated with the name of Montesquieu, belongs in this context. Whether this doctrine is structured monarchically or in a republican fashion, it is decisive that the powers are clearly separated by the basic law and are fixed in their respective functions and jurisdictions. Only under such conditions can freedom be made secure.[8]

It would seem that Montesquieu himself was undecided about the choice between a republic and a monarchy, but I am inclined to think that, in the last analysis, he preferred constitutional monarchy as it existed in England. For such a government, something else is very important besides the separation of powers: the existence of what Montesquieu calls intermediary powers. He particularly emphasizes courts like the French parliaments, estates and other local corporations, and related appurtenances of the "government with estates."

For each of the three forms of government one basic principle is characteristic: virtue for the republic, whether aristocratic or democratic, honor for monarchy, and fear for despotism. Laws must be derived from this basic principle, and they must be shaped in accordance with it. Alongside this basic principle the most diverse concrete conditions must be allowed for, whether geographic, cultural, or other. We see here that Montesquieu combines a rational principle, namely, that of the constitutional legal state, with various laws of nature in order to interpret the laws of each community as expressive of its "spirit." This "spirit"

[8] See for this also *Constitutional Government and Democracy* (3d ed., 1950), chap. x, and the discussion there of the transformation of the doctrine of the separation of powers from Locke to Kant.

is not made absolute as a working principle—as it is by Hegel—but remains relative, and in the last analysis it is subject to the abstract measuring rod of a rational justice.

Laws are further defined by Montesquieu as the necessary relations of things ("les rapports necessaires qui derivent de la nature des choses") and he adds that in this sense all beings have their laws: the deity has its laws, the material world has its laws, and animals and men likewise have theirs.[9] This concept of law has been much disputed; thus Destutt de Tracy declared that laws are not such relations but are rules of action prescribed by an authority which possesses the competence and the power to do so and therefore has a right to make such rules.[10] Clearly such objections go back to natural-law notions in the sense of Locke. They miss the point which is crucial for Montesquieu, for Montesquieu desires to liberate law and the laws from these rational fetters and to explain them by the nature of things. That is to say, Montesquieu wishes to understand laws in terms of their functions. As a result, he divides law into nine different kinds (XXVI): the law of nature, the divine law which is the law of religion, the ecclesiastical law or law of the church-exercised police function (canonical law), international law, the general constitutional law, the particular constitutional law, the law of conquest, civil law, and, finally, family law. Montesquieu believes that these laws constitute disparate legal orders, the principles

[9] This notion has, of course, as we have seen, very ancient roots, and was already fully developed by the Stoics. What is distinctive in Montesquieu's approach is the relativism with which he makes the laws depend upon environment: "Elles [les lois] doivent être relative au physique du pays, au climat glacé, brulant ou temperé; à la qualité du terrain, à sa situation, à sa grandeur, au genre de vie des peuples, laboureurs, chasseurs ou pasteurs. . . . C'est dans toutes ces vues qu'il faut les considérer" (I, iii).

[10] Destutt de Tracy, in a commentary in his edition of Montesquieu, remarks that "laws are not necessary relations originating in the nature of things. . . . The word law has its special and appropriate sense: . . . law means a rule of action, prescribed by an authority, invested with competent power and a right so to do. . . . This last condition is essential, and when it is not possessed, the rule is no longer law, but an arbitrary command, an act of violence and usurpation." The only reason for citing this critical comment is to show that Montesquieu is clearly opposed to the command theory of law.

of which must be clearly kept apart if one wishes to make sound laws. Divine laws must not prescribe what should be regulated by human laws, or vice versa, for they are different from each other not only in source but also in purpose and nature. Upon this general basis, Montesquieu establishes a whole series of important distinctions of the different fields of law. But these distinctions are not rigid. Particular social institutions such as the family may appear in two or more of these legal spheres. This depends upon the possibility of their possessing different aspects relevant to the law. But if one should ask how this distinction between the several spheres of law is to be accomplished, Montesquieu would answer: by the constitution or the basic law. He does not say so explicitly; rather he implies it by stating that this must be decided by the legislator. But when one remembers that in the Greek tradition the legislator, the *nomothetes,* was the one who established the basic law, I believe the inference is clear. Once again, Montesquieu returns to the problem of the spirit of a nation in connection with the limits of all legislation. It is a concept which bears a certain resemblance to the concept of the general will in Rousseau (see below, chap. xiv) and which corresponds to the modern notion of a system of values or beliefs.[11] Montesquieu argues that if it is a question of altering the habits and customs of a people one ought not to attempt it by laws, for such laws would appear too tyrannical (XIX, xiv). This is an injunction which it would have been well for quite a few of our contemporary legislators to remember. Particularly the dictatorial regimes of our times, including military governments, have tended to neglect it.

In conclusion, it may be noted that Montesquieu again and again stresses moderation as decisive for good legislation. Indeed, at the beginning of Book XXIX he declares that it would seem to him that he had written the entire work exclusively for the purpose of proving that a legislator should exercise moderation.

[11] See for this concept Talcott Parsons, *The Social System* (1951), and *Toward a General Theory of Action,* ed. Talcott Parsons and Edward Shils (1952), esp. Part II.

He cites Aristotle to the effect that the political as well as the moral good is to be found between the extremes. This idea is in a sense central for whoever would consider as the core of legal philosophy the constitution resting upon a separation of powers. Let us recall that in New England the man presiding in the town meetings is called "moderator." The Speaker of the English House of Commons likewise is such a moderator. Without moderation, we might state more generally, a constitutional order based on law is not capable of functioning, for such an order must compensate by soundness and caution for what it lacks in speed and readiness to decide. This aspect, though very general, is crucial for constitutionalist legal philosophy.

XIII. *Law as the Expression of "Pure Reason"*

FROM SPINOZA TO WOLFF

The tensions resulting from the establishment of the modern state and its concentration of power led to solutions in the rest of Europe very different from those in England. On the Continent the omnipotence expressed in the idea of sovereignty was moderated by the transformation of Christian natural law into a law of secular reason. Built upon ideas of the late Scholastics, this law of pure reason was made the basis of a reformation and renewal of many parts of the positive legal order. The development starts with Grotius, but its greatest representatives were Pufendorf, Leibniz, Thomasius, and Christian Wolff. In a way, we are face to face here with a particular German development.

I have discussed earlier (chap. viii) Grotius' view of sovereignty and have shown that the basic idea of his theory of natural law was to make it independent of all theology and to anchor it in a rational ethics. We might add here that Grotius conceived of man as a sociable being to whom life in the community was a natural desire. This idea Grotius shared with Aristotle, the Stoics, and Thomas Aquinas.

The view which Grotius had maintained was sharply rejected by Hobbes, as we have seen. For Hobbes, natural law was a code of purely prudential rules of conduct, and the decisive purpose of it was self-preservation. Much more radical was Baruch Spinoza (1632–77), who identified law with power.[1] He formulated his position in very sharp antithesis to any rational law by asserting that the natural law of every man is not determined by right

[1] *Tractatus Theologico-Politicus* (1670), chap. xvi. The references given in the text, inclosed in parentheses, refer to the edition by Van Vloten and Land entitled *Benedicti de Spinoza Opera* (1913), II, 83–331; in the same edition, *Tractatus Politicus* is found in II, 1–82. (The first names of these two editors are not given in the book.)

reason but by cupidity and power (259). The laws of nature, the regularities of nature, determine the actions of men. These natural laws are actually the law of nature; all behavior is shaped by them; they express the power of nature (6–7). With inexorable logic, Spinoza derived this conception from a conviction he had taken from Machiavelli that the rules of the law of nature, like those of mathematics, could be deduced only from the nature of man as it actually is; everything else is utopia. The virtue of rule is its security, that is to say, its success (*imperii virtus securitas*). Man, like all living beings, wants to preserve himself, and whatever he undertakes to realize this goal he does according to his right, i.e., the highest natural law. For everyone has as much right as he has power (8). There is nothing to be wondered at, for nature is not limited by human laws but by other laws which are infinite and which order all of nature, of which man is only a small part. Clearly, man is conceived by Spinoza as a purely natural being, and for that reason state and law are seen as the concentration of the power found in many individual men. Once such a sovereign state is founded, he who rules it has the limitless right which results from such limitless power (261 ff.). Breach of treaty is not only his right but in fact his duty, for he is responsible for the security of the state ("Pactum nullam vim habere posse, nisi ratione utilitatis, qua sublata pactum simul tollitur) (261). All of this by no means implies that reason has no importance. On the contrary, only the man who lives according to reason and his own free assent is free, and therefore that commonwealth is the most free the laws of which are based upon reason (263). It is upon this basis that Spinoza can assert that democracy is the most natural of all forms of government. Democracy leaves to everyone a part of his freedom and a part of his natural right. But in every form of government, the sovereign—whoever he be—has, as we said, a limitless right. If he refuses to obey God, he does it at his own peril, and whatever damage results will be his. But he does not violate a natural law ("nullo jure civili vel naturali repugnante") (267). It would be a severe misunderstanding of these doctrines if they were to be equated with the materialism of

Hobbes. All nature and its power are, for Spinoza, divine and hence animated by spirit. But the practical consequences of such a mystical idealization of reality are even more dangerous than Hobbes's outright materialism.

Spinoza's pantheism was so violently rejected by his contemporaries that his doctrine of natural law, based so blatantly upon power, did not have any concrete influence upon legal development. What happened instead was that the law of reason of Grotius and of the Thomistic and Neo-Thomistic philosophers was combined with the naturalistic conceptions of Hobbes into a new synthesis. This new synthesis increasingly emphasized pure reason as the only satisfactory basis for all law. The development is somewhat complicated and has given rise to many controversies.

Grotius had, as we have seen, made the sociability of man the ontological foundation of community and of all law. In contrast to him, Hobbes had stressed the war of all against all and the resulting insecurity and anxiety for one's self-preservation as the natural cause of state and law. The man who combined the two positions in a new conception was Samuel Pufendorf (1632–94). He did so by making sociability in conjunction with an original incapacity (*imbecillitas*) both the ontological and epistemological foundation of community, state, and law. This was not, as has at times been asserted, a rather artificial and eclectic combination of Grotius and Hobbes but contained a basically new notion regarding man as he is. For Pufendorf related the dual aspect of man's living together to his basic distinction of physical and moral beings (*entia physica* and *entia moralia*). Man is a participant in both of these worlds. By his incapacity, he stands in the world of nature with its dangers and necessities, but by his sociability, which is related to the sense of values, he participates in the moral world. Man is in this sense free, for even though his freedom commits him to the moral law, it does so only in the sense that he can choose and reject.[2] As a result of his explicit doctrine

[2] The main work of Samuel Pufendorf is the *De jure naturae et gentium libri octo* (1672). Besides this magistral work, two others need to be consulted for his legal philosophy, *De officio hominis et civis* (1673) and *Elementorum jurisprudentiae universalis libri duo* (1660).

of freedom, Pufendorf's thinking possesses a distinctly enlightened flavor. One might be tempted to identify the dualism of *entia moralia* and *entia physica* with Kant's notions of law and virtue, but it would be a great mistake to overlook the very real differences. For one thing, Kant's dualism rests upon a critical epistemology which is very far from the unquestioning faith in the power of reason characteristic for the men of the early Enlightenment. What is more important is that, in accordance with his critical evaluation of reason, Kant sees the natural causation and moral freedom merely as cognitional grounds for a distinction, whereas Pufendorf considers *imbecillitas* and *socialitas,* the incapacity and the sociability of man, as truly constitutive elements of human nature in an ontological sense. Therefore, human action and human judgment must be explained in the sense that both of these possibilities are continually struggling within man and that the drama of human legal relationships can be comprehended only by this struggle.[3]

The double-faced quality of human beings explains the dialectic of Pufendorf's thoughts, for in a remarkable way he combined a dogmatic and rationalistic legal doctrine with a theory of the state that was at once historical and political. A German legal historian put this very nicely when he wrote: "Pufendorf combines the attitude of a rationalist who describes and systematizes the law in the geometrical manner [*more geometrico*] with that of the historian who rummages through the archives and who explores the historical facts and personalities."[4] In other words, Pufendorf's combination of historicism and rationalism had its foundation in his view of the dual nature of man as both a natural and a moral being.

The very great juristic impact which Pufendorf's doctrine had, in contrast to those of Spinoza and Hobbes, rests, in my opinion, to some extent upon this sensible and unreflected recognition of

3 Compare for all this *Jus naturae,* Books I–II, esp. chaps. i–iii; *De officiis,* Book II, more particularly chap. i, pars. 1–6. In the latter Pufendorf's doctrine of persons is developed.

4 See Erik Wolf, *Grosse Rechtsdenker der deutschen Geistesgeschichte* (2d ed., 1944), p. 298.

the contradiction of man. Pufendorf developed within this framework a doctrine of the human personality which has had a great deal of influence and which has made it possible to see crime and punishment as necessary consequences of man's freedom. Otto von Gierke has rightly emphasized these aspects and has shown how much this emphasis upon personality is rooted in older notions of Germanic law. Pufendorf recognized the whole welter of such personalities, individual and corporative, private and public, simple and composite. Into this manifold of personalities the traditional juristic concepts are absorbed, and they receive through this linking with Pufendorf's doctrine of personality a new vitality and a great vigor resulting from their natural law basis, that is to say, their moral basis. For the purely rational concept thus becomes the expression of a social ethics which in historical perspective is seen as the whole of all values. One may doubt whether this can yet be called cultural history, but it is evident that a dangerous confusion of valuational and existential considerations is involved because within such a context it becomes possible to identify law with the actual conduct of men in society. The concept of the reason of state in Pufendorf is a very characteristic sign of these potential dangers.[5]

Pufendorf's philosophy of law is a decidedly juristic system. In spite of all the objections which have been raised against him and often not without justification, it remains true that Pufendorf was the first modern legal philosopher who not only sketched but carried through a comprehensive system of natural law. Within the framework of this systematization which comprised all of law, international law was given a very influential formulation as pure natural law. Pufendorf denied the existence of an autonomous international law.[6] Significantly, Pufendorf insisted that peace and

[5] Compare for this Friedrich Meinecke, *Die Idee der Staatsräson in der neueren Geschichte* (1925), Book II, chap. ii. Meinecke makes the historical works of Pufendorf the basis of the interpretation.

[6] Compare for this the American reprint of the *Elementa* and of the *Jus naturae* with their English translations because of the very illuminating Introductions by Hans Wehberg and Walter Simons. Compare particularly Wehberg, pp. xvi ff.

not war was the natural state of mankind (*Elementa,* Definition XV, § 15). The systematic basis of his system is his doctrine of action (*actiones*). The juristically relevant actions are moral actions (*actiones morales*) and must be distinguished from natural actions by the fact that the consequences of such moral actions can be attributed to the actor who can be held responsible for them. This basic thought he eventually developed in his system of *jus naturae* into the doctrine of the *entia moralia* which we have already spoken of, which gave him a broader philosophical base. It is very characteristic of the ethical and political thought of Pufendorf that he does not start in either of these works from law and the laws (in the *Elementa,* law and the laws are treated in two separate sections, VIII and XIII); instead he starts from the facts of human nature which are beyond the law. The sharp criticism of Pufendorf by Leibniz probably is due to the fact that Pufendorf did not explain these views in a philosophically convincing manner but assumed them on the ground that they were evident to common sense.

Gottfried Wilhelm Leibniz (1646–1716) places natural law within the general framework of his metaphysics.[7] All ethics and all human society are based upon this law of nature. The law of nature is a system of eternal ideas toward which the cosmos and its parts, the monads, are directed. And the law of nature and the laws of nature are intertwined. The monads each mirror the total cosmos, for, although they are quite separate and apart and have no way of communicating with each other, these monads are held together both among themselves and toward the cosmos by the pre-established harmony which Leibniz asserted. This pre-established harmony is a consequence of a reason which permeates the entire world and which is in fact the reason of God. As a consequence, Leibniz declared the actual world to be the best of all possible worlds—a statement which has yielded him in more pessimistic times much mocking comment but which does in fact

[7] The works of Leibniz are usually cited according to the edition of L. Dutens, the fourth volume of which (1768) contains his juridical writings. The great Academy edition is not yet far advanced. Unfortunately, he never completed his legal and political theory as planned.

follow quite logically from his general view. The law of nature is based upon the eternal idea of justice and can be derived from it both logically and deductively.[8] But Leibniz did not provide us with this deduction. It is not permissible to go back to his youthful writings for this purpose,[9] for in his youth Leibniz argued in terms of a nominalistic voluntarism like Pufendorf's, which he later (1770) entirely abandoned. There exists a schema in his early writings (*Nova methodus,* II) which describes the law of nature as on three levels and by nature oriented toward three principles: first, the *jus strictum,* or strict law, which is oriented toward the principle "hurt no one"; second, the *aequitas,* or equity, which is oriented toward the principle "give everyone his own"; and third, the *pietas,* or piety, which is oriented toward the principle "live honestly." It is evident that this is an attempt to organize the basic principles derived from Roman law according to metaphysical and religious notions. But it does not become clear what consequences result for the philosophy of law. It may well be doubted whether one would be justified in describing these hints in Leibniz as a philosophy of law in the strict sense. Leibniz' great accomplishment as a metaphysician, as a mathematician, and as a statesman and organizer of science has persuaded scholars to assign to him a position in the history of legal philosophy which is not justified by the intrinsic merit or originality of his contributions.

A similar observation might be made concerning another philosopher, Christian Thomasius (1655–1728), who in many other respects was very unlike Leibniz. Thomasius, however, in contrast to Leibniz, has had a very great influence upon the development of law; he stimulated greatly its rationalistic systematiza-

[8] "Doctrina juris ex earum numero est, quae non ab experimentis, sed definitionibus, nec a sensuum, sed rationis demonstrationibus pendent, et sunt ita dicam juris, non facti" (*Akademieausgabe,* 6th ser., VI [1930] 460).

[9] *De principio individui* (1663), *Nova methodus jurisprudentiae* (1668), *De arte combinatoria* (1666). The first two are now available in the Academy edition, 6th ser., VI, 3, 259.

tion. His main work[10] on the foundations of natural law is based upon a sharp distinction between law and morality. What is particularly important is the attempt of Thomasius to build the law of nature, conceived of as the law of reason, entirely upon common sense. This is perhaps the major concern of Thomasius in his *Fundamenta.* He hopes, he says in the Preface, to show human nature to be what it is commonly believed to be by most men; that is to say, he wants to follow common sense (*sensus communis*). Everyone, he claims, can detect and feel in himself what is essential for an understanding of the moral nature of man. In this connection, he explicitly refers to Hobbes as well as to Richard Cumberland. Thomasius praises Cumberland above all as the one who first clearly distinguished between revelation and the law of nature and who derived the law of nature purely from reason and experience. In this connection, Thomasius makes the radical statement that nothing is in the mind which was not previously in the senses. The law of nature is seen by Thomasius as a sum of counsels (*consilia*)—as it had also been interpreted by Hobbes. God is for the wise man more a teacher of what is by nature right than a legislator.[11] Bluntschli, consequently, rightly emphasized that Thomasius everywhere considers statutory law the original and highest source of all law.[12] This statutory law to Thomasius, as to Hobbes, is the command of the government.[13] Only such a command obliges, and the contract is based upon such statutory commands. It is within this context that Thomasius, like Locke, turns from the law of nature to natural rights. Right becomes an attribute of persons on the basis of which, with the consent of

[10] *Fundamenta juris naturae in quibus decernuntur principia honesti, justi ac decori;* besides this major work, his earlier *Institutionum jurisprudentiae divinae libri tres* (1687) is also of considerable significance.

[11] "Sapiens Deum magis concipit ut doctorem juris naturae, quam ut legislatorem" (*Fundamenta juris naturae,* I, v, 40).

[12] *Geschichte des allgemeinen Staatsrechts und der Politik* (1867), p. 198.

[13] "Lex est jussus imperantis obligans subjectos, ut secundum istum jussum actiones suas instituant" (*Inst. jur. div.*, III, i, 1, § 28).

the government, a man can have or do something.[14] In the more narrow sense, therefore, law is always a right within human society. For one can have a right only toward someone with whom one lives in society. A so-called natural law rests, therefore, upon a command of God, and we see here a recognition of the distinction between human and divine law.[15] At the same time, Thomasius interprets society in a strongly individualistic sense as a purposive association.[16] Naturally, the law is seen as essentially coercive, but it is seen upon the basis of the paradoxical doctrine of the coercive duty.[17] This sharp separation of positive law from all morals and ethics, and the consequent positivism of all law in the strict sense, has been considered the peculiar contribution of Thomasius to the philosophy of law.[18] Such a view overlooks the fact that this kind of positivism had already been clearly enunciated by Hobbes, that it was taken over by Thomasius, perhaps via Locke, and that it probably confirmed him in his own opinion.[19]

For the rest, Thomasius largely follows the systematization of Pufendorf, although he rejects Pufendorf's doctrine of the *entia moralia.* His enormous reputation does not rest upon his system, which lacks genuine originality, but upon his great courage and the vigor with which he stood his ground against the general prejudices of his time, more particularly against the persecution of witches and against torture. Thomasius was a true man of the Enlightenment and, like Leibniz, a passionate defender of toler-

[14] "Jus pro attributo personae sumtum est qualitas moralis activa ex concessione superioris personae competens ad aliquit ab altero homine . . . juste habendum vel agendum" (*Inst. jur. div.,* III, i, 1, § 82).

[15] *Inst. jur. div.,* III, i, 1, § 29, and *Fundamenta juris naturae,* I, v, 6.

[16] *Inst. jur. div.,* III, i, 1, §§ 100–101.

[17] Compare the critique in Hans Welzel's *Naturrecht und materiale Gerechtigkeit* (1951), p. 162, and Erik Wolf, *op. cit.,* chap. x, esp. pp. 369 ff.

[18] Welzel, *op. cit.,* p. 163.

[19] The connection between Thomasius and Locke is rightly emphasized by both Bluntschli and Erik Wolf. But I think that connection ought not to be overdone because, as we have seen, in the center of Locke's legal doctrines we find the constitutional theory (see above, chap. xii) of which there is no trace in Thomasius, who was a representative of enlightened absolutism.

ance and religious freedom. Besides that, he was the first to lecture in German. Germans, exaggerating somewhat, like to call him the "second Luther." What is true is that Thomasius was the legal, or shall we say juristic, pathfinder of the Enlightenment in Germany.

The very divergent doctrines of Leibniz on the one hand and of Pufendorf and Thomasius on the other, concerning the rational basis of law, were combined in a system of rational natural law by Christian Wolff (1679–1754). At least he made a valiant attempt so to combine them. Wolff would explain natural law, like all law, by duty. "No law exists without a moral obligation which precedes it, in which it is rooted, and from which it flows. There exist inborn human rights because there exist inborn human duties, they are for all men the same, because they are the consequence of human nature."[20] For this reason it is axiomatic for Wolff that all human beings are equal. No man has by nature the right to hinder another or to issue commands to him, and therefore all men are by nature free. Indeed, liberty simply means following natural necessity.[21] Wolff's emphasis upon man's striving for perfection instead of for happiness is merely a shift in emphasis which is already found in Leibniz. Yet this idea of a striving for perfection Wolff made, quite in keeping with the ideas of the Enlightenment, a main pillar of his system of natural law. Here again we have the heritage of classical antiquity, and more particularly of Socrates, Plato, and Cicero. Nonetheless, as a major basis for interpreting the law of nature, it is peculiar to the Enlightenment. Obviously there are links here to the philosophy of Kant. At the same time, the difference between law and morals is once again obscured, and the positivists of the nineteenth century who credited Thomasius with having drawn the distinction were annoyed by Wolff's abandoning it again. For basically, Wolff's system of a natural law based on reason is simply a system of morals. To be

[20] Compare the main work of Wolff concerning this matter, entitled *Jus naturae methodo scientifico pertractum* (9 vols., 1748–49), Book I, chap. i, § 26 (translated by Bluntschli, *op. cit.*).

[21] *Jus naturae,* Book I, chap. i, §§ 81 f.

sure, Wolff distinguished between a more perfect law, which is provided with the right to coerce, and a less perfect law. But his general doctrine of duties goes far beyond all jurisprudence.

Taken all in all, the philosophical content and the creative significance of these celebrated systems is quite disappointing, even if one concentrates upon the most important ones. Yet their practical impact was far-reaching and greatly diversified. In recent years the importance of these systems for the history of law, as contrasted with the history of the philosophy of law, has been receiving renewed attention.[22] It has been shown how the idea of a rational law of nature led to significant changes in the conception of a great many legal institutions. Pufendorf transformed the law of contract and of property, and he also stated the risks in commercial transactions differently. At the same time, obligations were systematized, and this systematization continues down to the present-day German civil code.

What is perhaps even more important is that the great codifications of the late eighteenth century rested upon this rational law of nature. Leibniz, like Bodin, had demanded such codification.[23] Beginning with the Prussian cabinet order of 1746, a number of codes were created: first in Bavaria (1756), then in Prussia (1794), and finally in Austria (1811). A German legal historian has described their nature as follows: realization of the law of nature, explicitness and completeness in order to anticipate legal argument, and resolution of doubtful points of legal interpretation not by the judge but by the legislator.[24]

The most celebrated code is of course that resulting from the French Revolution known as the *Code Civil* or the *Code Napoléon* (1804).[25] The *Code Civil* shows the systematization derived

[22] See Thieme, *Das Naturrecht und die europäische Privatrechtsgeschichte* (1947), and Franz Wieacker, *Privatrechtsgeschichte der Neuzeit* (1952); Wieacker gives many valuable references to other writings in the field.

[23] In a letter to Kestner, he states explicitly his hope that there would soon be created a new, short, clear, and adequate code.

[24] See Franz Wieacker, *op. cit.*, pp. 197 ff.

[25] See for this *The Code Napoléon and the Common Law World*, ed. Bernard Schwartz (1956), chap. i, "The Theological and Philosophical Background," by the author.

from natural law in perfect form. Private law is divided as follows: I. The law of persons; II. The law of things: (1) the law of property, (2) limited rights; III. Acquisition of property: (1) inheritance and wills, (2) obligations. It has been rightly pointed out that what distinguished the *Code Civil* from the German codifications is the spirit of "constitutionalism." Equality in the civil law, more particularly in regard to real estate and inheritance, freedom of the individual, and especially economic freedom, took the place of legal notions which were rooted in the feudal order and the concept of corporations in the older law. "Very decidedly we find everywhere the anti-feudal, egalitarian and centralizing tendency; it made possible the general supernational formulation which had wide appeal and enabled the *Code Civil* to march victoriously through the world of the nineteenth century."[26]

Considering the vast impact of these systems of natural law, one cannot help thinking that their importance is primarily not theoretical and philosophical but rather practical. They offered a method for limiting the prevailing absolutism as well as for rationalizing it. The relation between these systems and the peculiar kind of political order in Prussia and Austria has often been commented upon. Rulers of these large states, which at first had only a dynastic unity, found in such rationalism the tools for unification and for superseding feudalism and aristocracy, guilds and estates. What greatly aided such a development was that these views were no longer related to religious convictions and hence could not be restrained by them. The idea of a legal system derived from pure reason was thus linked with the thought of equality and freedom which became the motif of the French Revolution.

[26] Wieacker, *op. cit.*, p. 213.

XIV. *Law as the Expression of the General Will*

ROUSSEAU AND KANT

Kant called Rousseau the "Newton of the moral world." What he meant was that Rousseau had shown that man's true being was his ethical autonomy, that freedom was as much part of man as gravity was of matter, and that law and the state could be understood only in the light of this basic reality. This idea is not new in itself; we have encountered it in the legal philosophy of the Stoics and Thomas Aquinas. But it was given a new interpretation. The autonomy of man was interpreted to mean that a legal norm possesses truly legitimate binding obligation only if it has been created with the free participation of those who are subject to it and, furthermore, that only within the framework of the categorical imperative can such free decision be realized as an expression of human autonomy, as an indication of the general will (*volunté générale*). It is important that by Rousseau this general will is conceived of as the final authority in all decisions concerning law and hence is given a radically democratic and unlimited sense, whereas in Kant this general will remains subject to a general law of nature, in the sense of the constitutionalists.

Let us turn first to Rousseau. For Rousseau, as for Hooker, Locke, and Montesquieu, law is the center of all social life. This idea is not only decisive for his main work in our field, the *Social Contract,* or *Contrat social* (1762), but is given importance in a number of his other works, for example, *Émile* (1762) and the *Confessions* (1766–67).[1] A society without laws is not, in the last

[1] Incomparably the most important work of Rousseau for the student of legal philosophy is the *Contrat social,* of which many good translations are available; the most readily accessible is that in Everyman's, but recently the Oxford University Press has published a new translation by Gerard Hopkins,

analysis, a true community. It is treated as a marginal case in the sense of tyranny and despotism. Rousseau at the very outset of the *Contrat social* states his main problem: how the coercive power of governmental authority is to be understood. In his emotional and rhetorical way he exclaims, "Man is born free, yet everywhere he is in chains." Rousseau believes that he cannot explain how this has come about, but he can explain how this situation can be made legitimate. Such legitimation results from the fact that the laws have been decided by the general will.

Rousseau's central concept of the general will is somewhat equivocal, and there has been a great deal of argument concerning it. The decisive passages in the *Contrat social* are as follows:

> The constant will of all the members of the state is the general will; by virtue of it they are citizens and free. When in the popular assembly the law is proposed, what the people is asked is not whether it approves or rejects the proposal but whether it is in conformity with the general will, which is their will. Each man, in giving his vote, states his opinion on that point; and the general will is found by counting votes [IV, ii].
>
> The general will is always right and tends to the public advantage; but it does not follow that the deliberations of the people are always equally correct.
>
> Our will is always for our own good, but we do not always see what it is [II, iii].
>
> The general will . . . is always constant, unalterable and pure; but it is subordinate to other wills which encroach upon its sphere. . . . Even in selling his vote for money, a man does not extinguish in himself the general will, but he only eludes it [IV, i].
>
> Of itself, the people will always the good, but of itself by no means always see it. The general will is always in the right, but the judgment which discloses it is not always enlightened [II, vi].

---

who profited from C. E. Vaughan's careful textual criticism as offered in *The Political Writings of Jean-Jacques Rousseau* (2 vols., 1915). This translation appears in a volume entitled *The Social Contract* (1948) and has an interesting Introduction by Sir Ernest Barker. One cannot, however, disregard Rousseau's other writings, in view of the many obscurities and paradoxes in the *Contrat social*. The edition of his works I used is *Œuvres de Jean-Jacques Rousseau . . .*, by Mussay Pathay (1827). This edition is preceded by a valuable "Notice des principaux écrits relatifs à la personne et aux ouvrages de J. J. R." Text references are to book and chapter. For the principal works on Rousseau, see the Bibliography for this chapter.

There is evident in these statements a definite contradiction, for this will is apparently at the same time both transcendent and rational.[2] The doctrine of a rational will is very ancient and played a great role in classical antiquity and in the Scholastic period, as we have seen. But in the older forms, a rational will was not attributed to each individual man but depended upon the degree to which the rational was active in a particular man. In Rousseau, as a result of his radically egalitarian view of man, we encounter the Copernican turning point. All men are said to possess a rational will, and the general will is then seen as the expression of these willing individuals when they come together to legislate.

But this does not mean, as our quotations show, that Rousseau thought of the general will as the sum of the wills of the individuals composing the community. For these particular wills are not directed toward the general good but toward the good of the individual. A true law is always a general rule, and the central problem for every governmental order is how one can secure such laws. But Rousseau does not really solve this problem. He certainly does not solve it in the democratic sense of a majority decision, as has often been asserted.[3] Rousseau believed democracy to be suitable only for very small communities, for he would not allow or admit representation. In a famous passage in the *Contrat social* he speaks of an unwritten constitution which is engraved upon the hearts of the citizens and which, although continually changing, is the true basis of the political and legal order.[4] The contradictions here involved are the result, I believe,

[2] See for further detail my *Inevitable Peace* (1948), chap. vi. Derathé, *Le rationalisme de J.-J. Rousseau* (1948), has given a carefully reasoned argument in support of the rational interpretation of the general will. See also Ernst Cassirer, *The Question of Jean-Jacques Rousseau* with a penetrating Introduction by Peter Gray, surveying past Rousseau interpretations.

[3] For the limits of Rousseau's support of majority rule, see Derathé, *Jean-Jacques Rousseau* (1950), chap. v, § III. See also J. Talmon's challenging if somewhat one-sided *The Rise of Totalitarian Democracy* (1952) and chap. iv of my *The New Belief in the Common Man* (1941).

[4] Book II, chap. xii. This argument of Rousseau's related to the widely discussed problem of the so-called "agreement on fundamentals," now more

of the fact that Rousseau did not really resolve the problem of the rational will of an autonomous personality. Therefore the general will is suspended in mid-air and, on the one hand, reminds one of the general spirit in Montesquieu, on the other, of the majority will in Locke, but is neither one nor the other.

The problem of the rational will of an autonomous person was tackled by Kant, who solved it in the perspective of his critical rationalism. For Kant shows how and in what sense the autonomous wills of the individuals can be understood as constituents of the general will. This is accomplished by his celebrated doctrine of the categorical imperative.[5] The basic law of the pure practical reason which this categorical imperative embodies says in its most famous formulation: "Act so that the maxim of thy wills may at all times be valid as a principle of universal legislation." We cannot enter here upon the complex problems of this kind of formal ethics.[6] What is clear is that, if the individuals act in accordance with such a legislative categorical imperative, apparently a general law may result from their joint decision. For the principle which the categorical imperative provides in its application to the concrete instance is related to a general law.

The legal philosophy of Kant is contained in his late work, *The Metaphysics of Morals* (1797). Indeed, it is in the first part of this work that Kant treats of the metaphysical principles of legal doctrine. It must be borne in mind that Kant's arguments con-

---

academically discussed in terms of "value systems," "symbol systems," and the like. See for this issue my *The New Belief in the Common Man* (1941), chap. v, where the need for dissent is juxtaposed to this need for agreement.

[5] Kant's works are most conveniently studied in Ernst Cassirer's splendid edition *Immanuel Kants Werke* (10 vols., 1922). The eleventh volume contains a searching biography, *Kants Leben und Lehre* (1923). The Kant literature is, of course, very large; some other works are found in the Bibliography. Unfortunately, there does not exist a critical edition of his works in English, though there are many different translations of individual works. I have tried to bring some unity into this welter of conflicting glosses by my *The Philosophy of Kant* (1949), which offers a group of selections in reasonably uniform style, with an Introduction. On the categorical imperative, see especially Paton, *The Categorical Imperative* (1947).

[6] Max Scheler, *Der Formalismus in der Ethik und die materiale Wertethik* (3d ed., 1927), *passim*.

cerning law rest upon a sharp separation of theoretical and practical reason, of observation and action, of phenomenon and norm (the latter is also called *Noumenon* by Kant). His legal doctrine belongs, of course, to the realm of practical reason which finds its basis in the freedom and autonomy of man and its expression in the autonomous action. "Since the concept of law is a pure one, but is oriented toward practice, that is to say, the application to cases which occur in experience, a metaphysical system of law would have to take account of the empirical many-sidedness of these cases." Since this is impossible, one can develop only principles and not a complete system of law as a part of morals.[7] Kant considers it the duty of everyone to possess such a metaphysics of morals and furthermore declares that every man in fact possesses it "although ordinarily in a dark manner." Such a metaphysics cannot be based upon a doctrine of man (anthropology) but can be applied to such an anthropology. Its purpose is to show how and how far law is a pure norm. How does Kant differentiate between ethical and juristic norms? By pointing out that the ethical norm presupposes only an inner legislation which rests upon conscience. Apart from such conscience, every action is legal which is according to law, and such legality Kant juxtaposes to morality because it rests upon external legislation. "The theory of law and the theory of virtue are not distinguished by their different duties but rather by the difference of the legislation which links these impulses with the law."

Kant gives at the outset a number of definitions which one would have to repeat if one were to give a complete picture of the basis of his legal theory: obligation, imperative, duty, action, person, thing—the general connotation of each one of these basic concepts Kant defines carefully. But in the center he places the "highest principle of morals": "Act in accordance with the maxim

[7] *The Metaphysics of Morals* is presently going to be published in a new translation by Professor John Ladd, but since it is not yet available, the translations in the text are by the author. See also L. W. Beck's edition of the *Critique of Practical Reason and Other Writings in Moral Philosophy* (1949); he gives a longish extract from the *Foundations,* but hardly anything from the *Metaphysics.* They are also omitted from my own selections.

which at the same time can be considered valid as a general law." A law thus is a proposition which contains a categorical imperative, or rather which contains a command in keeping with and derived from the categorical imperative. In this connection it is important that Kant insists that the laws are made by the will, whereas arbitrary preferences determine the maxims. Only arbitrary preference is free; the will which is "directed toward law" cannot be called either free or unfree.

Upon this basis Kant declares that "the substance [*Inbegriff*] of the laws which an external legislation can comprehend may be called a legal theory." If it is actual, it is positive law. "The law is therefore the totality [*Inbegriff*] of the conditions under which the arbitrary preference of one may coexist with the arbitrary preference of another according to the general law of freedom." Thus every action is right which corresponds to this conception. "If therefore my action or, generally speaking, my state can coexist with the freedom of everyone else according to a general law then whoever prevents me [from taking that action] is doing me an injustice." All that is unjust is an obstruction of freedom, according to general laws, and the removing of such an obstruction is just. From this it follows that "law carries with it the right to coerce him who seeks to interfere with it." Hence, law can be seen as a mutual coercive obligation. From this basic consideration can be deduced the coercive order of the state as a necessary part of every legal order.[8]

Kant places at the beginning of his general division of legal theory an interpretation of the triad of natural law which relates it to legal duties. The three formulas of *honeste vivere, neminem laedere, suum cuique tribuere* represent, according to Kant, a division of law into internal and external legal duties as well as into those which can be derived by subsuming the latter under the former. But in the sequel, he reduces all innate rights to one, namely, freedom understood as independence from the arbitrary coercion of another. "It is the only one and original right which

[8] See "Einleitung in die Rechtslehre," in *Metaphysik der Sitten, Werke,* VII, 30 ff.

belongs to each man by reason of his humanity."[9] Thus the division of mine and thine becomes the decisive dichotomy of Kantian legal doctrine. All other distinctions can be reduced to this one.

Kant organizes the general discussion of law into that of private law, which is the law of the external mine and thine, and that of public law. The latter is primarily characterized by the fact that the laws of which it consists require general publication. It consists of constitutional and international law. Constitutional law is "a system of laws for a people, that is to say a multitude of men . . . who . . . need a constitution in order to partake of what is right."[10] International law corresponds to this Kantian conception of constitutional law, but it refers to nations. The two of them together lead to the idea of international constitutional law which Kant also called a law of world citizenship. It is obvious that Kant's idea of peace within a legal world order is clearly and unequivocally derived from his legal doctrine as rooted in practical reason, and certainly it is not, as has at times been asserted, a kind of sudden inspiration of an old man.[11]

In his critique of the Hobbesian doctrine of the state,[12] which is quite important for an understanding of the Kantian legal philosophy, Kant calls the original social contract an idea of reason from which the nature of human society can be deduced. He does not speak of a contract of submission, but every man is by this contract made secure in his general rights. He exchanges, so to speak, this security for a part of his arbitrary preference. Man has therefore unalterable rights vis-à-vis the state, and the constitution has as its purpose to make this sphere of freedom se-

9 *Ibid.*, pp. 38 f.

10 *Ibid.*, pp. 117 ff. (Part II, Sec. I).

11 See for this my *Inevitable Peace, passim,* and Kurt von Raumer, *Ewiger Friede: Friedensrufe und Friedenspläne seit der Renaissance* (1953), chap. vi, pp. 151–207, where the ideas of Kant and Genz are strikingly confronted.

12 Given in *Theory and Practice: Concerning the Common Saying: This May Be True in Theory, But Does Not Apply to Practice,* a translation of Part II is found in my selections, pp. 415 ff.

cure.[13] But it remains unclear how such a constitutional limitation of the head of the state can be made legally effective. If one takes this lack of clarity together with Kant's sharp rejection of all resistance to the laws, one gains the impression of a marked authoritarianism which is only formally modified by the insistence that the head of the state is obliged to act according to the categorical imperative.

In view of this authoritarianism, it is of very great importance that Kant most explicitly insists upon constitutionalism, which he juxtaposes to despotism in which one man has all the power. All constitutionalism rests upon the tripartite separation of powers into a legislative, executive, and judicial power, among which the legislative one is dominant. For according to Kant, following earlier writers, the executive power is concerned with the execution and application of the laws. This constitutionalism comprehends a monarchical, an aristocratic, and a democratic form, depending on to whom the legislative power is given by the constitution. For this legislative power is the true power to rule, or sovereignty. It is Kant's view that "the only truly legal constitution" is that of a "pure republic," and toward this kind of constitution all other kinds of constitutions gradually tend. "Every true republic is and cannot be anything but a representative system of the people, in whose name, as it unites all the citizens, the laws are taken care of by deputies."[14] We see here that the united people not only represents the sovereign but is the sovereign.

Kant's inclination to stress the authority of the "state" is limited further by his emphatic recognition of the importance of freedom of speech and the press, even in a highly authoritarian system.

[13] Kant, however, explicitly states that it is not feasible to say "that a man in the state has sacrificed a part of his innate external freedom for a certain purpose, but rather that he has abandoned the wild and lawless freedom entirely in order to rediscover his true freedom in a legal framework, that is to say, in a condition under law, because this new dependence is derived from his own legislative will" (*Die Rechtslehre,* par. 47, *Werke,* VII, 122).

[14] *Die Rechtslehre,* par. 52, *Werke,* VII, 149.

Even here "the sovereign understands that there is no danger in legislation permitting his subjects to make *public* use of their own reason and to submit *publicly* their thoughts regarding a better framing of such laws together with a frank criticism of existing legislation."[15] He argues that he may do so because, unlike the ruler of a free state, he "can say: 'Argue as much as you want and about whatever you want but obey.'" Nature, he believes, has implanted in men the need for free thought, and as such free thought spreads and influences more and more people, they become capable of "acting in freedom." The basis of such freedom of thought is the freedom of religion, which flows from the fact that religion as genuine belief cannot be forced.[16] The large-scale consultation of the public which the Prussian authorities conducted, before enacting the Prussian General Code, was quite in line with such notions, as it provided at least a minimum of public participation in the comprehensive legislation the Code embodied.

In sum, it is evident that, according to Kant and his idea of law, only constitutional democracy is in the position to create fully obligatory laws, that is to say, laws by which the individual is completely obligated. The contrast between law and ethics is completely bridged by a fully valid law. This notion sprang from but was not developed by Rousseau, who, by his vague idea of the general will, left the door open for dangerous innovations.[17] Some of these may be found in the legal philosophy of Hegel.

[15] *Was ist Aufklärung?* as translated in my *The Philosophy of Kant* (1949), p. 139.

[16] *Ibid.*, and pp. 134 ff.

[17] Talmon, *op. cit., passim.*

XV. *Law as the Expression of the Spirit*

HEGEL AND THE HISTORICAL SCHOOL

Hegel's philosophy of law stands in sharpest contrast to that of Kant, a fact often obscured by the term "idealism," which is applied to both. To be sure, Hegel too sees law within the framework of morals; both Hegel's ethics and Hegel's philosophy of law form a unity. They are treated in Hegel's famous *The Philosophy of Right and Law, or Natural Law and Political Science Outlined* (1821).[1] In this study of basic principles Hegel first investigates law, thereafter morals, and finally what he calls ethics (*Sittlichkeit*). Within the framework of the last topic, he finally describes the state as the crowning achievement of the whole and as the realization of ethics in the community. But these concepts of state, law, and ethics are no longer treated by Hegel "abstractly" or "generally" but are taken as developing concepts. They are treated "dialectically" so that we progress, from Hegel's point of view, from "abstract" law to the "concrete" state. Law, state, and ethics are expressions of a historical development which is the manifestation of a national spirit, and these national spirits in their entirety are manifestations of the world spirit. They must be understood as concrete projections of this world spirit. The world spirit is not something outside them, but in and through them it is what it is.

Hegel's state is the ethical community. It is not an institution for the realization of ethics but is this realization itself. If one

[1] Substantial portions of this work are included in my *The Philosophy of Hegel,* which I edited with an Introduction in 1953. Besides this basic work, the students of Hegel's legal philosophy should also give careful attention to his *Schriften zur Politik und Rechtsphilosophie* (Leipzig, 1913). For the main work in German, entitled *Grundlinien der Philosophie des Rechts oder Naturrecht und Staatswissenschaft im Grundrisse,* the most authoritative edition now is that by Johannes Hoffmeister, published as Vol. XII of the new critical edition of Hegel's *Sämtliche Werke* (Hamburg: Felix Meiner). The paragraph references in the text are to *The Philosophy of Right and Law.*

does not grasp this basic position of Hegel, Hegel's legal philosophy remains incomprehensible. For the general prevailing notion of the state is that of an institution or an institutional manifold in which those are united who possess the power to rule and hence the power to create obligatory norms. In a free and democratic society of course that means all the citizens as well as the government. But apart from this prevailing positivist notion of the state, it is natural for common sense to look upon the state as the actually existing structure of power and law which prevails or rules in a particular community. Thus the state of Hitler would be the apparatus which does really exercise the function of ruling as a matter of historical fact. But in Hegel's view, only that is truly a state which can be understood as realizing ethics. It may hence be doubted whether much would be left of Hitler's apparatus for rule if it were subjected to this kind of criterion.

Hegel's conception of law is intimately linked to his metaphysical views concerning the role of religion and of the spirit, which is God's spirit. Ethics is the concrete world of the norm, of societal life. This concrete ethical world seems to Hegel more important than the abstract subjectivity of mere morality. What nowadays is spoken of in the social sciences and philosophy as the system of values of communities is very close to what Hegel had in mind by this concrete ethical world. By contrast, mere morality is the realm within which the independent will takes effect; within it the person is pure subject. Ethics on the other hand is more concrete because it is more objective, but it can be realized only through or in the state. Hegel tells a rather revealing anecdote at a crucial point in his *Philosophy of Right and Law,* and this, I think, may be considered important, for such anecdotes are not frequent in his writings. He says: "To a father who asked how he might best bring up his son, Pythagoras answered: 'By making him the citizen of a state with good laws' " (§ 153).

Ethics in Hegel is defined as the idea of freedom. It is the "living good," or to put it another way, "the concept of freedom which has become the existing world and the nature of self-consciousness." Man can therefore live a truly ethical existence in freedom only within the ethical realm of the state. For "the state is the actual reality of the ethical idea" (§ 257). If one interprets this statement of Hegel as meaning that the actually existing governmental apparatus is the realization of the ethical idea, there may be derived from this notion the basis of a total and eventually a totalitarian deification of power. But this view is not at all that of Hegel. Indeed, for Hegel such deification of power is blasphemy. In a famous footnote to his *Philosophy of Right and Law,* he sharply condemns the work of a contemporary who had expounded this point of view. That the more powerful rules, must rule, and always will rule, Hegel declares to be a dangerous heresy to which must be opposed the doctrine of the power of the just and the ethical. He comments bitterly that, according to such a doctrine, "those who are more powerful by their knowledge of law do rightly by plundering the people who need protection." As contrasted with such doctrines of power, Hegel insists upon the veneration of the law as the basis of all true ethics: "How infinitely important, how divine it is, that the duties of the state and the rights of the citizens, just as the right of the state and the duties of the citizens, are *legally* determined."

Abstract law is to a very considerable extent what had in the past been called the law of nature or natural right (*jus naturale*), that is to say, those rights of the individual which are based on his being an autonomous person. Hegel in this context treats of property, contract, and torts. Under the latter he also puts fraud and crime. "A person must give himself an external sphere of freedom," he writes by way of giving a first definition of property. Only thus can a person exist ideally. And hence property is defined as the sphere of freedom of man, as that which is immediately different and separable.

This abstract law derives its existence from the sphere of what is relative, that is to say, from the mutual relation of needs and the work to fill them. Only thus is it generally recognized, known, and willed, and by thus being known and willed, it achieves validity and objective actual reality (§ 209). What this means is that law is not only something rational, nor is it something only willed, but it is something which is willed as something rational. It is the expression of a rational will. It becomes positive law by the statute which declares what shall be law (§ 211). "Right and law become through such determination positive law." The valid laws of a nation, Hegel says very significantly, do not cease to be its customs by dint of their being written and collected. He cites as an example the English common law, which, he thinks, is contained in statutes as well as in unwritten laws. He adds what so often is forgotten, namely, that this unwritten law is also written; he mocks at the many tomes which one has to read in order to determine what law is and compares the resulting confusion with the situation in late Roman law. He questions the position of the judge under the common law, which seems to him often too important and too nearly legislative. But to deny to a nation the capacity for legislation, as Savigny had done, and thereby to deny that its jurists possessed the capacity to make a code "would be one of the greatest insults which can be leveled at a nation or the legal profession of it."[2] In this context, Hegel emphasizes that such a codification does not mean that new laws are being made but that the existing content of legal customs and legal norms is rendered fully rational. Therefore, Hegel insists upon the importance of publishing the laws, which Thomas Aquinas, Hobbes, and Kant, among others, had already stressed. It is an idea which recurs again and again as people stress the role of law in connection with government. But all of this does not mean that such legislation, such a codification, is something absolutely finished, a final product which is not capable of further development. Finite states such as are treated in private law are continuous approximations to a desirable state, and what is general reason in its perfection must not be confused with what is general for the intellect. "Le plus grand ennemi du Bien c'est le Meilleur"—this, Hegel says, is the judgment of common sense.

Courts have for Hegel a very great importance, although he does not wish to allow them a legislative function, as we have just seen. Yet a court has the task of recognizing the law as right which

[2] *The Philosophy of Hegel*, ed. Friedrich, p. 275.

is expressed in the laws, and of putting it into actual practice. Regardless of how courts may have developed historically, regardless of how great a role patriarchal relationships and power may have played, for Hegel this is unimportant for the understanding of the essence of the matter. The institutions of law and state are in themselves rational and necessary. And therefore the work of the courts must be handled publicly, and it is desirable that juries be established so that the accused can have confidence in the decision and not feel that he is delivered up to impersonal laws.

Although Hegel attributes to the police and to corporations an important partial function in the realization of the legal order, all his thought on law ultimately leads to the state, for the state is "the actuality of the ethical idea." In this connection, Hegel distinguishes three aspects of the legal interpretation of the idea of the state. First, it has immediate actuality in the constitution, or what he calls the inner law of the state. Secondly, it shapes the relation of the states to each other in international law, or the external law of the states, as Hegel calls it. And third, it is the general idea as the spirit which becomes actualized in the process of world history. By these notions the state is not only seen as shaped by law through and through, but it is placed within a cosmic context of universal significance. The legal philosophy of Hegel culminates in a sketch of the philosophy of history precisely because each individual state can be comprehended only by the role which it fulfils in the general march of the spirit in history. The legal idea of the state is thus spiritual power which is legitimized by a higher order of being. This spirit is the "absolute judge," and all attempts to form a supernational court are, like a lasting peace, only relative and limited. "The only absolute judge, which always prevails and against all particulars, is the spirit which is in and by itself and which presents itself as the general and as the effective operator [*wirkende Gattung*] in world history."[3] With this last step, Hegel once again dissolves all binding and fixed norms, and everything that seemed so secure and legally

[3] *Ibid.*, p. 284.

ordered becomes fluid, is oriented toward the chance of success, and is judged in its light. The state, as the legal order of the people, is animated by that spirit which is called the world spirit and has stepped upon the stage of world history. It is in the last analysis justified in all that it does or does not do by this world historical calling which to Hegel seems a theodicy. As a consequence, we get a metaphysical "reason of state" which deifies the state on the premise that it is the one state which the world spirit has called at the particular time.

The critics of the Hegelian philosophy of law and the state have frequently stopped at his deification of the state. But this is unwarranted, for the state and its law are ultimately merely means for the realization of the idea of the world spirit. This idea of the world spirit is freedom, which is the true object of the realization of the world spirit in world history. Like Montesquieu, Kant, and other liberal philosophers of law, Hegel places at the head of his entire philosophy of law the idea that man must be free. For this is man's true being, and in becoming conscious of his true being man finds his true destiny. For this reason, law for Hegel receives its meaning by the fact that through it freedom is made possible by providing law with the order within which it can operate. This is mainly a thought related to Greek antecedents. We read at a decisive place in Hegel: "The basis of law and right is altogether the *spiritual,* its starting point the *will* which is *free.* Freedom constitutes its substance and its end, and the legal system is the realm of actualized freedom, the world of the spirit created by the spirit as its second nature" (§ 4). And further: "*Right* and *law,* then, result from the fact that any human existence is an *existence of free willing beings.* Right and law are altogether freedom as an idea" (§ 29). (The italics are Hegel's.)

Hegel explicitly rejects what he calls the liberal view of freedom which Kant had expounded and which culminates in the proposition that the legal community is characterized by the fact that "the freedom, that is to say arbitrary preference, of each one can coexist with that of every other one according to a general law." This so-called law of reason, and the negative determination of freedom related to it, are rooted according to Hegel in the view which has become general since Rousseau that the will of the individual with its peculiar arbitrary preferences is the first thing, whereas, according to Hegel, it is the rational will which comes first. It is obvious that this criticism is not very much to the point if one bears in mind what was really Rousseau's doctrine of the general will and Kant's of the categorical imperative. But Hegel's reference to the terror of the Jacobins (§ 29) suggests the true political controversy. Reason applied as an external standard to human affairs stands in diametrical opposition to a reason which is immanent in these affairs and which unfolds through them. Hegel's freedom is one which is contained within the law, which unfolds as part of the dialectic of history, and thus "freedom constitutes its substance and determines it."

Hegel's view of law and right, which is evidently thoroughly rationalist, must not be confused or equated with that of the historical school as represented by Hegel's great contemporary, Friedrich Carl von Savigny. Hegel stood in sharpest opposition to Savigny. We have already mentioned how unequivocally Hegel rejected the passive attitude and the traditionalism of the historical school. Its dislike for legislation and codification Hegel considered entirely wrong. Yet, like it, he considered law "as something sacred," but he did so because law is "the existence of the absolute concept of self-conscious freedom." Here once more we are confronted with the problem of the dialectic which is the moving principle of the concept, or rather, conception. "This dialectic is not an external activity of a subjective thought, but is the very soul of the content which organically puts forward its branches and roots." And furthermore, "science has only the task of making conscious this inherent rationality of the objects" (§ 31). What is decisive here is the notion of an imminent destiny. The dialectic of law is the recognition of "the soul of law."[4] Law is

[4] The Neo-Hegelian philosophy of law as represented, for example, by Joseph Kohler, *Lehrbuch der Rechtsphilosophie* (3d ed., 1923) has attempted to eliminate the dialectic from Hegelian philosophy of law. The same was undertaken by the English Neo-Hegelians as represented by B. Bosanquet, *Philosophical Theory of the State* (1899). Regardless of how one judges such

thus the realization of freedom. If someone should ask how this freedom is to be understood, Hegel would refer to the law. Only there can one see what any man is called upon to do as a free man. Therefore, we should like to quote, by way of a conclusion, a very general statement which Hegel placed at the end of his general reflections: "To consider something rational does not mean to apply reason to such a matter from the outside and thus to work upon it [*bearbeiten*] but to recognize that the object is by itself rational; here it is the spirit in its freedom, the highest summit of self-conscious reason, which gives itself reality and creates itself as the existing world; science has only the task of making conscious this labor of reason" (§ 31).

This imminent regularity of social development and structuring was destined to receive an interpretation at the hands of Karl Marx and Friedrich Engels very different from that of Hegel. But both Marx and Engels built upon the Hegelian notion of a rationality inherent in the things that unfold in the drama of their dialectic, so that nothing remains for man but to try to understand these relations and to comprehend their inherent development.

But before we turn to Marxism, it is necessary to consider in somewhat greater detail the so-called historical school founded by Gustav Hugo (1764–1861) and developed to its fullest flower in Germany by Friedrich Carl von Savigny (1779–1861).[5] In England, where the historical school flowered somewhat later than in Germany and to some extent under German influence, the most eminent representatives were Sir Henry Maine (1822–88)[6] and

efforts, it is difficult to see why Radbruch should be justified in claiming that such a Neo-Hegelian philosophy of law has "little to do with Hegel" because "Hegelianism without dialectic is no Hegelianism." In the recent literature which is influenced by the renaissance of Hegel's studies, the most important contribution is Franz Rosenzweig, *Hegel und der Staat* (1920). See further references in the Bibliography. Cf. also the fine chapter in Huntington Cairns, *Legal Philosophy from Plato to Hegel* (1949), chap. xiv.

[5] Concerning Savigny, see Adolf Stoll, *Friedrich Karl von Savigny* (3 vols., 1927–29). Concerning Hugo, compare Fritz von Hippel, *Gustav Hugo's Juristischer Arbeitsplan* (1931), and the literature cited there. Cf. also Erik Wolf, *Grosse Rechtsdenker der deutschen Geistesgeschichte* (2d ed., 1944), chap. xii.

[6] His most important work is *Ancient Law* (1861).

Frederick William Maitland (1850–1906). The latter was greatly devoted to Otto von Gierke (1844–1921).[7] In all these writers, but more particularly in the earlier German group, the romantic notion of the spirit of a people is vigorously alive. Unlike Hegel, these men treated national spirits as self-contained entities without any subjection to a world spirit. For in the historical school, the turn to historical positivism takes place. According to Savigny, there exists "an organic connection between law and the nature and character of a people." For "what unites them into a whole is the common beliefs of the people, the same sentiment of inner necessity, which excludes all thought of an accidental and arbitrary origin."[8] According to such an idea, customary law is the truly living law. As compared with it, legislation is unimportant; it is good only insofar as it is of a declaratory nature. But there is in Savigny a point of view, a strange fissure, which is akin to the contradiction in Hegel's attitude toward the national spirit. For Savigny was by no means ready to treat all national legal forms as equivalent. On the contrary, the Roman law stood for him above all other legal systems as an example and a norm. His main work was devoted to the "purification" of medieval Roman law from the "admixtures" of a later time. This is philosophically paradoxical, since these admixtures were the very notions by which the national spirit of the Germanic peoples (if it existed) must have become manifest. Out of this contradiction there developed a sharply divergent dualism of the schools in German legal historical scholarship. On the one hand, we have the Germanistic school, devoting itself particularly to German legal history; this school was founded by Karl Friedrich Eichhorn (1786–1854), further developed by Jacob Grimm in the full spirit of romanticism, and

[7] Gierke's most important work was *Das deutsche Genossenschaftsrecht*, 4 vols., of which partial translations into English have appeared, more particularly Sir Ernest Barker's *Natural Law and the Theory of Society* (1934). Maitland's work, by contrast, ranged over a wide field and was primarily distinguished by great editions to which he brought in his introductions an extraordinary grasp of the intellectual setting within which the history of law occurs. Cf. *Constitutional History of England* (1908).

[8] *Geschichte des römischen Rechts im Mittelalter* (6 vols., 1815–31), Foreword. See also *Das Recht des Besitzes* (1803); the latter is in many ways the most extraordinary juristic work in the German language.

found perhaps its most outstanding representative in Otto von Gierke. On the other hand, we have the men who, in the spirit of Savigny himself, continued to cultivate the history of Roman law and who, of course, had distinguished representatives, such as Ihering and Sohm, as well as the great legal historians of Italy and France.

We do not find a legal philosophy in the strict sense in these legal historians, although Gierke, for one, several times defended the natural law with considerable animation. This historicism is part of a pronounced academic and professorial self-confidence which asserts that the learned jurist is "the carrier and the interpreter of the national spirit."[9] For in the progress of culture, so Savigny once declared, the law which lived before in the consciousness of the entire people "becomes the consciousness of the jurists by whom the people are now represented in this regard."

The body of thought in which the historical school was rooted is to a considerable extent derived from Edmund Burke (1727–97), the great English liberal, the enemy of the French Revolution, the eminent theoretician of conservatism. His decisive basic concepts, like "tradition" and "prescription" and "immemorial custom," made him interpret the English constitutional and legal system as a creation of the English national spirit, which he praised in speeches and writings of great oratorical polish. To recognize this is to understand that the historical approach to law in England has its important native founders, like Sir Henry Maine, its greatest representative, who might well have written without any reference to the German historians. In any case, there is a striking ingredient in Sir Henry which relates him to the prevailing English positivism. It gives his historical studies a comparative slant which made him formulate a number of famous generalizations, among which the best known is the one about status and the law. He tried to show that in the development of law there is to be observed in all legal systems a steady progression from status, as characteristic of the relation between persons in a primitive soci-

[9] Georg Dahm, *Deutsches Recht: Die geschichtlichen und dogmatischen Grundlagen des geltenden Rechts* (1951), p. 151.

ety, to contract, as the natural form of such relations in a developed society. For this reason, Maine looked upon freedom of contract as a kind of crowning achievement of legal development. The more recent trend showing a marked renewal of regulation and limitation of the freedom of contract was not yet apparent, of course, at the time Sir Henry Maine wrote. It is interesting, incidentally, that when Maine wrote *Ancient Law* in 1861 he anticipated to a certain extent the ideas which L. H. Morgan (1818–81) was to set forth concerning the kinship grouping of primitive societies. Morgan's most pre-eminent work, *Ancient Society* (1877), was based upon the notion that culture had developed in a comparable manner everywhere through successive stages of savagery, barbarism, and civilization.[10] Many of the writings of the historical school show an inclination toward philosophical skepticism which is the natural outlook of many historians. Central concepts which are important are introduced as principles into the discussion without critical evaluation, as if they were generalizations empirically derived from the material at hand.

In conclusion, it must be said that although the historical school, like Hegel, operated with the conception of a national spirit, the use made of this concept was profoundly different. Whereas in the historical school it served as a vague unifying principle, providing a kind of general bracket for the study of legal institutions and their evolution in detail, the national spirit in Hegel was treated in a personalized fashion and was given the function of expressing a universal freedom, a principle designated as the manifestation of the world spirit. The hostility between the two was therefore profound and can perhaps be put no more effectively than in terms of a proposition which Hegel advances at the end of his *Philosophy of History*. "We have confined ourselves," he writes, "to the consideration of that progress of the idea, and have been obliged to forego the pleasure of giving a detailed picture of the prosperity, the periods of glory that have distinguished the rise and fall of nations, the beauty and the grandeur of the character of individuals, and the interest attach-

[10] Cf. E. A. Hoebel, *The Law of Primitive Man* (1954), *passim.*

ing to their fate. Philosophy concerns itself only with the glory of the idea mirroring itself in the history of the world. Philosophy escapes to the calm region of contemplation from the weary strife of the passions that agitate the surface of society; that which interests it is the recognition of the process of development which the idea has passed through in realizing itself, the idea of freedom whose reality is the consciousness of freedom and nothing short of it."[11] Such a statement with its cavalier indifference to the details of historical experience was, and was bound to be, anathema to the great historical school. The dialectics of this conflict have profoundly affected legal thought ever since.

[11] *The Philosophy of Hegel,* ed. Friedrich, pp. 157–58.

XVI. *Law as Class Ideology*

MARX AND ENGELS

In his critique of the Hegelian legal philosophy, Marx greatly stresses the contrast of idealism and materialism. He wrote his critique in 1844, and this is worth remembering because the famous phrases from the Preface to *Das Kapital* are basically merely a repetition of his original viewpoint. It is not without interest that Marx formulated his critique of Hegel in relation to the philosophy of law, which of course implies a philosophy of politics. He enunciated at the same time, together with Engels, in *The Holy Family* his kinship with the English philosophers of a materialist point of view, more particularly Bacon and Hobbes.[1] The conception of law as an expression of power, which we have already had occasion to study in these philosophers, is of central importance for Marx.

Law is seen by Marx and Engels, as by the entire Marxian movement, essentially as a part of the ideological superstructure which rises above the material reality of the control of the means of production. Thus Engels wrote: "The particular economic structure forms the real basis by which the entire superstructure of legal and political institutions and of the religious, philosophical, and other production [*Herstellungsweise*] of every historical period must in the last analysis be explained."

Law is therefore not oriented to the idea of justice but is a means of dominance and a tool of the exploiters who use it in the interest of their class. It is the task of the critic of the existing

[1] Marx's *Kritik der Hegelschen Rechtsphilosophie* is not, unfortunately, available in English translation, whereas *Die Heilige Familie* (1845) is; *Das Kapital* (1863?), in the three-volume edition published in 1906 (Chas. H. Kerr Co.), is not very specific on problems of law and politics. Engels' late works, cited below (n. 11), need to be consulted.

legal system, as of the existing society, to unmask it as a façade and to recognize its role as part of the ideology of a class.[2]

This attitude of Marx (and of Engels, too) is rooted in a thought derived from Hegel that man in an industrial society is alienated from himself. In Hegel's *Phenomenology of the Spirit* there is a very remarkable discussion of rule and servitude and of labor as divestiture and appropriation.[3] But whereas the phenomenon of lord and servant is treated by Hegel as an existential reality, Marx gives it a revolutionary and utopian turn. He argues that the alienation can be eliminated by the proletariat's seizure of power. A decidedly eschatological attitude[4] brings it about that Marx hopes for the creation of genuine community via the establishment of the dictatorship of the proletariat. What is important for us here is that law is a very important aspect of this alienation, this formalization of all communal life. It is therefore quite characteristic that Marx and Engels should hold that law would become unnecessary and superfluous in a communist society.[5]

Marx and Engels describe the state in the *Communist Manifesto* (1847) as an executive committee: "The modern state is

[2] The comment which Radbruch set forth in his *Rechtsphilosophie* (3d ed., 1932), p. 19, has not been able to prevail against communism and must be seen as a social-democratic gloss. The quote from Engels is found in *Die Entwicklung des Sozialismus von der Utopie zur Wissenschaft* (1882); the translation is my own.

[3] This particular part of Hegel's work has aroused a good deal of interest in recent years. There is a very widespread tendency to translate Hegel's terms *Herr* and *Knecht* as "master" and "slave," but these translations are a distortion of Hegel's thought. The German word *Herr* means "lord" or "ruler," and the German word *Knecht* means "servant." There are perfectly good words for master and slave in German: the one would be *Meister,* and the other would be *Sklave.* See for all this my *The Philosophy of Hegel* and more especially the short extract given there from the *Phenomenology of the Spirit.* Incidentally, these sections were most brilliantly commented upon by Alexandre Kojève, *Introduction à la lecture de Hegel: Leçons sur la phénoménologie de l'esprit* (1947).

[4] Cf. Jacob Taubes, *Abendländische Eschatologie* (1947), and Karl Popper, *The Open Society and Its Enemies* (1945), Vol. II, chap. xxiv.

[5] The development of this component of Marx's thought is the subject of a very penetrating study by Heinrich Popitz, *Der entfremdete Mensch: Zeitkritik und Geschichtsphilosophie des jungen Marx* (1953); Popitz shows very clearly the relation to Hegel.

nothing but a committee for managing the common affairs of the entire bourgeois class." Since at that time free general elections were not yet common, it was possible to defend such a viewpoint.[6] But it is necessary to understand this formulation also as a vivid expression of Marx's opposition to Hegel: it is the sharpest rejection of the ethical nature of the state, which Hegel had asserted.

Marx and Engels did not find an opportunity to treat the specifically legal questions in any detail. Perhaps this is in part explained by the fact that they expected, in the classless society of the future, the spontaneous co-operation of a liberated mankind. Thus we read in the *Communist Manifesto:* "When in the course of development class distinctions have disappeared and all production has been concentrated in the hands of the vast association of the whole nation, the public power will lose its political character. In place of the old bourgeois society with its classes and class antagonisms, we shall have an association in which the free development of each is the condition for the free development of all." Significantly, law is not even mentioned in this concluding statement of the *Manifesto.*

But evidently the radical rejection of property represents a position of greatest importance in regard to the philosophy of law. For property played a central role in the development of the philosophy of law of the preceding centuries, as we have seen. Not only liberals but writers like Bodin described property as a realm of private autonomy removed from the inroads of even the absolute state. They all conceived the protection of this sphere to be one of the most important aspects of any legal order. This doctrine, which was developed out of ideas already present in Scholasticism, namely, that private property is inviolable, obviously suited the predominant interest of the rising middle classes with which the lawyers who promoted these conceptions were closely linked. Bodin and Althusius, Grotius and Coke, Pufendorf and Locke—they all belong in this context. The whole development rests upon a conviction, which was repeated again and again

[6] Cf. Alfred G. Meyer, *Marxism: The Unity of Theory and Practice* (1954), and Harold Laski, *The State in Theory and Practice* (1935).

and was never seriously questioned, that property provides the essential safeguard for the freedom of the individual. The free man can be only a man of property, and for a long time it was believed that therefore only a man of property ought to participate in political life. Hence not only in Europe but in America, property qualifications remained a universally accepted condition for participation in elections until far into the nineteenth century.

Occasionally, protests against the emphasis on property had been raised, as in the peasant wars whose German part Engels characteristically described in a monograph,[7] by the Anabaptists, by the Diggers during the English Revolution, and by Babeuf and his friends in the French Revolution.[8] With these last ones there began the socialist movement which, in the course of the nineteenth century, became stronger and stronger—represented in France by men like Saint-Simon, Fourier, and Proudhon. Proudhon called property "theft." All these critics of the current concept of property made their attacks in the name of freedom; that is to say, they rejected the traditional linking of property and freedom. The reason was a very simple one: the traditional view started from those who possessed property and then asserted that their freedom and independence rested upon this property. The socialist movement turned the tables and asked what would be the condition of freedom for those who did not possess property and who therefore lived in continuous dependence upon those who did. The demand for the abolition of the property which held them in servitude was the logical consequence of this outlook. It entered into a ready connection with the democratic view which understood freedom as the participation in political life, as the Greeks had done. What this means is that freedom is not a freedom from the government but freedom in and through the government, or "state," as the continental Europeans say. This is indeed the social-

[7] *Der deutsche Bauernkrieg* (1875); no English translation of this significant study seems to exist.

[8] See Perez Zagorin, *A History of Political Thought in the English Revolution* (1954), chap. iv; George H. Sabine, *The Works of Gerrard Winstanley* (1941), Introduction; and (for Babeuf) J. Talmon, *Totalitarian Democracy* (1952), Part III, pp. 167–247.

democratic viewpoint as expressed in the English Labor party[9] and in the social-democratic parties of Europe, wherever they have liberated themselves from Marxist orthodoxy. For orthodox Marxism does not accept such a democratic solution of the problem of freedom.[10] Starting from its conception of the state as an instrument of class interest, communism demands the overthrow of the existing political order and expects that the dictatorship of the proletariat which follows will make the state and its class divisions disappear. According to a famous formula of Engels, "the state withers away." Perhaps it would be worthwhile to cite here the sentences which precede this particular statement because in these sentences the entire Marxist legal and political philosophy is very well expressed:

Whilst the capitalist mode of production more and more completely transforms the great majority of the population into proletarians, it creates the power which, under penalty of its own destruction, is forced to accomplish this revolution. Whilst it forces on more and more the transformation of the vast means of production, already socialized, into state property, it shows itself the way to accomplishing this revolution. *The proletariat seizes political power and turns the means of production into state property.*

But, in doing this, it abolishes itself as proletariat, abolishes all class distinctions and class antagonisms, abolishes also the state as state. Society thus far, based upon class antagonisms, had need of the state. That is, of an organization of the particular class which was *pro tempore* the exploiting class, an organization for the purpose of preventing any interference from without with the existing conditions of production, and therefore, especially, for the purpose of forcibly keeping the exploited classes in the condition of oppression corresponding with the given mode of production (slavery, serfdom, wage labour). The state was the official representative of society as a whole; the gathering of it together into a visible embodiment. But it was this only in so far as it was the state of that class which itself represented, for the time being, society as a whole; in ancient times, the state of slave-owning citizens; in the Middle Ages, the feudal lords; in our own time, the bourgeoisie. When at

[9] See Adam Ulam, *Philosophical Foundations of English Socialism* (1951), for a broad philosophical appraisal.

[10] See Meyer, *op. cit., passim,* and Plamenatz, *The English Utilitarians* (1949), *passim.*

last it becomes the real representative of the whole of society, it renders itself unnecessary. As soon as there is no longer any social class to be held in subjection; as soon as class rule and the individual struggle for existence based upon our present anarchy in production, with the collisions and excesses arising from these, are removed, nothing more remains to be repressed, and a special repressive force, a state, is no longer necessary. The first act by virtue of which the state really constitutes itself the representative of the whole of society—the taking possession of the means of production in the name of society—this is, at the same time, its last independent act as a state. State interference in social relations becomes, in one domain after another, superfluous, and then dies out of itself; the government of persons is replaced by the administration of things, and by the conduct of processes of production. The state is not "abolished." It withers away.[11]

What is to be thought of this alleged withering-away of the state has been made clear by the development in the Soviet Union. However, it must be borne in mind that the Communist leadership, and more particularly Stalin, has explained and excused the developments in the U.S.S.R. by claiming that the withering away is being prevented by the fact that the socialist state, this dictatorship of the proletariat in the Soviet Union, is opposed by a hostile capitalist world against which it must defend itself. Yet from the standpoint of the philosophy of law, it seems very improbable that if this capitalist world should disappear, the Communist world state would wither away and the prophesied age without state come into being. The power struggles within the Soviet Union have shown that the state, that is to say, the political order and the distribution of power, is not only a question of economic interests and behavior including the control of the means of production, but it is also a question of personal predominance and the realization of viewpoints which may be occasioned by ideological and technological disagreements. The very extensive law of the Soviet Union shows that the Marxist starting position, as sketched by Engels, represents a sort of class ideology, that the

[11] F. Engels, *Socialism: Utopian and Scientific* (1882), where the other quotations are also found. I am quoting the translation published in the Marxist Library, Vol. II, and made by Edward Aveling (1935). See also Popper, *op. cit.*, Vol. II, esp. chap xvii.

views of government and law are part of this ideology and cannot claim any kind of scientific value.[12]

But in spite of this oft-repeated criticism, the Marxist analysis of the existing views of law and the state has contributed considerably to the philosophy of law. This analysis has, if one takes it seriously—which unfortunately is frequently not the case—brought it about that the social conditions to which law is related and which it tries to shape are recognized as relevant to the kind of understanding which the legal philosopher seeks. I have indicated in my Introduction that only a conception of the law which is concerned with social reality and human experience can have philosophical meaning. This does not mean that such a conception should be pushed as far as it is in the so-called interest jurisprudence represented by men like Philipp Heck. Law is not only a compromise between separate interests, though it is among other things such a compromise. There is a variable factor involved here, and different historical periods present different kinds of balance between the two. The more generally the existing foundation of the social order is accepted, as was the case in the United States until recently and in Europe during the nineteenth century, the more law can be treated *as if* it were only a compromise of existing interests—the reason being that the deeper foundations, the "fundamental agreements," are not questioned.

Marx and Engels, and more particularly the latter, also fertilized the philosophy of law by directing attention to those philosophical problems which are derived from anthropological and ethnological research. In a late work, *The Origin of the Family, of Private Property and the State,* Engels, basing his arguments upon the researches of the American anthropologist Lewis H. Morgan,[13] had come to assert that there was at the beginning of

[12] Alfred G. Meyer, *Leninism* (1957). See also H. Berman, *Justice in Russia: An Interpretation of Soviet Law* (1950), and A. Vishinsky, *The Law of the Soviet State* (1948).

[13] *Ancient Society, or Researches in the Lines of Human Progress from Savagery through Barbarism to Civilization* (1877). Morgan to some extent built upon J. J. Bachofen, who had stressed the importance of matriarchy in *Das Mutterrecht* (1861).

mankind a kind of aboriginal communism (*Urkommunismus*). According to this view there must be placed at the beginning of the social development of mankind a communist society in which the group marriage demanded by Plato was predominant. Even though these views are completely obsolete today and have been replaced by a much more differentiated view of human development,[14] it cannot be denied that the study and understanding of the origins of law have gained greatly in realistic appraisal of scientific evidence as the result of the Marxist challenge.

Finally, it should be noted that Engels recognized only one historical right, namely, the right of revolution. What he asserts is that every legal order contains as an essential ingredient the right of being overthrown. All modern states, he claims, without exception rest upon this right.[15] For this reason, Engels believes that the right of revolution is "in the general consciousness recognized so firmly that it can not be upset." At the present time, one could probably assert the exact contrary. Not one of the existing constitutional states recognizes such a right, and in many of them there exist very detailed and rather far-reaching laws which are devoted to identifying this alleged right as illegal and to preventing its exercise in every conceivable way. This is true not only of constitutional states but to an even higher degree of the totalitarian ones, and particularly of the Soviet Union. Although the state has admittedly not yet withered away, there seems to be very little confidence in its vitality and its capacity to preserve itself on a pacific basis. For that reason, a very extensive penal law has been developed to cope with the enemies of the established order.[16]

The materialistic and Marxist philosophy of law rests, in the last analysis, upon the view that the movements of the dialectic as they occur in human thought are merely a reflection of a dialectic

[14] Cf. Alexander Rüstow, *Ortsbestimmung der Gegenwart,* Vol. I (1950), and P. W. Schmidt, *Das Eigentum in den Urkulturen* (1937).

[15] This position is most clearly stated in Engels' introduction to Marx's *Klassenkämpfe in Frankreich* (1895); the quotation is found there.

[16] See Berman, *op. cit.*; Vishinsky, *op. cit.*; C. J. Friedrich and Z. Brzezinski, *Totalitarian Dictatorship and Autocracy* (1957), pp. 186 ff. and *passim.*

which is at work in reality. Thus Engels could assert that scientific socialism could develop only in Germany because "here the classical philosophy had kept alive the tradition of a conscious dialectic."[17] Indeed, Engels claims that it was the greatest merit of German philosophy to have again taken up dialectics "as the highest form of reasoning." In this connection, Engels praises Hegel most highly while at the same time designating his philosophy "a colossal miscarriage"; that is to say, "this way of thinking turned everything upside down and completely reversed the actual connection of things in the world." The reason for this was, according to Engels (and Marx), that Hegel was an idealist: "to him the thoughts within his brain were not the more or less abstract pictures of actual things and processes but conversely things and their evolution were only the realized picture of the 'idea' existing somewhere from eternity before the world was." Since Hegel connected the idea of a steady development of mankind with the discovery of an "absolute truth," he got involved in internal and incurable contradictions. The only escape was materialism, not the metaphysical materialism of the eighteenth century (such as that of Helvetius) but only the dialectic materialism which recognizes in history "the process of evolution of mankind" and whose task it is to discover the laws of movement of this process. Philosophy as such is no longer needed; only the theory of the thought and its laws remain. "Everything else is subsumed in the positive science of nature and history." This kind of materialism sees everything as evolution and development; it demands of each science that it "make clear its position in the great totality of things and of our knowledge of things." When that is done, "a special science dealing with this totality is superfluous and unnecessary." As a result, the notions of the law and government within the context of dialectical materialism become a shallow positivism which would see the science of law in analogy to natural science as a purely empirical collection of data and their analysis.

In close parallel, the view of history is a view of class struggles,

[17] Engels, *op. cit.*, where the other quotations are also found.

with the exception of the original community.[18] And in turn the classes themselves are interpreted as purely economic power groups. The classes are products of the relations of production and commerce. They are purely economically conditioned. This again is a very important insight, although a partial truth. For undoubtedly economic groups have played a very great role in history, including the history of law. But it is entirely wrong therefore to assert that they have shaped history exclusively. Even if such a phenomenon as conquest and "superimposition" is placed at the beginning of all higher culture, as one recent writer does,[19] such an event or process cannot be understood either in its origins or its consequences as an exclusively economic one. It is more probable anyhow that, apart from force and coercion, the propensity of man to form communities has all along played a decisive role. Law has always in the long process of the evolution of mankind been a means for the defense of the economically weak as well as a means for exploitation. The labor movement of our time has very extensively utilized law, as giving it this chance, and continues to do so in the democratic constitutional states. The conclusion is inescapable that, in spite of the great value which the Marxist insistence upon the ideological aspects of law and its class character had, the insistence of the materialist dialectic philosophy of law that these aspects exhaust the nature of law is unsound.

It is a paradox of recent developments that the unmasking of the ideological aspect of law has vitalized the demand for a just law. In a sense this is not surprising, because beneath the surface of the allegedly positivist and scientific atitude of Marxism there lives a passionate consciousness of value and of normative preference. If one inquires what in broadest philosophical terms is going to be the objective realization of the coming social order, it is

[18] See M. M. Bober, *Karl Marx' Interpretation of History* (1927). See also F. Engels, *The Origin of the Family, Private Property, and the State* (International Publishers, 1942).

[19] Rüstow, *op. cit.*; cf. my comments in "The Political Thought of Neoliberalism," *American Political Science Review*, XLIX (1955), 514 ff.

clear that it is social justice. From the *Communist Manifesto* to the programs of the Internationals, the work of Marx and Engels is founded upon a fervent desire for true law which fully realizes justice as an ideal concept. Their faith in the possibility of such a definitive realization of justice is the very core of their philosophy of law. Such faith gives their philosophy its apocalyptic character. This faith is idealistic in the most extreme sense, and for that reason it demands a very large degree of coercion and force for its realization. Here we may discern the deeper dialectics of the Marxist philosophy of law which has been unfolding before our eyes in the twentieth century.[20]

[20] See also H. B. Mayo, *Democracy and Marxism* (1955), *passim.*

XVII. *Philosophical Liberalism*

IHERING AND STAMMLER

The challenge to the philosophy of law which the position of Marx and Engels contained when it claimed that law is merely a matter of interests did not immediately cause a counter-movement in the philosophy of law. Only its practical manifestations in the Marxist labor movement brought forth a number of philosophical opponents. In the second half of the nineteenth century there developed a considerable literature which consciously or unconsciously was oriented toward this problem, more especially in economics and sociology (Max Weber, Pareto, Simmel). The basic viewpoint of these sociologists is, from a political standpoint, liberal and reflects the older liberal views. But instead of the large number of writers who might be examined, we shall concentrate upon two German philosophers of law who have exercised a very broad juristic influence, namely, Ihering and Stammler. By doing so, we do not wish to imply that other writers, more particularly French thinkers, did not also put forward very significant philosophical positions.

It has been said of Ihering that he was at once the fulfilment and the end of the historical school. In his work, *The Spirit of the Roman Law*,[1] he undertook to show how a concrete national spirit is realized in the legal institutions of a people. What Hegel had asserted in accordance with his dialectic, what the historical school had assumed as a hypothesis, Ihering tried to prove in concrete historical fashion. But history cannot be so simply determined, and the conflicting historical positions tend to confuse the conception of law which is to be demonstrated in such an analysis.

The legal philosophy of Ihering is focused upon two poles, pur-

[1] Rudolph von Ihering, *Der Geist des römischen Rechts auf den verschiedenen Stufen seiner Entwicklung* (3 vols., 1852–65); *Der Kampf ums Recht* (1872); *Der Zweck im Recht* (2 vols., 1877–83).

pose and struggle. It is the struggle, the fight over the purposes, which may be realized in law, out of which law emerges. But it remains an open question how these purposes are motivated, whether they are derived from class interest or from other components of human purposiveness. By that, the Marxist conception of law as merely oriented toward economic purposes is questioned. Ihering, like the typical liberal that he was, thinks of the several possible purposes as homologous and resulting from individual determination.

As a consequence, Ihering makes human personality and its freedom central to his legal philosophy. The position of a person in the world rests upon three propositions: I am here for myself; the world is here for me; I am here for the world. Ihering declares that "the entire legal order rests" upon these three basic principles. But further than that, he would claim that the entire ethical world order rests upon them.[2] It is very characteristic that the "I" is thus the very center of the entire philosophy of law. The purposes which this "I" seeks to realize in keeping with Ihering's principle are the result of his will. The will is conceived by Ihering to be autonomous in the sense of Kantian and post-Kantian philosophy. "Will," he says, "I call the capacity or potentiality of a causality of one's own vis-à-vis the external world." He calls this "an independence of the will from the law of causation," and he means this, in the same sense as Kant, not as a separateness and apartness but as an autonomy (*Selbstgesetzlichkeit*) which absorbs and digests influences coming from outside and transforms them into its own purposes. Ihering throws the gauntlet of liberal conviction at all determinists when he proclaims the decisive importance of personal conviction. "There are no terrors or tortures which man has not employed in order to break the will of another, but the moral power of conviction, the heroism of duty, of personal affection, of religious faith and of patriotism has withstood them all. The witnesses for the unbreakable strength of wills count by the millions." This Ihering feels proves "that the will is not subject to the law of causation but only to the law of

[2] *Der Zweck im Recht* (3d ed., 1892), p. 67.

purpose."[3] His statements sound like a prophetic anticipation of what has proved true under totalitarianism, and hence in a sense they amount to a philosophical anticipation of the limits of the Marxist approach to law and government.[4]

A legal philosophy which thus emphasizes the "I" and the autonomous personality has to face the question of how a harmonization of the existing laws can be brought about. "How can the world exist," Ihering asks himself, "in view of the egoism that wants nothing for the world and everything for itself?" He answers that the world employs egoism by paying it the wages which it demands. He develops a doctrine of "a coincidence of purposes," the crowning of which are law and the state. We find in this coincidence of purposes the realization of the principle "of linking of one's own purpose with the interest of others." Ihering is of the opinion that all human life is based upon this formula; government, society, commerce, and all intercourse depend upon it. If such an interest does not exist, it must be created. There are "organized" and "unorganized" purposes, but the organized purposes are incomparably more important, are incorporated in associations, co-operative groups, and society, and reach their summit in the state. The legal order is the organization of the state's purpose, or rather of the multiplicity of the state's purposes. Within the state, the most diverse interests fight for their realization, and they find in it their mutual adaptation, their coincidence, and thereby also their partial satisfaction. Evidently Ihering's *The Purpose in Law* (*Der Zweck im Recht*) is dedicated to the realization of a liberal and free society.

But in order that this order be realized there must everywhere exist a will for self-preservation. Therefore, the fact of self-denial becomes for Ihering a serious problem. He rejects pure egoism as too one-sided, but he equally pointedly rejects Kant's doctrine of the categorical imperative because this doctrine contains the

[3] *Ibid.*, pp. 24–25.

[4] Regarding the concept of "islands of separateness," see C. J. Friedrich and Z. Brzezinski, *Totalitarian Dictatorship and Autocracy* (1957), chaps. xxii–xxvi.

postulate of absolute elimination of the self, because it expects of the will that it be motivated by the respect for a logical category, the moral law. For Ihering the will is real, and what is needed "in order to move it is a real pressure." This pressure is exercised only by interest.[5] This interest is even at work in those actions which are customarily called altruistic, for even here the self-denial presupposes an interest, and such action is oriented toward the self. Ihering therefore concludes: "There is no such thing as acting for others without the actor at the same time wanting to do something for himself." Only this need not be an egoistic purpose. In order to master the problem, Ihering undertook to develop a system of human purposes. This system he presented as a "theory of practical life." He distinguishes two large groups of interests: the interests of the individual and the interests of the community or society. The first are egoistic purposes of self-preservation, and they have three major forms, the physical, the economic, and the legal. The purposes directed toward the society or community are social purposes, he thinks, some of them being also of an egoistic nature and determined by reward and punishment. But they also rest upon the fact that the individual has "a sentiment of the ethical meaning of his existence"; that is to say, the individual has a sense that he is "meant to serve mankind" according to Ihering's third principle: I am here for the world. This side of human purposiveness Ihering calls ethical self-preservation. The sense of duty and love are its two forms.

It is evident that we are here dealing with a general approach which is philosophically rather naïve and somewhat eclectic, for in it idealistic, utilitarian, and historical elements are combined by what one might call a juristic common sense. The legal philosophy of Ihering demanded a renewed examination of the basic problems which it suggested. More particularly the problem of method, which was implied in the notion of a double causality, urgently called for clarification. Rudolf Stammler was the man who devoted himself to this task and developed a legal philosophy which was based on a Neo-Kantian foundation. What Stammler

[5] *Ibid.*, pp. 49–51.

did was to develop once again the idea of a "right" law in contrast to all positivism, whether of a historical or an analytical nature. This right law is just law and, in the philosophy of Stammler, is erected upon the axiom that every right, like every other value, is subject to the question which asks, Is this right? In three great works he developed and supported this viewpoint in great detail.[6]

At the outset it is important to be in the clear as to what Stammler means by "right" law. He explains that it is "a particular kind of positive law" (p. 22);[7] that is to say, it is "that law which in a particular situation coincides with the basic idea of law altogether" (p. 15). But this does not mean that the right law is natural law. "Right law does not stand outside positive law as some kind of norm with non-legal demands upon the law; it is conceptually not at all identical with a law that may be desired in contrast to one which has historically come into being" (p. 23). In other words, right law constitutes a specific difference, a kind of standard for distinguishing what among all existing law is right law. For this reason, Stammler observes that the standard he has in mind may be applied to the law of the past and to the law of the future as well as to the law of the present. "Right law is positive law, the content of which possesses particular objective qualities" (p. 23). Under which conditions is this the case?

Law as the necessary condition for the lawful conduct of social life is "a coercive attempt at the right"; that is to say, all positive law is an attempt to be right law. Even if we admit that a tyrant or a mob may use law only for arbitrary and subjective preferences, such a situation "does not suspend the notion of a legal order which objectively aims at the right" (p. 31). For "law as a

[6] *Wirtschaft und Recht nach der materialistischen Geschichtsauffassung* (1896; 5th ed., 1924); *Die Lehre von dem Richtigen Rechte* (1932; 2d ed., 1926); *Lehrbuch der Rechtsphilosophie* (3d ed., 1928); compare also his *Theorie der Rechtswissenschaft* (2d ed., 1923). Searching criticism of Stammler's position can be found in Erich Kaufmann, *Kritik der neukantianischen Rechtsphilosophie* (1921), and Julius Binder, *Rechtsbegriff und Rechtsidee* (1915), the latter writing in a Hegelian perspective.

[7] All the quotes are from Stammler's *Die Lehre von dem Richtigen Rechte* (1902), and the page of this first edition is given in parentheses.

means in the service of human purposes requires for its justification the proof that it is a right means for a right purpose." That it is merely wanted does not suffice; "it is always the same concept of right law with uniform characteristics which confronts the merely positive norm" (p. 39). But this does not mean that right law can be derived from ethics or morality. Ethics must be sharply distinguished from law. In the sense of Kant and of Protestantism, ethics is essentially related to conviction, in contrast to law, which fixes the rules for external conduct.[8] But even though law and ethics must be sharply distinguished from each other, they nonetheless stand in a close relation to each other. Right law requires ethics, for only ethics produces the right attitude in rulers and ruled, namely, the commitment to the "ought," which is necessary for the realization of right law. Conversely, ethics cannot get along without right law because without the rules of right conduct it cannot be active, that is, it cannot be actual.

Stammler recognizes the notion of right law in general legal concepts such as good faith, reasonable discretion, good morals, and so forth. All of them lead to the question regarding the method of judging which is required for their application. There is, according to Stammler, in all these cases only one answer, namely, "that the citizen, the consultant or the judge must consider which norm will give the right answer to the controversy" (p. 42). But how are they to achieve this goal? Again, according to Stammler, there is only one way—"the critical reflection about the lawful end of the legal order" (p. 45). This reflection must not be realized by applying a judgment from outside, like that which refers to good morals, but must "be taken from the legality that is immanent in law" (p. 50). This attitude, which is several times repeated by Stammler in different contexts, has been critically examined by a number of writers. Gustav Radbruch, for example, declared that Stammler had "stated the task of legal philosophy rather than solved it," and he added that Stammler's

[8] How important the Protestant position was for Stammler one can see from the fact that, again and again, and particularly at decisive points, he cites Martin Luther and he does so as an essential part of the text.

doctrine "is not so much a philosophy of law as a logic for a philosophy of law" and "a very meritorious prolegomenon to any possible philosophy of law but not the structure itself."[9]

Contrary to all natural law, the value of which Stammler nonetheless defended against its positivist enemies, right law is to be understood as a generally valid method. The purpose of this method is to judge necessarily changing material of empirically conditioned legal rules and to determine it in such wise that it acquires the quality of what is objectively right (p. 116). Such a method is, for Stammler, "a procedure which is oriented toward the whole. It is the sum of rules according to which a certain matter of either cognition or will is determined or judged in a fundamental way with regard to its uniform understanding" (p. 118). Stammler is well aware that the understanding of such a method may be progressively achieved. But its validity is absolute until an error has been proved.

The result of the search for a universally valid method may be summarized by saying that the right law which regulates co-operation in a community is, in its idea, "a unitary method of weighing separate and individual purposes in relation to the final purpose of the community" (p. 196). For what unites all possible purposes of persons who are legally joined together is the final purpose of a "community of free-willing men" (p. 198). This formula Stammler calls "the social ideal." All right law is oriented toward it. Stammler understands this social ideal, in other words, as a measuring rod. "To define the concept of the rightness of a legal proposition one needs to determine it in relation to social regularity: the content of a norm of conduct or behavior is right if in a particular situation it corresponds to the notion of the social ideal" (p. 198). Not the perfection of the individual nor yet his freedom, but the community of free men is the purpose and the end.

Yet though the rightness of a legally willed decision is measured by its correspondence to the social ideal, this ideal must not be

[9] Gustav Radbruch, *Rechtsphilosophie* (3d ed., 1932), p. 24.

understood as a design which is the same one for all and can be realized as such. Further, "the idea of a community of free-willing men is not itself again a legal proposition" (p. 202). Rather this notion of a social ideal "means really the unity of the conditions in terms of which the opposition of the legal content may deserve the predicate of being right with justification" (p. 209).[10] These conditions are set forth in the form of principles which for Stammler follow logically from the social ideal. He identifies altogether four such principles. Of these, two are related to the mutual respect and two to the participation in such a community of free-willing men. The principles of respect are, first, that content of a will must not be subject to the arbitrary preference of another and, second, that any legal requirement may exist only in the sense that he who is obligated by it can yet be his own neighbor. The principles of participation, on the other hand, are, first, that a legally obligated member may not by arbitrary decision be excluded from the community and, second, that all legal power of disposition may be exclusive only in the sense that he who is excluded may still be a neighbor to himself.

We cannot enter here into a critical discussion of these principles, but their mere formulation may show that we are dealing with decidedly liberal principles. For even though the individual as such is not postulated as the exclusive and final purpose, as he was in the older liberalism of Wilhelm von Humboldt or John Stuart Mill, and even though the community of these individuals takes the place of the individual as such, this community is seen as essentially directed toward these individuals. To be sure, Stammler asserted that these standards and methods were purely formal; we can recognize by a closer inspection that they are decidedly value-oriented. Stammler seeks to escape from this consequence by interpreting the right law, which he develops as a form of legal matter, this legal matter being the historically exist-

[10] These "conditions" are not seen by Stammler as causal conditions but rather as logical "forms of every possible experience" in the sense of the Kantian critique of the understanding.

ing law. But this historical law is in turn form, the stuff of which is concrete social life.[11] Stammler's formulations are typically idealistic. He claims that the form of the content of a thought is the unity of the persistent elements of it, in contrast to the specific features which may be observed in its content, the concrete phenomenon. Law therefore is not something which is added to the particularities of social life like something which is imposed upon them from the outside, but is given in this very life and its conditions. But how does law then relate to custom and mores? I think that for Stammler custom and mores are, so to speak, indirect legal rules, conventional rules, that is to say, the effective validity of which is determined by law. In other words, these customary norms lack the element of autonomy which the law of the positive kind possesses; they also lack its permanence. They are "a fleeting stuff" (p. 235). Law in any case assumes that the content of such conventional rules "harmonizes with the principles of right law" (p. 237).

What follows from all this in the sense of neo-liberalism is that the economy does not live as an independent entity which the state and the legal order interfere with but which might exist without such legal order as a thing separate and apart. Rather the economy exists only "as a legally regulated working together" (p. 243).[12] For these reasons, a completely centrally directed economy (*Einheitswirtschaft*) and a completely competitive economy (*Wirtschaft freier Beiträge*) are marginal concepts. It is a methodological error "to think of the social existence of man as a coexistence of several individuals whose natural freedom the state

[11] The distinction between form and matter or stuff which Stammler employs is, in his opinion, that of Aristotle. This interpretation appears rather problematical, but I cannot here explore the problem. Compare the writings of Kaufmann and Binder cited above (n. 6) for this purpose.

[12] This idea is highly characteristic for neo-liberalism as expressed particularly among the writers who belong to the group publishing the annual *Ordo,* though they seldom speak of this connection. See *Ordo-Jahrbuch für die Ordnung von Wirtschaft und Gesellschaft* (7 vols. since 1949). Compare also my article "The Political Thought of Neo-Liberalism," *American Political Science Review,* XLIX (1955), 509 ff.

interferes with by force" (p. 247). The concept of a legal regulation is the very condition of the concept of society and equally of an economy. For this reason it is not possible to draw generally valid limits, as had been attempted by Humboldt, because the limits between state, government, and society are determined according to the particular situation within the framework of the social ideals which right law offers. How far Stammler was prepared to go in this direction is seen in his assertion that "the idea of a struggle for survival inside the legal association and among the members of the community as a possibility is the most extreme error; for only a common and joint struggle against the adversities and scarcities of man's living conditions can be considered right" (p. 251).

What has been said shows that Stammler's idea of right law must not be equated with the idea of justice, no matter how close the relations between the two seem to be.[13] For besides justice, equity as the moderation or *epieikeia* of Aristotle is an important source of right law. On the other hand, right law must not be misunderstood as a creation of the state, for the state is based upon law which logically precedes it. Here too we can discern the markedly liberal basic attitude of Stammler. But, as we have said, his outlook is no longer purely individualistic; it sees the individual as a communal being. The precision of Stammler's argumentation, which we have tried to let speak for itself by numerous quotations, must not deceive us and make us overlook the fact that the marked formalism of Stammler's thought, in the sense of Kant's critical rationalism, is subject to philosophical objections of the kind formulated by Max Scheler.[14] On the other hand, it is

[13] This happened in the English translation of Stammler's *Lehre von dem Richtigen Rechte,* which is entitled *The Theory of Justice* (1925); the same error is found in Haines, cited below, chap. xix, n. 1. In both cases, the philosophical basis of Stammler's argument was not clearly grasped as resting upon the Kantian critique of reason. Compare particularly *Die Lehre von dem richtigen Rechte,* pp. 248–50.

[14] Max Scheler, *Der Formalismus in der Ethik und die materiale Wertethik* (1913 and 1916; 3d ed., 1926).

important to recognize that Stammler succeeded in showing clearly what the logical premises of all legal thinking are; for by doing so he shook positivism to its foundations. From Stammler, the road leads, on the one hand, to relativism and skepticism as I intend to discuss them in the next chapter and, on the other hand, to a revival of the natural law which I will treat in chapter xix.

XVIII. *The Decline of Legal Philosophy*

RELATIVISTS, FORMALISTS, AND SKEPTICS

If we sense in Stammler and in the Kantian schools generally an element of skepticism, this trend is greatly strengthened in positivism, because positivism implies at bottom, at least with reference to philosophy, a markedly skeptical outlook. For what do the several positivists say but that to philosophize makes no sense and has no value? Beyond that, the positivists insist that what matters is the systematic and empirically reliable analysis of the positive legal materials as they are presented in statutes, ordinances, decisions, and administrative practice. But how is such analysis to proceed? How are we to choose among the vast masses of material and how are we to organize them? The skeptic may, in answer to such a methodological question, develop a purely formal attitude based upon a critical appraisal of the limits of human understanding, or he may turn to common sense, the *communis opinio doctorum* and similar notions. These variations of common sense, like formalism itself, hide rather than solve the philosophical problem because the question is precisely where the standards for evaluation of the common men whose common sense is being acclaimed come from? They can be of religious or philosophical or cultural origin. Presumably, this viewpoint may be very naïve or hypercritical. Only the latter is of interest here. Skepticism results from a multiplicity of systems and a richness of philosophical education. This was the situation in classical antiquity, and it has been the situation in recent times. If such positive skepticism leads to scientific labor and the analysis of positive legal materials, it may be combined with scholarly achievement of the first order. Only if it is extended to scholarship as such does it become hostile to scientific work in the general sense.

A subtle variant of skepticism is relativism. Among recent philosophers of law, relativism has been most impressively expounded by Gustav Radbruch (1878–1949). He shows in his philosophy of law[1] very clearly how relativism emerged from Neo-Kantianism. The decisive position is that of the skeptical notion concerning the discovery of truth. To put this point specifically concerning law, the proposition is advanced that absolute judgments about law are not discoverable, that is to say, not demonstrable. Radbruch develops this position as do most of the Neo-Kantians on the basis of a sharp separation of the existential and the normative grounds, of the "is" and the "ought" (*Sein* and *Sollen*). "The philosophy of Kant has shown us the impossibility of deducing from what is that which is valuable, that which is right, that which ought to be. Never is something right merely because it is or because it was—or even because it is going to be" (p. 6).[2] But the correctness of the second of these statements does not prove the correctness of the preceding one. Certainly nothing is simply and only valuable because it is, but, though that is so, it may still be possible to deduce something concerning the value or lack of it of a particular thing or action from what is or what is not.[3] The actual is very relevant for the sphere of values, and not only because values determine actions and because their consequences may be different from what was expected. The relevancy which can be demonstrated in many connections actually is the result of the many-sidedness of the world of values and the problems connected with its inner order, that is to say, with what is sometimes called the hierarchy of values.

The conviction that values are completely autonomous leads

[1] The last of these editions which Radbruch himself edited was the third one (1932). The fourth one was published in 1950 and in a number of important points questioned his earlier relativism. See for this the Introduction by Edwin W. Patterson to *The Legal Philosophies of Lask, Radbruch, and Dabin,* translated by Kurt Wilk (1950). For the extended literature concerning Radbruch, consult a thoughtful study by Fritz von Hippel, *Gustav Radbruch als rechtsphilosophischer Denker* (1951), where this change in position is discussed with great care.

[2] The figures in parentheses refer to pages in Radbruch, *Rechtsphilosophie,* (3d ed., 1932).

[3] One is reminded here of the older discussion about whether the consensus of mankind proves a certain legal rule to be right, as Hooker thought, or does not, as Locke was inclined to feel (see chaps. ix, xii). For a further discussion of the problem of fact and value and their relation to theory, law, and justice, cf. my *Man and His Government* (1963), chaps. ii, xv, xvi.

Radbruch to the parallel conviction that they are not demonstrable. Prime values spring from the metarational ground of human willing. Radbruch says one can clarify one's thought regarding them, one can try to understand their consequences, but one cannot demonstrate them to another man by rational argument. And since all law in the last analysis depends upon such a value notion because it is determined by the idea of justice toward which law is oriented, a philosophy of law can merely seek to discover these several values and the scales of values and to indicate them more clearly, but it cannot resolve the contradiction between these values. This means, with reference to the present time, that the positions of the several parties are relative: "Since therefore the philosophy of law is on the one hand the intellectual reflection of the struggle of the political parties, the struggle of the political parties in turn appears as a grandiose discussion of the philosophy of law" (p. 9). To put it another way, since propositions concerning the ought are arguable and demonstrable only with reference to other propositions concerning the ought, ultimate propositions concerning the ought are capable of being "confessed" but not of being "scientifically known." But what happens when the ought as posited encounters facts which were not anticipated? Has not socialism in our time made precisely this experience? And is it impossible to communicate to other persons the nature and significance of this experience?

Radbruch calls the position which he represents a "method" and says that it proposes "merely to ascertain the correctness of a certain value judgment in relation to a certain highest value judgment, that is to say only within the framework of a certain general value and world view, but that it does not propose to ascertain the rightness of this value judgment, that is to say of this general value and world view" (p. 11).[4] "If the philosophy of law does

[4] Radbruch at this point in his discussion mentions as the most important representatives of relativism Georg Jellinek, Max Weber, and Hans Kelsen. I discuss the last one at the end of the chapter. Radbruch was in his thinking closely linked to Emil Lask, who in his *Philosophy of Law* (1905) laid the foundation for a culturally relativistic philosophy of law. Lask's viewpoint, as Radbruch himself says, has been decisive for his own thinking. See for all this the work cited above, n. 2. It is evident that there are connections here with

not wish to stop at the arbitrary preference of a particular system, it has no other choice but to develop a system of systems without taking a position between them" (p. 25).

But however valuable such a recognition of the many-sidedness of the world of values and of their cultural conditioning may be, the man who is seeking truth and justice will not be prepared to rest content with it. He will ask what the common element of all these value systems is, since all of them are willed by man.[5] Thus one can ask with Stammler what the continuing and presumably self-identical meaning of right law is. It certainly is possible to proceed in an empirical and comparative way in trying to answer this question, or one might try to derive it by a psychological analysis from human nature, or one might deduce it from the essence of *ratio* according to formal considerations, or one might combine a number of these ways. But there is no particular reason for denying that any one of them may lead to rational conviction.

Radbruch undertook to analyze the order of such comprehensive systems of values. Among them there is one of particular importance, namely, that which distinguishes the several groups of values depending upon whether one gives priority to the individual values, the collective values, or the creative values (*Werkwerte*). Radbruch distinguishes accordingly individualistic, trans-individualistic, and trans-personal positions. (Other relativists like Jellinek contrast individualism with universalism.) In an abbreviated formula, Radbruch says that one could put it this way: to the individualistic position, freedom appears as the final end; to the trans-individualistic, the nation; to the trans-personal, culture. Radbruch suggests that one recognize the parallel between this triad and the triad of society, collectivity, and com-

American tendencies of the present, more particularly with cultural anthropology and the views of law and justice which have been influenced by it. Compare Clyde Kluckhohn, *Mirror for Man* (1949).

[5] The basic problems of such a panhumanism I have suggested in my book, *The New Belief in the Common Man* (1941). It is also the core of the important critique of relativism which Arnold Brecht has developed in a series of articles which have now been united in a volume entitled *The Political Philosophy of Arnold Brecht* (1954).

munity (pp. 54, 55). From the standpoint of legal philosophy, such systematizations are useful as a starting point, but they fail us at the very point where the task of philosophy begins (when religion no longer can satisfy man's metaphysical interest), namely, at the point where we have to give a rational ground for a decision in favor of one or another of these positions (even if such rational ground cannot be conclusively demonstrated). For as I said at the very beginning of this study, every philosophy of law is oriented toward and comprehended within a specific general philosophical view. The general philosophical view which is involved in relativism is, as I have said, skepticism, and skepticism is clearly that philosophical position which is most difficult to defend. It shines in the criticism of others but cannot effectively defend its own position because having raised general doubts concerning all possibility of knowledge and understanding, it is exposed to these selfsame doubts.

Upon this philosophical foundation rests Arnold Brecht's very significant critique of the relativistic philosophy of law. Brecht starts from the position that the value of justice is determining all law—a proposition which Radbruch himself makes central in his reflections, clearly following the Neo-Kantians. For Radbruch, "law is the reality which has the meaning of serving the value of law, the idea of law." And again, "The idea of law can be no other than justice." In a decidedly idealistic formulation, justice is given an absolute value alongside truth and beauty. This central position of justice follows from the further definition of law as "a sum of the general arrangements for human coexistence" (pp. 29–30). But whereas Radbruch explains everything that may be said concerning justice, beyond these very general statements, as relative to the particular form of the actual or intended human coexistence, Brecht shows that the idea of justice implies certain very general requirements which he calls postulates. These postulates are in Brecht's own words:

> First, *truth*. In the objective sense justice demands an accordance with truth; in the subjective sense it demands an accordance with what is thought to be true. . . .

Second, *generality* of the system of values which is applied. It is unjust to select arbitrarily a system of values from one case to another.

Third, *treating as equal what is equal under the accepted system.* It is unjust to discriminate arbitrarily among equal cases ("arbitrarily" signifying in contradiction to the accepted system).

Fourth, *no restriction of freedom beyond the requirements of the accepted system.* It is unjust to restrict freedom arbitrarily ("arbitrarily" again meaning in contradiction to the accepted system).

Fifth, *respect for the necessities of nature* in the strictest sense. It is unjust to inflict punishment for non-fulfilment of a law or command which is impossible of fulfilment.[6]

To explore the aspects of the several systems of values is not possible here, but for a rejection of relativism one of Brecht's postulates is sufficient if it can be considered demonstrable in principle. It seems to me that both the last and the first postulate can certainly be thus demonstrated. Brecht himself is satisfied with general indications of the feeling for what is right (*Rechtsgefühl*) and common sense, according to which something cannot be just which is based upon untruth. A judicial decision is considered by everyone unjust when it is based upon facts which in actuality are untrue. Likewise, a statute is condemned as unjust when it does not correspond to demonstrable facts, etc. One could demonstrate Brecht's thesis by comparing the several systems of law. A system of law in which what is actually untrue is asserted to be just does not exist, in my opinion, provided it is recognized that the untruth is understood by those who live under and support the system. The position may also be formally demonstrated by considering the meaning of justice which attributes equal things to equals, for the concept of equality presupposes that what is asserted to be equal actually is equal. We must content ourselves with these hints. They show that what is involved here is not so much truth as truthfulness—truthfulness taken not as a personal quality or virtue but in the sense of a recognition that certain kinds of meaning correspond to each other.

[6] Brecht, *op. cit.*, pp. 35–36. Cf. also the discussion of justice in my *Man and His Government* (1963), chap. xv.

But if such an "absolute" meaning of justice, that is to say, a meaning not derived and hence not relative, can be asserted, a breach is opened into the fortress of relativism, for one can now ask further how the truth, which is so important, can be secured. Law is thus referred to those social realities which are immediately relevant to law. This is the very position which the "pure theory of law," as it is expounded by Hans Kelsen, firmly rejects.[7] In many respects, this pure theory of law is the most consistent doctrine developing the basic positions which are involved in skepticism and positivism. But instead of doing it as philosophical relativism had attempted to do, by systematically relating law to social reality, the pure theory of law seeks to solve the problem of norms by excluding all social reality. Kelsen too starts from Kant's separation of the is and the ought, but he pushes it to a radical extreme so that basically all connection between these two worlds of the is and the ought are denied—a position which goes far beyond that which Kant himself took.[8]

It is well known that Kant, much to the dismay of his purely logical interpreters, resumed the tradition of natural law in his ethical and legal doctrine. Indeed, in a sense he is the man who gave to this position its final form (see above, chap. xiv). Law as the bridge between ethics and politics was thus integrated in the total configuration of the world. Pure theory of law resulted from

[7] See Hans Kelsen, *Hauptprobleme der Staatsrechtslehre* (1911), *Reine Rechtslehre* (1934), *Allgemeine Staatslehre* (1925), and more particularly *Der juristiche und der soziologische Staatsbegriff* (1928); see also Bibliography. For this whole school, consult William Ebenstein, *Die rechtsphilosophische Schule der Reinen Rechtslehre* (1938), where the other representatives of this school are treated. Ebenstein, in my opinion, gives proper recognition to the importance of Stammler for the pure theory of law. Rightly, Ebenstein points out (p. 44) that the pure theory of law is a philosophy of law in the sense of a "theory of the science of law in a transcendental meaning." See also Kelsen's recent volume, *What Is Justice?* (1956), which gathers and implements a number of his important recent articles in legal philosophy.

[8] Compare Ebenstein, *op. cit.*, p. 110. Ebenstein also shows how strong the influence on Kelsen was of Hermann Cohen and his interpretation of Kant in terms of a logic of cognition. (Kelsen himself has fully recognized this.) Ebenstein claims that Franz Weyr was the most penetrating representative of the philosophical foundation of the pure theory of law. Compare for this Weyr's *Rechtsphilosophie und Rechtswissenschaft* (1921). Alongside this, one should take into account two phenomenological interpretations by Felix Kaufmann and Fritz Schreier, whose works are cited in the Bibliography.

an effort "to develop a normative theory of normative cognition which would parallel the theories of cognition concerning natural phenomena in Kant."[9] Such an effort is very much opposed to the view of Kant, who did not wish to subject the laws of freedom to the predestination of the laws of nature. For law is here shown as a world of things analogous to those in nature. This world must be ordered by the normological effort of legal science which is thus unified. Such an undertaking appears at first sight quite meaningful, since Kant had replaced the ontological concept of an object by a concept of relations. For law is a realm of relations. But this realm in Kant is subject to the concept of freedom as its prime hypothesis. The concept of freedom and not the concept of the norm corresponds, according to Kant, to the hypothesis of causation which dominates nature. A norm is therefore already a transposition of this hypothesis of freedom into some kind of "realization" or "actualization" (*Verwirklichung*).

The radical separation of the is and the ought, of the existential and the normative realm, to which corresponds the separation of substance and form, produces the decidedly formal outlook of the pure theory of law which does not, so to speak, wish to soil itself with the dirty concrete world. Yet the pure theory of law, since it not only is positivistic but also radically extends the positivist tendency toward a neutrality in respect to values, strictly insists that it is concerned only with the positive legal order. Law is seen in its actual details as a content with regard to which the theory of law develops the essential concepts of law (*Rechtswesensbegriffe*), according to which the content of law (*Rechtsinhaltsbegriffe*) must be arranged and ordered. Thus the pure theory of law becomes a theory of potential law within which all actually existing law is seen as "accidental" (*zufällig*). As a consequence, one representative of the theory could say that "the pure theory of law is only a part of logic."[10]

Like all positivism, the pure theory of law is in sharpest opposi-

[9] Ebenstein, *op. cit.*, p. 24 and elsewhere.

[10] See Fritz Schreier, *Grundbegriffe und Grundformen des Rechts* (1924), p. 81. I have followed the usage established by Kelsen of speaking of the *reine Rechtslehre* as a pure *theory* of law, but within my own frame of refer-

tion to all natural law. The natural law appears to Kelsen either as an ideological façade for the existing legal order or as an ideological façade for its criticism. He cannot admit the challenge of natural law because it contradicts the unity of legal science, for the unity of method is, according to some philosophers, the first postulate of every science. But apart from criticizing this proposition which I consider highly doubtful, one might ask whether natural law may not be absorbed into this unity. What prevents us from treating the norms which it contains together with the norms of the positive legal order as a whole? Kelsen does not answer this question in any other way than all positivists; he says that the particular given positive law is *the* law which it is the task of science to understand, that this positive law consists of coercive norms which are created by *the* "state," and that therefore a set of norms which is in conflict with the norms willed by the state cannot be recognized.[11] If one asks upon what the validity of these norms of the positive law rests, Kelsen and his school answer: upon the basic norm (*Grundnorm*). This basic norm is a norm which states that one should obey a parliament, a monarch, etc. Why this should be so remains an open question. This decisive question remains unanswered, with the result that the "state" or the makers of the *Grundnorm* are made into an axiomatic absolute, with the further result that peace is asserted to have greater value than justice.[12] Kant, in spite of all his emphasis on the value of peace, never took any such position, for even though he postulated a kind of basic norm, he allowed this to rest upon a "natural law"; that is to say, he demonstrated it in terms of the law of nature. Kelsen, by contrast, speaks of "contenting one's self" (*Sich-Bescheiden*). This self-contentment expresses itself in a purely hypothetical assumption of this basic norm. The importance of the basic norm must be seen in the fact that by it and through it the

---

ence it would be more correct to speak of the "doctrine of pure law," for the adjective qualifies the term "law" and not the term "theory"; furthermore the term "theory" is more exact than the term *Lehre* in German.

[11] Kelsen's main work on this question is *Die philosophischen Grundlagen der Naturrechtslehre und des Rechtspositivismus* (1928). See also numerous articles (cf. n. 7 above.)

[12] Cf. Ebenstein, *op. cit.*, pp. 90 ff.

unity of the system of norms is given. For the basic norm is "that norm the validity of which cannot be derived from a higher one." And a system of norms is given by its relation to a basic norm: "All norms, whose validity may be traced back to one and the same basic norm, form a system of norms, or of order."[13] But this question concerning the validity of norms is not to be understood psychologically or sociologically or politically, but strictly normatively. With such a proposition the problem of validity is not solved but turned into a tautology. Here we can see the danger of splitting the world into two halves, that of the is and that of the ought. The basic norm actually is presupposed to be valid. Within the realm of the constitutional order, the consequences are very odd. "If we ask why the constitution is valid, perhaps we come upon an older constitution." Ultimately, we reach some constitution that is the first historically and that was laid down by an "individual usurper" with some kind of assembly. Even the will of such a usurper is ground for a basic norm which in that case says, "Thou shalt obey." Thus Kelsen concludes that "the validity of this first constitution is the last presupposition, the final postulate upon which the validity of all the norms of our legal order depends" (p. 115). It is therefore "postulated that one ought to behave as the individual or the individuals who laid down the first constitution have ordained." The absurdity of this position results from Kelsen's attempt to be at the same time a radical positivist and a radical normativist. The refusal to consider historical, sociological, and political realities when the validity of the norms is under discussion amounts to a denial of the philosophical problem when this refusal is combined with the refusal to recognize either a rational or a revelational basis as the starting point. "The basic norm of the legal order prescribes that one ought to behave as the fathers of the constitution and the individuals authorized by the constitution command." The desire of man to understand the meaning of legal obligation is not satisfied by such a doctrine.

[13] See Kelsen's *General Theory of Law and the State* (1945), p. 111. In this work, Kelsen "intended to re-formulate rather than merely to republish thoughts and ideas previously expressed in German and French" (see p. xiii). The page references in the text refer to this edition.

He neither learns the natural ground for norms which he is asked to obey nor is he given a firm conviction or a faith. In its place we find a bland recognition of bare power and the application of force. The most striking expression for this is Kelsen's identification of state and legal order: "The state as a juristic person is a personification of the [national] community or the national legal order constituting this community." Between state and law there is basically no difference: "The community consists in nothing but the normative order regulating the mutual behavior of the individuals" (p. 183). Not how the individuals actually behave but how they ought to behave—this and nothing else is the community. Apart from the vicious circles and tautologies which are contained in these propositions (how can the state personify what it is?), it is important to understand clearly that this readiness, indifferent to all values, to designate every power to command as an "order of norms" (*Sollensordnung*), that is to say, as something valuable, may be meaningful for a time which is peaceful and unified in its value judgments, but it becomes doubtful in a time which is torn by conflicts over values.

Kelsen himself escaped from the implied indifference by referring all such problems to "sociology" and then defending the basic values of liberal democracy as, for example, constituting the "sociological concept of the state" (*Staatsbegriff*). Nor can there be any doubt, in light of our general analysis, that the pure theory of law is a radical form of liberal thinking on law, as its derivation from Kant clearly indicates. But our analysis also reveals the weakness of such liberalism when confronted with the basic challenge of totalitarianism.

Besides the law of nature and the philosophical positions which are akin to this doctrine, Kelsen with equal vehemence struggles against the sociological school of jurisprudence. This viewpoint, which in Germany was represented by Max Weber, Eugen Ehrlich, and others,[14] has had many followers, especially in America.

[14] See Eugen Ehrlich, *Grundlegung der Soziologie des Rechts* (1913); besides that, Max Weber, *Wirtschaft und Gesellschaft* (1925), particularly pp. 387–513, and *The Theory of Social and Economic Organization,* translated by A. M. Henderson and Talcott Parsons and edited with an Introduction by Talcott Parsons (1947), esp. pp. 324–82. The page references in the text refer to the German edition; the translations are my own.

Ehrlich, an Austrian, was one of the first to stress the importance of going outside the formal system of law, especially as represented by the Continental codes, in order to discover the operative rules of conduct prevailing in various sectors of society. His stress was on the actual living processes, as compared with logical concepts and abstract norms. His was a significant challenge which was carried forward by a number of jurists in other countries; in the United States this view coincided with an increasing recognition of social realities in judicial decisions and pleadings before courts, as epitomized by Brandeis' famous brief before the United States Supreme Court in 1908. Its greatest theoretical proponent was Roscoe Pound.[15] But the systematic exploration of the sociological setting within which legal phenomena occur did not remain the province of jurists alone. Max Weber places law within the context of the social and political reality. He calls an order law "if it is externally guaranteed by the chance of physical or psychic coercion resulting from the actions of a specialized staff of men who are directing their actions toward forcing the obedience or punishing the violation of such an order." Evidently we find here, besides the application of force, which is equally important for the pure theory of law, the stress upon the existence of a bureaucratic staff and its behavior. Law is therefore "a complex of factual conditions determining real human actions."

This viewpoint is closely akin to that of the skeptics and cynics who have significantly contributed to recent American philosophy of law—the so-called realists.[16] They were "realists" not in a philosophical, but in a popular, sense of the term, a "next step" (Llewellyn) after sociological jurisprudence. Rather, they were pragma-

[15] *Muller* v. *Oregon,* 208 U.S. 412, 28 Sup. Ct. 324 (1908). For Pound's programmatic statement of the case, see "The Scope and Purpose of Sociological Jurisprudence," in *Harvard Law Review,* XXV (1911–12), 512 ff.

[16] I would name particularly Jerome Frank, Thurman V. Arnold, and Karl Llewellyn. For the last named, all the more important papers are now gathered in the posthumously issued *Jurisprudence* (1962); see also his *The Common Law Tradition* (1961). For Arnold, see *The Folklore of Capitalism* (1937) and *The Symbols of Government* (1935); for Jerome Frank, *Law and the Modern Mind* (1930). Cf. also Max Radin, *Law as Logic and Experience* (1940). Some have protested against the expression "cynics," but Llewellyn explicitly claimed that the realist position was "cynicism." Cf. "On Philosophy in American Law," *Pennsylvania Law Review,* LXXXII (1933–34), 212.

tists; but their philosophical ecclecticism and enthusiasm for the novel made them hospitable to psychoanalysis as well as to behavioristic trends. Furthermore, they were predominantly "scientistic."[17] Their weakness as philosophers of law did not prevent them from making very significant contributions to legal methodology. They liberated much of American jurisprudence from obsolete formulas perpetuated in traditionalism and formalism by ruthlessly critical analyses of judicial verbiage and, like sociological jurisprudence, invited lawyers to look beyond the narrow confines of their technical craft to what social scientists in related fields were doing.[18] In these writings, law is more or less identified with the activity of judges or of all governmental officials and their decisions and judgments. In this school, there is recognition only of the factual reality and a complete disregard for the normative content of all law. Thus this point of view is the precise obverse of the pure theory of law, but, like the pure theory, it leads to an emphasis upon power as decisive. At this point we encounter the connection between the philosophy of law and the science of politics which is discussed below (see chap. xx).

In conclusion, we can say that the positivists, whether relativists, purists, or realists, all represent a turning-away from the philosophy of law as such. In its place we find a ready acceptance of power as the factual creator of norms; regarding power and its activity philosophy has nothing to say, for "science is free of values." I may be permitted therefore to put at the end of this chapter a sentence of Kelsen in which he describes what may be expected of him who has freed himself of all metaphysical thought. He finds behind the positive law not the absolute truth of a metaphysics nor the absolute justice of a law of nature. "He who lifts the veil and does not close his eyes faces the Gorgon head of power." This is exactly what we have experienced.

[17] Cf. the penetrating assessment by Morris R. Cohen, "A Critical Sketch of Legal Philosophy in America," in *Law: A Century of Progress, 1835–1935* (1937), II, 266 ff., esp. 303 ff. Cohen points out the importance of Arthur F. Bentley's *The Process of Government* (1908), in this connection.

[18] A critical appraisal in terms that fit my general analysis was offered years ago in particular response to Llewellyn's views and is reprinted below as Appendix II.

XIX. *The Revival of Natural Law in Europe and America*

To speak of a revival of natural law is not quite accurate, since natural law had never quite disappeared from European and American legal thought.[1] That it should do so is out of the question, if for no other reason than the attitude of the Catholic church. Catholic doctrine considers natural law a part of the *philosophia perennis* and has firmly embodied it in the theological dogma of the church. I do not propose to interpret this side of the question, since what we find here are essentially refined presentations of the doctrine of Thomas Aquinas and other Scholastics which I have already discussed.

From a strictly philosophical point of view, natural law is brought forward again as an antidote to positivism. This happened soon after the turn of the century, at about the same time in Italy, France, and Germany. The revival of natural law was connected with names such as del Vecchio, Geny, and Krabbe and, in a wider sense, also Duguit and Hauriou.[2] Since that time the literature has become very voluminous, as is indicated in the Bibliography. If one asks what led to this strengthening of natural-law thinking, one finds that a number of causes have played a role. Among these, the steady expansion of governmental activity is of decisive importance. That is as true for America, where the Supreme Court has become the mouthpiece for the criticism of

[1] That is explicitly stated by Charles C. Haines in his *The Revival of Natural Law Concepts: A Study of the Establishment and of the Interpretation of Limits on Legislatures with Special Reference to the Development of Certain Phases of American Constitutional Law* (1930). Cf. also the systematic review of natural-law models by Erik Wolf, *Das Problem der Naturrechtslehre: Versuch einer Orientierung* (1955), and A. P. D'Entrèves, *Natural Law: An Introduction to Legal Philosophy* (1951).

[2] For the work of these authors, see the Bibliography. Some may object to the inclusion of Hauriou and Duguit in this group of writers, but I agree with Haines that they should be seen in this perspective. Duguit's espousal of preconstitutional basic rights would suffice for that.

much regulatory legislation, as it is for Europe. Not only the Marxist movement but also general legislation for an ever-increasing expansion of state activity (statism) has raised the question as to how far such a development ought to be permited to go.[3]

But the several representatives of this natural-law thinking usually do not wish to return to the "eternal verities" of an unchangeable law of nature such as were taught in the seventeenth and eighteenth centuries. Such thought played a considerable role in the past in the decisions of the United States Supreme Court. At certain times the court, or at least some of its judges, wanted to develop the concept of due process of law in terms of such eternal principles and gave corresponding emphasis to certain basic rights, such as equality before the law and the unalterable principles of a free society. Giorgio del Vecchio also inclines toward this view. The prevailing tendency, however, is to treat natural law as changeable. In a famous formulation by Stammler, natural law is understood as a law with changing content. Geny and Duguit have stated similar positions explicitly.[4] The concrete content of natural law, according to such views, would change with time and circumstances but would be oriented toward the idea of law which demands that it is right law.

This point of view, which as we have seen rests upon Kant's critique of the reasoning process, overlaps with another outlook which seeks to understand natural law in terms of the laws, natural or otherwise, of social behavior and social events. The development of psychology and of the social sciences suggests that in place of a presumably known, in any case presupposed, unalterable human nature there are now the insights of these new sciences of man based upon scientific research. This approach is particularly pronounced among those who advocate a sociology of law, such as Ehrlich and Max Weber. In the United States, the idea was put into another form by Roscoe Pound when he spoke of law as social engineering. This idea of law as social engineer-

[3] Cf. for this, William E. Rappard, *L'individu et l'état dans l'évolution constitutionelle de la Suisse* (1936), *passim.*

[4] See Haines, *op. cit.*, pp. 260 ff., 288 ff.

ing is incidentally not a new one, as is sometimes assumed; it had already appeared at the beginning of the seventeenth century.[5]

As I have just shown (see above, chaps. xvi–xviii), a sociology of law which seeks to discover the laws determining the social relations upon which law is built has a definite connection with the Marxist view of law, which it fights with its own weapons, so to speak. For the sociologists ask: Are the natural and historical conditions of law as asserted by Marx and the Marxists actual and true? Is only class interest operative in the creation of law, or does it play a predominant role? We can see here that the inquiry is put in terms of scientific truth which would uncover gradually what is always true. The social sciences are directed toward ascertaining and understanding recurrent phenomena, and thus have replaced divine revelation or abstract reason, in the sense of rational understanding of the nature of law and justice. The social sciences are working out empirical generalizations, based upon established matters of fact.[6] But theirs is nonetheless a truth of lasting validity. Duguit too is looking for this kind of explanation when he thinks of the higher law not as ordered by the state but as created by the collective conscience of the people. His view that the declaration of human rights and the basic principles of the constitution rest upon some such foundation is part of this trend of thinking. For this higher unwritten law, if it is not to remain a vague, romantic notion, must be capable of being made more distinct by an insight into the working of social relations. Krabbe's doctrine of the feeling for right as the basis of all law shows a similar range of problems. Krabbe himself deduced from his doctrine that a positive law which is in conflict with this higher law is "unconstitutional" (*verfassungswidrig*), and that therefore it is desirable that a judicial process be available in order to suspend such statutes. For if such a procedure does not

[5] Cf. my Introduction to *Politica methodice digesta of Johannes Althusius* (1932).

[6] See my "Political Philosophy and the Science of Politics," in *Scritti giuridici in memoria di Piero Calamandrei* (1957), and chap. xxv of *Constitutional Government and Democracy* (2d ed., 1941).

exist, a right of resistance must be recognized. Quite similarly, Duguit wrote, "To refuse to obey a law which is contrary to what is right is entirely legitimate."[7] Others, like Geny, were satisfied to declare that such a statute would, in the course of time, turn out to be unenforcible.

Here we see the more specific juristic problems presented by these new doctrines of natural law. These problems can most readily be comprehended by considering their political significance, in spite of the fact that this political significance is often contradictory. Since time immemorial, men have utilized the law of nature or similar notions of a higher law to fight the existing law because they were fully conscious of the conservative nature of positive law which embodies the status quo. Rational thought based on natural law has also been pitted against positive law, because positive law was believed to be contrary to "eternal" verities when these verities, such as the system of free competition or capitalism, seemed to serve the purpose of defending the status quo against unwelcome innovations. But in spite of this contradiction, both viewpoints have a central idea in common. It is the notion that one may apply standards of evaluation to statutes willed by any legislature including one popularly elected, and furthermore that such standards are rational standards whether they are derived from metaphysical or empirical and scientific reasoning. Whatever position one might be prepared to take with reference to this philosophical standpoint, for the concrete structuring of the legal order it is in such doctrines of decisive importance, whether the consequence is that judicial review of statutory enactments is derived from it *or* that individuals, groups, and authorities resist unjust enactments.

All these tendencies, which appeared well before the First World War, have been reinforced by the emergence of totalitarianism and dictatorship. Many who formerly rejected a right of resistance without hesitation are today inclined to recognize such a right of subjects against a government whose power is devoid of genuine authority. This is as true for England and America

[7] *Traité de droit constitutionel* (1928), Bk. III, p. 661.

as it is for continental Europe.[8] In accepting the legislation of these totalitarian dictatorships, whether fascist or communist, as law, positivism has gone astray. To proclaim that a law is a norm merely because Hitler has willed it violates the most elementary sense of right. This same thing is equally true of the arbitrary actions of totalitarian parties. In the face of that kind of positive law, only a standard valid outside and beyond the law can protect the law. In the secure days of constitutional order during the last century, there was a general inclination to transfer such standards, even when recognized, from jurisprudence into ethics or religion. The lawless rule of totalitarian power has made it evident that jurisprudence once again must consider the development of such standards as one of its most essential tasks. At the same time, it should be remembered that "neither Hitler nor Stalin would have regarded themselves as positivists, both having been fanatical dogmatists with no respect for truth or reason."[9]

But the recognition of this task does not mean that it is solved. A return to the old law of nature consisting of eternally valid principles is excluded if for no other reason than because the concept of nature upon which it was founded is no longer acceptable. Even if one looks upon nature as an order created by God, a view which orthodox Catholicism shares with others, the knowledge and understanding of this order have so much changed that it is no longer possible to try to understand this nature as a system of a few very simple and generally valid mechanical laws in Newton's sense. We cannot here enter into an analysis of this change in the view of nature, but it is clear that little if anything is achieved if one proclaims that the natural law to be developed must be a changing one. For one thing, those who wish to defend the legality of totalitarian power structures would readily proclaim such change and thereby pervert the legal order.[10] Second,

[8] See H. von Borch, *Obrigkeit und Widerstand* (1954), and Oscar Jaszi and John D. Lewis, *Against the Tyrant: The Tradition of Tyrannicide* (1957). Cf. also the interesting symposium, *Widerstandsrecht und Grenzen der Staatsgewalt*, ed. Bernhard Pfister and G. Hildmann, with contributions by Johannes Spörl, Ernst Wolf, Alois Dempf, and others (1956).

[9] Cf. William Ebenstein, in *Natural Law Forum*, V (1960), 157.

[10] Fritz von Hippel, *Die Perversion von Rechtsordnungen* (1955).

the question as to what is right law can be answered only if, in the face of a change, a persistent requirement or "idea" can be asserted. If right law is now this, now that, here this, here that, the demonstration that it is right law can be achieved only if it is oriented toward the rightness of fixed norms of some kind. Stammler was vividly aware of this when he insisted upon research into law as such. But as I noted and as Radbruch pointed out, Stammler outlined the task but did not solve the problem. He gave a critique of legal reason, a kind of propaedeutics of the problem, but the problem remains. Formalism and the Kantian philosophy are very much emphasized in these writers, considerably in contrast to Kant himself, who progressed to very definite and concrete legal norms derived from his conception of a natural law based on practical reason (see above, chap. xiv). This turn to legal procedure, to the research into what is essential for creation of any kind of real law, represents an approximation to a tendency which had for a long time been characteristic of the English-speaking world, namely, an emphasis upon procedure as decisive for the rule of law. The criteria for determining whether law is right law are very general rules of procedure, and these rules of procedure do claim for themselves general validity in the sense of the old natural law. For this reason we cannot concede what Geny stated as a criticism of Stammler, namely, that the concept of right law cannot be applied to the positive law of a particular country. Stammler himself, to be sure, left this problem aside, but it is evident that one can apply his general criteria and presumably ought to do so. This has often been overlooked because writers, including Stammler, have been too unconditionally committed to the dichotomy of the is and the ought. We have seen that this is even more true of the pure theory of law. But in my view the world of norms, the world of values, is imbedded in the world as a whole, as Kant himself pointed out in the *Critique of Judgment.*[11]

Thus the problem of the law of nature presents itself in all its complexity. For proper criteria, of a general nature, as to what

[11] *Werke,* ed. Cassirer, Vol. V; cf. also the brief extract in my selections, *The Philosophy of Kant* (1949), pp. 265 ff.

ought to be law, there is a road to law as it actually exists. The philosophy of law of today is face to face with this problem.

I should like to emphasize among the more recent philosophies which point in this direction in the field of legal theory and politics the rather extraordinary doctrine of Leonard Nelson.[12] Starting from Kant's position, Nelson places the philosophy of law within the general context of metaphysics. It is a part of the practical philosophy in the sense of Kant; that is, it belongs to the world of the norms. For Nelson, like other Neo-Kantians, distinguishes sharply between the existential and the normative realm. But the ought is not methodologically seen in analogy to existence, as is the pure theory of law, but is understood in its free autonomy. Nelson develops in a strictly logical and decidedly abstract manner first a formal and afterward a material theory of law. The formal theory is concerned exclusively with the form of a law "abstracted completely from its content." The formal theory of law "develops a requirement of a lawful situation. . . . It asks what are the conditions which a social situation or state must fulfil when it is to be thought of as a lawful situation without logical contradiction" (pp. 34–35). The basic concept of the formal theory of law, as of all theory of law, is of course the concept of law. This concept is defined by Nelson as "the practical necessity of mutual limitation of the spheres of freedom in the mutual relation between persons." From this it follows that rights must be defined as duties, for "duty is nothing but the practical necessity of limiting free choice" (p. 40).

Before Nelson comes to determine the law as such, he deduces from these definitions the analytical principles of a formal theory of law. He discovers them by investigating the formal characteristics of a legal proposition. "If we abstract from all content, there remain certain requirements which a proposition must fulfil in order to be a legal proposition at all. . . . A legal proposition

[12] See Leonard Nelson, *System der philosophischen Rechtslehre und Politik* (1924). The page references in the text are to this book. The translations are my own, since this work is not available in English; fortunately, his system of ethics has been translated by Norbert Guterman and published under the title *System of Ethics* (1956).

states that in the mutual relation between persons some have a right toward others in so far as these others are subject to the requirements of law" (p. 42). By analyzing this general proposition, Nelson arrives at a number of very general and formal principles which I cannot develop here in detail. Universal validity and differentiation, autonomy and objectivity, legal coercion and freedom, rigorism and indeterminism—they all are grounded in the fact that a subject of duties can only be "a rational being," and I may add that Nelson defines reason as "capacity to imagine a law" (p. 46). In this connection I must particularly mention, against all positivist tendencies, that "no arbitrary proposition can contain a ground of obligation" (p. 49). For "a legal obligation is only possible if it can be recognized by the insight of the legally obligated one himself. The concept of a law which is not recognizable by the subject is self-contradictory." Coercion follows logically from the fact that "there exists no right to violate a right." On the other hand, any kind of coercion which is not itself legally necessary would prevent the satisfaction of a rightful interest. For this reason, more coercion than is necessary for protecting the right of all must not be used. This conclusion is connected with the principle of *rigorism,* that is to say, the limiting importance of the value of law within the realm of values: "every possible value which collides with the requirements of law is excluded" (p. 53). On the other hand, the possibility of applying the concept of law disappears when there do not exist certain positive values. Thus, "the applicability of law is always conditioned by purpose," but "the necessity of law itself is not conditioned by any purpose whatever" (p. 54).

The synthetic principle of the formal theory of law can now be stated thus: "There exists a rightful law," and this proposition "is the only synthetic premise" which Nelson admits in the general theory of law. Upon its basis he develops a series of subsumed formulas which contain inherent necessities: (1) the communication of thoughts by language, (2) a certain distribution of property, (3) the possibility of a lack of legal insight, and (4) the possibility of a lack of good will. From these he derives certain postulates, such as that "rational beings will recognize in their intercourse a certain language" or that "rational beings will recognize a certain distribution of property." Publicity of the law and certainty and security of the law are further postulates.

This concludes the formal theory of law. As far as the material theory is concerned, its possibility and necessity follows, according to Nelson, from the existence of the formal one. Because law is objective, the law that is right must have a certain content. This law which is right can be stated as follows: Justice is law—a formulation which for Nelson means that justice ought to be law. Justice is the rule for the mutual limitation of the freedom of the individuals in their interaction. "Justice means nothing else but personal equality" (p. 85). This is a law which addresses itself to persons. It does not exclude preferential treatment, but it demands that such preferential treatment be conditioned by corresponding differences of the persons. It is evident that we are here confronted by a metaphysical proposition which is akin to the doctrines of Aristotle concerning justice and equality. Nelson derives from this law according to right a number of postulates again: (1) the law of contract, (2) the positive law of the distribution of property, (3) the material equality of the distribution of property, and (4) the criminal law. It is evident, even without further exploration of the acute and strictly logical deductions of Nelson, that with these formulations we are once more confronting the problem of the law of nature.

Nelson starts with the proposition that the natural law of earlier days is "impossible." He then states that his eight postulates are not material propositions of natural law but are only "criteria for judging any possible positive legislation" (p. 106). But Nelson does not stop with this position, which is obviously similar to that of Stammler. He proceeds to develop a formal law of nature which is oriented toward "the ideal of human dignity," for from it follows the existence of "inalienable rights." Nelson in this connection clearly states that what he means by "inalienable" is "that the consent to the violations of the interest which determines the content of the right by him who has the right does not excuse the other from the duty of respecting this interest" (p. 115). This formal natural law is implemented by a substantive one which follows from the content of the formal ideal of human dignity. For this human dignity consists in "rational self-determination" according to which "the rational being actually becomes what according to its concept it potentially is." For from such rational self-determination follows the social ideal of personal freedom, and if we combine this ideal with the rightful law we arrive at the conclusion: "All rational beings have the right to an equal external possibility to achieve self-determination." The inalienability of the right of rational self-determination means or implies the right of intellectual freedom. This right of intellectual freedom and the corresponding unrightfulness of any paternalism leads Nelson to a proposition which he places, as the only proposition of this kind—the natural-law rule par excellence—at the end of his entire theory of law: "The same external possibility for all to achieve education shall be secured by public law, and the intellectual freedom of everyone from artificial interference shall be likewise protected" (p. 122). In this proposition the liberal and libertarian philosophy of law of Leonard Nelson culminates. It led him to the rejection of democracy as a species of intellectual paternalism, but this conclusion, which certainly we find confirmed in certain contemporary democratic forms of corruption and disintegration, in truth refers only to the despotic kind of absolute democracy which is not limited by any constitutional order, such as is frequently believed to be the essence of democracy in continental Europe. For Nelson's philosophy of law, profound and clear as it is in itself, does not grasp the nature of the constitutional order. For him, the constitution defined too generally is "the sum of the rules by which is determined how in a society the rightful law shall by force be made valid." The constitution determines who shall be legislator, who judge, who executive or regent (pp. 174–76). Such statements miss the true nature of a constitution (see chaps. xii, xiii, xxiii). But in spite of this serious flaw, it must be admitted that Nelson succeeded in developing a new basis for a law of nature, more especially since

I would like to consider his axiomatic postulates for the evaluation of a positive legal order as a kind of law of nature, simply because they contain admittedly a doctrine of justice. For, in my opinion, a doctrine of justice is equivalent to a law of nature whether taken formally or substantively. This is certainly true in the historical perspective. Therefore, Nelson's philosophy represents a very important achievement for the further development of the philosophy of law. For if justice is relevant as a standard for law, the central error of all positivists is recognized, and the totalitarianism which develops out of such positivism is basically refuted.[13]

To sum up, the "revival of natural law" is not easy. For what has really been revived is a strong sense of the need which gave rise to the doctrine of natural law in the past: the need for a standard of justice by which to evaluate the positive law, a standard firm and yet not subject to the criticism which destroyed the older natural-law doctrines. This is a broad philosophical problem to which only the Catholic tradition has a coherent metaphysical answer. Something more will be said on this score in the systematic part which follows.

[13] See M. D. Forkoseh (ed.), *The Political Philosophy of Arnold Brecht* (1954), pp. 83 ff.

PART TWO

Systematic Analysis

XX. *Justice, Equality, and the Common Man*

The evolution of the philosophy of law, imbedded as it is in the evolution of philosophy as a whole, revolves around certain problems which recur again and again. Among these problems, that of justice in relation to law is of central importance. For it is apparent that the law, or rather legal rules, ought to be just but often is not. Law is related to justice without realizing it unequivocally. It is not possible to deny the character of law to that law which is unjust, as Cicero and the Middle Ages had done. But it is equally impossible to identify justice with the law, as Hobbes and the positivists want us to do.[1] Rather, justice can be understood only if it is taken to be a state toward which the law is oriented as an approximation. Such an approximate realization is a dynamic process which takes place in time; it is dominated by forces struggling within the general framework of the political order for their effectuation (actualization). One may consider justice an idea, attribute to it absolute reality, as Plato and Hegel did, and assume that knowledge and understanding of it are possible only partially and only by way of very hard philosophical work. In that case, politics appears in the last analysis to be the task of the speculative, metaphysical philosopher who constructs intellectually the ideal political and social order. All actual politics then appears as a turgid corruption of such a politics of intellectual knowledge and vision. Or, one may consider justice as resulting from general religious or philosophical views of the world at large. In that case, one may define justice in the sense of one or another of these views, as is done, for example, by Catholic

[1] In the imprecise speech of everyday discourse it is possible to do so and to identify law and justice, if, as is often the case, justice is simply understood as a judge's or another official's following and observing the existing statutory norms and general customs. We are not speaking of justice in this sense, any more than we are talking of justice, subjectively, as a quality or virtue of persons. For further systematic elaboration, see my *Man and His Government* (1963), esp. chaps. xv–xvii, and *Transcendent Justice* (1964), *passim.*

natural law, and may thus enter into the struggle between rival ideologies. In other words, one may enter politics, in the highest sense. Or one may seek to understand, through detailed observation, the different notions of justice as they are expressed in the rival party ideologies and then to interpret the idea of justice at work in these ideologies. One would thus generalize from the continually shifting compromise among these rival viewpoints and try to discover their meaning in the very process of their mutual assimilation.[2] But even when no such parties exist, the argument about justice decisively molds the face of politics. Conversely, politics provides the basic *problema* for all philosophizing about justice.

If we ask what it is that has divided the philosophers and parties and continues to do so, we discover that an aspect of the problem which Aristotle considered the center of the discussion continues to arrest attention. It runs through the discussion and arguments for hundreds of years like a red thread. It is Aristotle's doctrine concerning the relation of justice to equality, and the distinction between distributive and corrective justice derived from this relationship. Surely such a distinction is basic to all thought concerning the problem of justice and law. And since it is distributive justice which decides who shall be equal to whom—a peculiarly political problem—the basic problems of politics are raised when distributive justice is being considered. What distinguishes the radical democrat from the more or less aristocratic or plutocratic man is that he builds his approach upon the idea of strict numerical equality. The range of problems here implied occurs at all times and in all places. From time to time this basic theme of all politics finds expression in the title of a statute, as in that of the "equalization of burdens."[3] Admittedly

[2] The relativism which Radbruch and others have advocated must not be confused with such an undertaking; see chap. xviii, above, and the balanced and thoughtful discussion by Arnold Brecht in *The Political Philosophy of Arnold Brecht* (1954), pp. 21–72.

[3] The law for the equalization of burdens, *Lastenausgleichsgesetz* (1952), was enacted by the German Federal Republic to distribute more evenly the damages resulting from the war.

the central question here is who is to be treated as equal to whom.

One could take the position—and the relativists do so—that nothing can be determined concerning equality from a philosophical standpoint. The reason given for such a position is that equality cannot be proved philosophically. But what can be proved regarding man if proof is meant to take the form of a coherent logical demonstration? If the demand for such demonstration be discarded and a humanly possible probability be accepted as sufficient for the purpose of a rational solution to the problem, then a good deal can be said and shown regarding equality. Kant, for example, sharply condemned all inequality based upon birth as unjust. It is often overlooked that this kind of inequality and the resulting privilege rests upon biological misconceptions which find their most blatant expression in the term "blood." Blood has, as is well known, very little to do with genetics; we now know that you can pump a man full of the blood of another, without affecting his character or nature at all (except in relation to some disease of the blood). We are faced with a similar situation in regard to inequalities based upon wealth; in this case, economic misunderstandings are the basis of the mistaken views.

If one starts from the premise that men *ought* to be largely equal to each other, that they should be "equal before the law," the question of equality is at once transferred to the political realm. For it now becomes decisive just who makes the laws. Rousseau made, as we have seen, equality before the law the pivotal point of his doctrine, and Kant developed this position philosophically by arguing that only such rules as apply normally to the same human situation are recognized as law, or at any rate can be expected to be enforced.[4] Both therefore put the making of laws into the hands of all who are thereby recognized in their basic equality as members of the legal community. But Rousseau as well as Kant made this position questionable by not wanting

[4] This position, though related to the older Ciceronian and medieval doctrine (that a law contrary to the law of nature is no law in the strict sense), must not be confused with it; it is a greatly refined and more tenable version of the older doctrines. For Cicero and Thomas Aquinas, see above, chaps. iv, vi, and the literature cited there.

to recognize a general rule as a law unless it was oriented toward a general source: the general will in Rousseau, the categorical imperative in Kant. These sources as such are not clearly determined, that is to say, self-evident. Who then is to make that determination? *Qui custodiet custodem?* The rational answer to this question remains open. The development of modern politics in the West has given a fairly unequivocal, conventional answer, however, which has achieved a remarkable degree of universal acclaim. It is the majority of the *people* who decide about laws and their value—a people who are organized under a constitution which they have given themselves.

By such a reference to a popular decision the problem of justice is by no means solved but is merely transferred to another level of discourse. This level is the politics of a constitutional democracy. Only if it can be asserted that in every free community there exists a sufficient number of responsible and conscientious persons who seek to find a compromise between conflicting interests can the problem of distributive justice which decides what is equal and what is unequal be resolved. For if it were simply a matter of finding the diagonal in a parallelogram of forces in the political arena which would decide what is equal and what unequal, then the deeper tension (*Spannung*) would be suspended, and a naked positivism à la Hobbes would oblige us to discover justice in the existing laws. This is not the case. For there exist just laws in which, beyond the conflict of the interests, the will and the understanding of the community-conscious citizens has brought about a "higher" synthesis. On the other hand, there exist many laws which are unjust or laws which are neutral in relation to justice because they are nothing but a compound of interests. The American doctrine of the common man, the community-conscious citizen who decisively shapes politics in the free community, is built upon an understanding of the foregoing reflections. This doctrine places the autonomous man in the center of the argument about how justice is found.[5]

[5] David Riesman, in his challenging study *The Lonely Crowd* (1950), although arguing that most Americans are today mere opportunists, shaping

Yet the prevailing doctrine of the common man is usually stated too much in accordance with utilitarian rationalism. Thus, the view of Thomas Paine, the most strident voice of the American Revolution, is based upon an unlimited faith in reason. There is, in this rationalism, a certain stress on empirical evidence, but it is untouched by Humean and Kantian "criticism." Common man and common sense are seen as mutually supporting each other, as they do in Locke's and Thomasius' writings (see above, chap. xiii). In the light of modern psychological and sociological research, it is no longer permissible to build upon such a foundation.[6] It has become certain beyond peradventure that in their social relations almost all men are to a large extent co-determined by interest and passion. The Kantian notion of a community of men who act according to the categorical imperative cannot become a reality. It is well that this should be so. For a good part of what matters for man is imbedded in such interests and passions. To put it another way, shared values are being realized in this sphere of interest and passion.

Nor do we need this radical faith in reason for the conduct of a civilized community according to law. Man participates in the political community with only a part of his being. Many of the "higher" values such as are manifest in religion, art, and learning play only a small role in the sphere of politics. The criticism of democracy which is rife everywhere today has been misdirected because it started from the assumption that the common man must decide *everything* in a democracy. Yet we must recognize that law and justice do play a decisive role in politics. Still, the legislation of a community deals only with the questions of exter-

---

their conduct in accordance with what they believe to be generally acceptable—a view which is rather dubious when one considers the American farmer or worker, to say the least—nonetheless recognizes the presence of an "autonomous man" with whom he identifies himself. Actually, the crowd phenomenon Riesman analyzes is a recurrent one near the seats of wealth and power in saturated and aging cultures.

[6] Cf. for all this my *The New Belief in the Common Man* (1942), *passim.* See also the Prologue and Epilogue to the later version, *The New Image of the Common Man* (1951), for a discussion of other views.

nal order which are common to all citizens. In order rightly to interpret that communal sphere in a constitutional democracy, it is necessary to distinguish it clearly from religion, art, and the private sphere and personal interests of the individual. The traditional rights, such as religious liberty (separation of church and state), freedom of self-expression (more especially academic freedom), and the rest, try to do just that. These rights have been too often seen only in their relation to the individual facing the "state," highly significant as this relation is. They have a functional importance also in limiting the tasks of politics to a sphere in which the common judgment of common men is more likely to be valid than that of any self-appointed elite.

It is important that we are dealing here with a *relative* matter. The common man is not even presupposed to be collectively infallible, as the rationalist faith of the eighteenth and nineteenth centuries tended to assume. The common judgments of common men, these judgments which deal with the concerns of the community, are fallible enough. There is merely a *probability* that such judgments will be more nearly right than those of an elite which is not made responsible to these common men. This proposition does not exclude the lucky chance that an elite may *not* act in accordance with its interests and passions; it merely argues that the appearance of such an elite is highly improbable.[7]

Another point of crucial importance for an understanding of the role of the common man is that this man is not some hypothetical "average" man. The common man is every man insofar as he participates as a free citizen in the decisions about common

[7] Plato himself, the great defender of the idea of such an elite, especially in his *Republic*, v, seems to be more than doubtful about its coming into being and takes refuge in the famous royal lie. See above, chap. iii. Cf. also Karl Popper's elaborate criticism of these Platonic notions, *The Open Society and Its Enemies*, I, 106–37. John Wild's attempt to refute Popper's position in *Plato's Enemies and the Theory of Natural Law* (1953), while effectively trimming off some of the more extravagant claims of Popper (and other critics), especially the proposition that Plato was a "totalitarian"—an amazing view considering Plato's bitter hostility toward tyranny—does not seem to me to succeed in refuting the conclusions about Plato's elitism. Nor is this surprising, because they are very patent. See also David Grene, *Man in His Pride* (1950), esp. chap. x.

concerns, that is to say, insofar as he acts outside his profession or special function. What this means is that what men have in common must not be confused with what today exposes man to the danger of becoming a mass man.[8] For mass man is the diametric opposite of the common man. He is the man without a community, an atom afloat in the vast aggregations of the modern metropolis, devoid of the values and convictions which characterize a community.

The notion of the common man is not only that of man in the community, of communal man. It also involves the notion of the community of mankind, of the common *in* man, of that which all men have in common. This shows that the concept and the image of the common man are rooted in natural-law notions. To put it another way, one might say that this kind of political outlook implies that only if human nature exhibits certain traits essential for communal life as common to most men can constitutional democracy be considered a workable scheme of government. That experience supports this view to a considerable extent is shown by the political life of those people who are organized in this fashion, namely, Britain, the Dominions, Switzerland, and the United States. It is also reinforced by the findings of modern psychology and sociology. In spite of all the differences between communities of men, man shows himself as a being capable of a measure of rational communal co-operation and one whose behavior exhibits considerable regularities. These regularities are to be found in the very sphere of external legislation which is essential for the community.

In the extended discussions about the role of the rational in man, the problem of justice has always played an important part. Since Plato, when faced with this question, constructed his utopia of an "ideal" commonwealth, philosophers and other students of human nature have tried to determine what kind of reasoning was needed for deciding about justice. Plato did not wish to admit the

[8] This confusion is the crucial weakness in Ortega y Gasset's well-known *The Revolt of the Masses* (1932). Cf. my comments, *The New Image of the Common Man,* Prologue.

judgment of anyone but the true philosopher; he therefore wanted to intrust the leadership in the community to him. In his original conception, as we have seen above (chap. iii), the laws hardly played a role. Only late in life[9] did Plato, in the *Laws,* place major emphasis upon the role of legal enactments. Even then, these laws were the creation of a philosophical elite which appears more or less accidental in its hierarchical position. That these notions hark back to ancient Greek folklore and the founder myths of most Greek *polis* communities is well known. Basically, Plato's outlook is characterized by a very "exclusive" conception of reason; only a few men are endowed with it to a sufficient degree to matter. The Stoics followed the Platonic notions in this respect, at least in the beginning, though the idea of human equality gradually reduced the built-in elitism.

A fundamental change in outlook was brought on by the coming of Christianity. But it took a long time and great struggles for the original challenge to take root and manifest itself in institutional changes. Even today this argument about human equality continues, elaborated by modern psychology and anthropology. In the course of these controversies it has become increasingly clear that the rational in man is only *one* component, but a very general and common component which is by no means limited to an intellectual elite. Rather, we find on all levels of a community men whose behavior and actions (including their communal activities) are codetermined by rational considerations. This common man can be effectively activated only if he is given the opportunity to participate in the creation of the law within the framework of democratic community life.

If the connection between man and the creation of law is thus understood, then it follows that justice is indeed an objective reality, transpersonal and not subjective, but it follows also that justice must be understood as a changing reality. Its changes occur in response to the dynamic process of politics, and justice needs to be comprehended within the context of politics. "Justice must

[9] Cf. Grene, *op. cit.*, chap. xiii, and the comments in Werner Jaeger, *Paideia,* trans. Gilbert Highet (1944), Vol. III, Book IV, chap. x.

forever be realized anew," Rosenstock-Hüssy has said, and he added: "Not the thoughts of the clever or wise, but the talk of the people create the law. . . . Thus a genuine, necessary right will be called for and implored [*beschworen*], until it becomes law."[10] This process of creating law is the task of the community in its wholeness and strength, its manifold forms as well as its unity; the process results from the interaction and co-operation of all the vital elements of such a community.

Since justice then remains an "open" question, I may add a concluding remark about injustice. It is a remarkable fact that men's feelings are more sharply aroused by the sense of injustice than of justice. Whatever may be the psychological reasons for this fact, the ontological ground upon which it rests is the value system to which a man is attached. It may be the personal or the associational, the national or the universal, value that is involved. If this value is clearly threatened, the injustice of the threatening action will be sharply felt and, if possible, resisted. When viewed from this angle, the conflicts over justice which rend a community are really differences in what is sensed to be unjust. One claims that it is unjust to take his property, another that it is unjust that his children should starve; one argues the injustice of putting his white child next to a black one in school, the other rejoins that it is unjust that his black child should be denied equal opportunity for education. These and thousands of similar situations show that justice and injustice cannot be related to any *one* value, be it equality or any other, but only to the complex value system of a man, a community, or mankind.

[10] Eugen Rosenstock-Hüssy has provided the broad sociological background for these views in his *Soziologie* (1956).

XXI. *Law, Authority, and Legitimacy*

The relation between law and politics, which finds expression as much in the contrast as in the interdependence of law and justice, creates the problem of authority. Authority is of decisive importance for every legal and social order. An order cannot be made to function without authority. An order cannot be built upon power alone. These crucial propositions have been obscured time after time by erroneous notions about democracy. If a democracy is seen not as a constitutional order but as an anarchic utopia or as pure majority rule, the conclusion is easily reached that all authority is noxious, even reprehensible, and in any case bad. Thus, we hear about "authoritarian order" or "authoritarian states," expressions signifying that an order or a state is bad and tyrannical. Yet it is precisely tyranny, and more especially totalitarian dictatorship, which lacks authority, as Plato well knew and clearly stated.[1]

Auctoritas in its original meaning can, according to Mommsen,[2] not be precisely defined, but means primarily an "augmentation." This augmentation meant politically a confirmation of the people's act of will by a *senatusconsultum*, a counsel of the elders. *Patrum auctoritas,* the authority of the fathers, was therefore "more than advice and less than command, the kind of advice which one cannot properly disregard," such as "the expert gives to the layman, and the leader in parliament to his followers." This notion that a judgment is "augmented" when it is confirmed by the counsel of elders is of great importance because it rests upon a principle which is the basis of all genuine authority, especially the authority of the law. In the English and American legal tradition, this authority is typically provided by the judge, the man who is "learned in the law" and who has mastered the "artificial reason of the

[1] Cf. my study "Authority, Reason, and Discretion," in the yearbook of the American Society for Political and Legal Philosophy, *Nomos,* Vol. I: *Authority* (1958).

[2] Theodor Mommsen, *Römisches Staatsrecht,* III, Part II (1888), 1033–34.

law" to an exceptional degree (see above, chap. x). Only by such authoritative assimilation of the willed statutory enactment, by its being fitted into the system of legal principles upon which the common law rests, does such an enactment become fully law.

The rational aspect of the problem of authority has frequently been overlooked, particularly among positivists, and consequently positivism has entertained the view that it is possible to base the law upon an act of will alone. The results of this outlook have proved themselves to be thoroughly disastrous. This trend of thought in part goes back to Hobbes, in part to Rousseau, both of whom see the decision, the act of will of the sovereign, as the essential and basic legal act (see above, chaps. xi, xiv). The reason for this set of notions is that authority has been confused with legitimacy by these writers and their following. To give an influential contemporary writer as an example: Max Weber built his theory of the forms of rule or governance (*Herrschaftsformen*) and of law upon the concept of legitimacy, without making clear what is to be understood by legitimacy. His basically positivistic attitude—and his protestations against positivism must not deceive one about his basic positivism—is clearly revealed in his failure to develop a theory of legitimacy. In his treatise on the economy and society[3] he undertook to show what guarantees the legitimacy of a legal and social order and what causes those who work within it to consider it a legitimate order. Weber wrote: "The legitimacy of an order may be guaranteed: (1) purely internally [i.e., subjectively] in three ways, namely (*a*) purely emotionally, that is by emotional devotion; (*b*.) rationally: by a faith in the order's absolute validity as an expression of ultimate values (moral, esthetic or others); and (*c*) religiously: by the faith that salvation depends upon its [the order's] maintenance; or (2) also (or only) by the expectation of specific external consequences, that is by

[3] Max Weber, *Wirtschaft und Gesellschaft* (2d ed., 1925), chap. i, pars. 6–7, chap. iii, pars. 1–2. The translation given of these passages by Talcott Parsons and A. M. Henderson, in *Max Weber: The Theory of Social and Economic Organization* (1947), while highly suggestive, is too interpretative for the present purpose, as it interpolates the translators' own view.

interests; but these expectations are of a particular kind."[4] It is evident that this approach stresses the psychological aspect of legitimacy; legitimacy is guaranteed by "devotion," by "faith," or by "expectations." These psychological factors undoubtedly play a great role, as they do in all human relations. But the psychological aspect is merely a transitional phase, so to speak. To determine the meaning of such a situation, it is of decisive importance to ask upon what such devotion, such faith, or such expectations are based. This question raises the problem of authority. Authority itself, however, is described by many authors of positivistic and naturalistic tendency as something psychological, and in circular reasoning legitimacy is in turn used in these definitions. Thus we are told that "authority is the expected and legitimate possession of power."[5] Obviously, it is not possible to achieve clarity by such a *petitio principii.*

It is, first of all, important to differentiate clearly between legitimacy and legality.[6] An order is legitimate when it is recognized as rightful; its legality is provided by its having a basis in positive law. For this distinction it is essential to recall the discussion of the last chapter about law and justice. For when law as right (*Recht, droit*) is primarily seen as characterized by the "chance of enforcement" and hence by its dependence upon a "staff" of functionaries who are concerned with this enforcement, the contrast between legitimacy and legality, as we have stated it, remains confused. Law must not be seen as operating only in the one dimension of the state but in the many dimensions of the community if we are to comprehend legitimacy as an objective datum. Legitimacy is related to right and justice; without a clarification of what is to be understood by the rightness and justice of law, legitimacy cannot be comprehended either. Hitler's rule was legal, but it was not legitimate; it had a basis in law, but none in right

[4] See Weber, *op. cit.*, p. 17.

[5] Harold Lasswell and Abraham Kaplan, *Power and Society* (1950), p. 133.

[6] This problem was formulated with particular acuteness and precision by Carl Schmitt, *Legalität und Legitimität* (1932); cf. also Guglielmo Ferrero, *Pouvoir* (1942), esp. chap. iii, which deals with the four principles of legitimacy.

and justice. This rule possessed unheard-of power, but it lacked authority to a large extent.

I repeat, the question as to the objective meaning of legitimacy leads to the problem of authority. And therefore we must avoid basing authority upon legitimacy. The will of those who participate in the community's common concerns must be augmented not only by those who are "learned in the law" but also by those who know about right and justice. What this means is that the will even of the majority must be related to the "higher reason" of a system of values—values that are not seen as purely subjective preferences. Authority cannot be based upon the positive law, because this law itself needs authority. The authority of law is subject to considerable oscillation, as is the authority of all communications. Briefly stated, the authority of a communication, be it a command, a counsel, or a thought, rests upon the communicator's capacity for reasoned elaboration. All genuine authority is based upon such rationality of the utterances which are said to be authoritative.[7]

But this rationality must be taken broadly, in the sense of a critical rationalism. We have seen above (chap. xiv) how a critical evaluation of reason influences legal thought. The Kantian legal philosophy was the result of such an effort, as was that of David Hume. But authority can be based upon the system of Thomas Aquinas just as well as upon that of Kant, or indeed of Marx. For critical rationalism has taught us that all comprehensive systems of thought possess a metarational basis. It is not possible for finite human reason to grasp, let alone understand, the infinite reaches of the real world. But within the limits set by such a metarational framework of ideas, values, and beliefs, human reason can elaborate any utterance made, and it is the potentiality for such reasoned elaboration that lends authority to the utterance. Hence not "devotion" or "faith" or similar psychic phenomena provide genuine authority, nor legitimacy either, but the

[7] Further elaboration of this discussion in my article cited above (n. 1) and the earlier paper "Loyalty and Authority" in *Confluence* (1954), pp. 307 ff.; cf. the similar view of Bertrand de Jouvenel, *De la souveraineté* (1955; English trans., 1957), esp. Part I, chap. ii.

"augmentation," the reinforcement by reason, of the communications which bind men into a community, as such reason expresses itself in the judgment of the old, the learned, and the wise. Only by such a relationship to reason, that is to say, only by reasoned elaboration in terms of the community's ideas, values, and beliefs, is authority added to the exercise of power, whether autocratic or democratic. Power thus reinforced by authority acquires the capacity to create law that is right and just by making it legitimate.

It is possible to make this process, these phenomena, more concrete and vivid by considering the relation between parents and child.[8] In the beginning, the child is helplessly subject to the pure power of the parents. But this power is gradually reinforced by authority and eventually replaced by it, if the parents know how to develop an understanding in the child. The authority of the parents rests upon the fact that the child gradually acquires an understanding of the sense of parental commands and regulations. It finds that when it questions such an order the parent is able (and willing) to give a reasoned elaboration of the whys and wherefores. Eventually parental authority is superseded by the authority of school, community, and so forth. (This is, of course, not always the case.) The power of the parents may continue to be exercised without such reasoned elaboration, and hence without an increasing understanding and sense of participation on the part of the child. In that case, there develop those difficult relations which rest upon an apparent authority but actually depend upon force, whether physical, economic, or psychic, that is to say, naked power. If that happens, the community of the family fails to develop, and all too often such a situation leads to serious disturbances in the personalities of the human beings involved in it.

The authority of a legal order develops similarly as a result of

[8] It is interesting that this seminal situation of parent and child recurs a number of times in the volume cited above (n. 1). Conversely, the failure to grasp the full implications of this problem was responsible for the more extravagant things done under the heading of "progressive" education, though this movement was right in some important respects because it raised the problem of genuine as against false authority sharply.

an increasing insight into its rational nature. The fact that it is capable of reasoned elaboration becomes increasingly clear to those who are members of it. This authority is founded upon transpersonal norms, whereas power and force belong to the realm of nature. Since these two realms are not completely separated from each other (see above, p. 182), transitions from one to the other occur. The actual power which exists gives to him who wields it a greater chance to argue what he considers right more convincingly; he possesses greater access to the means of communication which enable him to persuade by reasoned elaboration. Conversely, the authority of a communication and of him who issues it increases its chance to become operative, that is to say, to be enforced. But these transformations of power into authority and of authority into power must not deceive us and make us forget that the two are essentially different from each other, because they rest upon different and often antithetical bases.

In conclusion, we might say that the authority of law rests upon its reasonableness—that is to say, its justice—that the legitimacy of a constitution, a statute, or a decision rests upon its rightfulness, and that its legality rests upon its accord with the positive laws. The same may be said of the "bearers" of authority, legitimacy, and legality, the rulers or sovereigns. Their legality is a question of positive law, particularly of constitutional law, if there is such a law; their legitimacy is a question of right and justice, and their authority a question of reasonableness, that is to say, their ability to realize the ideas, values, and beliefs of the community's members.

XXII. *Law and Order*

THE PROBLEM OF THE BREACH OF LAW

In the philosophical speculations concerning law and right, law has recurrently been presented as oriented *either* toward justice *or* toward order. Indeed, the question as to which of these values has priority in dealing with the law cannot be gainsaid. For happy as is the situation in which the just law can be applied by a wise judge to a case which is fully covered by it, one cannot deny that laws are often unjust, judges unwise, or the law at hand not unequivocally applicable to the case. In these instances, the problem presents itself as to whether the maintenance of the legal order ought to have priority or not. Cases like the celebrated Sacco and Vanzetti one serve as striking reminders of this unwelcome yet all-too-frequent issue. At all times, there have been many voices which would insist upon the priority of maintaining the legal order. Positivism is virtually forced to do so. This attitude is easily understandable in quiet and orderly times, such as those in which positivism was the order of the day, for the general contentment and the stability of all values reduce the probability of such conflicts to a minimum.

The situation changes in times of great revolutionary upheavals and cultural crises characterized by the fact that important groups within a legal community are attached to rival faiths or worldviews. Yet it is in precisely such times that the legal order is especially imperiled, and hence it becomes more urgent that such order be maintained.[1] The result is a sharp conflict of opinion in which the value of justice becomes identified with that of order in terms of specific rival conceptions of law and right, because the

[1] See Sebastian De Grazia, *The Political Community: A Study of Anomie* (1948). This book raises a vital issue. The term "anomie," from the Greek *nomos*, of course, was first employed by Emile Durkheim to designate a state where basic values and beliefs are disintegrating or largely gone; see *Le Suicide* (1897) for its development. De Grazia builds on this foundation.

supporters of the rival positions insist that only in an order consonant with their own view of what is right and just can justice be realized.

Only in this perspective can one fully understand the problem of constitutional loyalty, which has become very pressing in all constitutional systems. For a constitutional loyalty enforced by criminal law rests upon an identification of the value of order and justice: the argument, the controversy about what is just, is interrupted or prevented on the ground that such a controversy would endanger the constitution, that is to say, the basic legal order. An analogous situation is presented by all those processes which are designated as "purging," such as epurations, denazifications, and the like. In these cases the persons who are being purged are being punished on the ground that they have destroyed the legal order by an alleged concept of law and justice which presumably was a desire for lawlessness and injustice. For was it not this group which had previously "eliminated" a large number of law-abiding citizens on these very grounds of alleged right and justice? Apart from the broader aspects of these processes, there is involved here a conflict which springs from the essence of law, linked as it is to the two values of justice and order. Ideally, the legal community should be ordered by justice; it should be a just order. This conflict may be regretted, glossed over, defended, or condemned, but regardless of such judgments it occurs because it is rooted in the very nature of law. Only if one has comprehended this conflict in its full dimension and depth is it possible to gain the necessary perspective on situations like the Nuremberg Trials.[2] For in these trials the legal conviction of the victorious powers created for them the instrumentalities with which to realize their view of law and justice. This was done in an imperfect way, to be sure, and many mistakes in details were made which might have been avoided had the Allies themselves been more united in their outlook. As it was, the Western powers had

[2] See the documentary evidence, *Trial of War Criminals before the Nuernberg Military Tribunal under Control Council Law No. 10,* Vols. I–XIII (1951), esp. Vol. III, "The Justices Case," and Vols. I and II, "The Doctors Case."

to take into consideration the legal views of their Communist brethren, which were as far removed from their own as were the views of those they were seeking to adjudge. Had the Soviet representatives really insisted upon their concepts of procedure and the law, the trials would, of course, have become impossible. As it was, the psychic impact of the trials was weakened, but the basic issue of justice and order was involved, just the same. It is an ancient principle of law that the judgment of a duly appointed judge is valid, regardless of his moral qualities.

The conflict between the value of order and that of justice raises the issue of the breach of law. Former views have been content, in the manner of positivism, to interpret a breach of law simply as the violation of a specific legal command, more especially a statutory provision. If one thinks of law as essentially a matter of command, and particularly as the command of a sovereign will, then the phenomenon of the breach of law is indeed essentially a contravention of such a command. It is different if law is seen as subject to and oriented toward the standard of justice. For if justice must be continually created anew, by a creative process which seeks to realize what is right in the law, if therefore, to speak figuratively, justice is understood as a lodestar rather than as a goal to be achieved, the breach of law becomes problematical. An enactment, even a constitutional enactment such as the Eighteenth Amendment, may lead to violations of such positive law on a large scale, and yet a breach of law in the sense of right may not be involved. For it is the very question of whether such a provision, such an enactment, is right which is at issue. This sort of nullification of law is a much more common occurrence than is customarily admitted, particularly in the field of personal relations (and in politics). Thus we find in many legal systems provisions concerning sexual intercourse (fornication), adultery, and other matters of personal conduct which correspond only very imperfectly to the notions of what is right that are current among the members of the legal community. Hence the saying that they are "honored in the breach"; that is to say, what is right is being recognized in the violation of such provisions of the positive law.

The same sort of conventional disregard can be observed in "political" fields, such as electoral laws, party finance, and the like; as in the case of personal relations, the possibilities of effective enforcement are very limited. In these fields of law, the "unwritten" law and right consists in the recurrent violations of the written law, particularly of the statutory enactment.[3]

One can appreciate this pluralism of the sources of law and the breaches of law which result from it without accepting the extreme view of philosophical radicalism, as presented by Godwin and Thoreau, among others. As is well known, Thoreau took the position in view of slavery that the just man could not accept so unjust a law as that legalizing slavery, that he would have to refuse to pay the taxes in support of such a legal community, and that he must resign himself to the fact that "the place for a just man in such a community is the jail."[4] John Brown, as everyone knows, went even further in such radical rejection of the legal community; he tried to force the abolition of slavery by an armed revolt. In spite of the fact that this revolt was roundly condemned at the time and was immediately suppressed, John Brown became a symbolic figure during the Civil War and a kind of popular hero.[5] We can see, in these well-known events, a typical case where positive law and right were in such deep conflict that a breach of law could appear as a defense of what was right; it shows the limits of a legal order, founded upon past enactments.

Besides the breach of law resulting from non-recognition of the claim to justice of an existing positive legal rule, there exists also the kind of breach of law which violates a rule of law acknowledged as right. This is the particular sphere of the criminal law,

[3] These phenomena have led the "realists" to their position of claiming that the actual practices are the "real" law. Cf. Llewellyn as quoted above, chap. xviii, and Jerome Frank, *Law and the Modern Mind* (1930). The discussion in the text is greatly complicated here by the English terminology where "law" does not readily lend itself as a term for the presentation of the distinctions set forth, as they rest upon the *Recht-Gesetz* and *droit-loi* dichotomy.

[4] Henry David Thoreau (1817–62), *Resistance to Civil Government* (1849).

[5] Cf. the philosophically unique epic by Stephen Vincent Benét, *John Brown's Body* (1927).

though even here a conflict of the kind just discussed is at times involved. According to older views, the guilt of the person to be punished is to be found in the disturbance of the legal order. The criminal must answer for the fact that he disturbed the public order, whether he realized it or not (ignorance is no defense). But in order to protect the accused against arbitrary punishment, the principle was developed—and this principle was by no means an innovation of liberalism—that a penalty could be inflicted only on the basis of a law which was "on the books" at the time the presumed crime was committed (*nulla poena sine lege*).[6]

In the light of these general principles, there has been much discussion about the nature of punishment and penalty. Great schools of criminal law have sprung from these controversies. Originally, the penalty was seen as atonement; it took the place of revenge and was measured out in accordance with the desire to re-establish the balance between the members of the legal community which had been disturbed by the crime. An eye for an eye, and a tooth for a tooth—this formula of the Old Testament, which resembles the formulas in many another primitive law, expresses this outlook very well. In contrast to such primitive notions, which still play a role even in the legal thought of the most civilized societies, several theories have been developed which discuss the penalty in regard either to its cause or to its effect. The expounders of the contractual theory have seen the consent, whether tacit or expressed, of the criminal as the ground (cause) of the penalty, while those who have favored a theory of retaliation (*Vergeltung*) have grounded the meaning of a penalty in the

[6] The principle of *nulla poena sine lege* is seemingly violated by the war crimes trials, and for the very simple reason that the crimes committed by the totalitarians are in many cases so extraordinary that a law forbidding them did not exist. However, a large number of Nazis have been brought to trial under German criminal law since 1945 and given heavy sentences for the many common crimes, such as murder, which they committed or caused to be committed. It is arguable whether it would not have been better to proceed in this fashion from the outset rather than to punish people for belonging to a party or other organization or for expressing certain opinions, as the denazification courts did. A really searching exploration of the issues involved remains to be undertaken. There is a considerable German literature on the subject, of course, but party political views intrude in too many of these writings.

conception of a transcendent justice—the sort of justice that Aristotle described as "corrective" (see above, chap. iii). It can be stated in terms of a rule of law (*rechtsstaatlich*), as was done by Kant, who went so far as to justify even the death penalty as a rightful retribution to be demanded by the reason of each member of the legal community. Besides this theory of retaliation, that of intimidation has played a considerable role. According to this theory, penalty must be explained by considering that not only the criminal but also others who might otherwise be tempted to commit a particular kind of criminal act should be deterred from it by the fear of the penalty to be expected. The psychological assumptions upon which this theory rests are dubious, to say the least; it has often been observed, of both criminals and others, especially children, that the penalty, or perhaps the danger represented by it, provides a temptation to commit the act it is designed to prevent. For the majority of men this may be untrue, for the average person is certainly deterred from many minor infractions of the law by his fear of the penalty.

Alongside these older theories, the notion has gradually gained ground that the person committing a breach of law is abnormal, is a sick person.[7] Sociological and psychological studies have suggested that the criminal act is not an isolated phenomenon but must be seen as part of the human situation and therefore must be understood as grounded in the person's physiological and psychological nature as well as in his social setting. This view of crime leads to the conclusion that the penalty is a means of improving or bettering the person involved in the criminal act. By such means one must try to influence him. Alongside such notions, the "technical" thought of protecting the community may play a role. Yet these two approaches are diametrically opposed to each other when their philosophical foundation is considered. The

[7] This approach, which is currently being looked upon as "progressive," tends to deprive the criminal of his "dignity" as a responsible human being. This aspect of the matter was already noted by Friedrich Nietzsche, who comments upon it in the section "Vom Bleichen Verbrecher" in *Also sprach Zarathustra* (1883); however, Nietzsche here recognizes the "sickness" of the criminal as one aspect of his predicament.

contrast becomes evident when we take into account the criminal law of totalitarian societies, which continue to operate with concepts of law and right when actually their approach is dominated by regard for the requirements of maintaining their system in power. Here we find that the pretense of "re-educating" the man who has been arrested by the police, by which phrase is meant that he is to be made into an adherent of the system, serves as the basis for applying to the alleged perpetrator of a crime techniques designed to destroy his psychic self.[8]

Recently an attempt has been made to deduce the penalty as a necessary consequence from the coercive nature of law and thus to see it as direct coercion (*unmittelbaren Zwang*). "A penalty is simply a substitute for the failure to enforce obedience."[9] But law, understood as right order, as it must be in a free and democratic society, is not adequately interpreted if its coercive character is stressed. The assertion is untrue that only the administrator of the law, not the member of the legal community, is to decide whether a particular provision or enactment applies to a particular situation. Yet, the positive law does, in a measure, coerce the individual member of the legal community. This coercive character results from the member's participation in the decisions of the community as a whole, as was shown by Rousseau and Kant (see above, chap. xiv).

If we review the long discussion about crime and punishment and its many ramifications, we are led to the conclusion that each of the theories of the nature of penalty and the related problem of the breach of law has clarified some *one* aspect of the matter, but that only when taken together in their entirety do they give a realistic picture of these phenomena. A breach of law occurs in the fully developed legal community when a group or an individ-

[8] The discussion in Radbruch, *Rechtsphilosophie,* pp. 164 ff., which deals with these matters, unfortunately is handicapped by confusing the goals of security and improvement.

[9] See Walter Burckhardt, *Die Organisation der Rechtsgemeinschaft* (1927); a similar position is taken by Kelsen in *Theory of Law and the State* (1945), pp. 50 ff. Accordingly, Kelsen recognizes only retribution and prevention as purposes of criminal law (*ibid.*).

ual cannot or does not wish to recognize the authority of the legal proposition he violates, that is, when by his act he rejects the value judgments involved in the law he challenges. The penalty is frequently accepted quite consciously by those who commit such a breach (consent theory), is felt by the majority who accept the value judgment as a just retribution for the breach (retaliation theory), but causes others who may also question the controversial value judgment to avoid the penalty by obeying the law (intimidation theory), makes those who have already been punished once obey the law the next time (reform theory), and finally induces the administrators to strengthen their enforcement machinery (security theory). Evidently, the several aspects of the breach of law and its penalty are elucidated by the several theories, but only their combination enables one to understand the entire situation. This conclusion may be illustrated by the example of the traffic light. When several cars late at night wait until red turns green, although there is nowhere a traffic policeman in sight and no car is approaching from the crossroad, one can be sure that the several motives which are stressed by the several theories each play their role in determining the behavior of the drivers. One waits because he is quite satisfied with this traffic regulation; another, because he fears the penalty which a policeman who might suddenly appear would inflict; a third one has recently been punished and has sworn to improve, while a fourth has just read a sign saying, "At intersections, expect the unexpected."

The problem of breach of law and penalty is presented in its most poignant form by the death penalty, which has recently been abolished in a number of states. It is indeed difficult to see how a legal community which rests upon the full participation of all members can inflict this penalty. It is not so much a matter of consenting to this punishment, whether one accepts or rejects it,[10] but rather a question as to whether it can be justified. He who is

[10] Rousseau and Kant have both asserted that this consent exists; their oversubtle arguments were skilfully dissected and criticised by Radbruch, *op. cit.*, par. 23.

familiar with all that modern psychology and the social sciences teach us about man's nature cannot consent to so radical a penalty as death, particularly if he denies the immortality of the soul. Since every member of such a legal community shares the responsibility for what is being done by the government, it is not to be wondered at that a civilized majority considers the death penalty an unnecessarily harsh procedure. These thoughts are reinforced by the fact that one can only very rarely be certain that no error of judgment has occurred. Since the death penalty cannot be undone if such an error should come to light, it seems better not to inflict it. Experience also teaches that the death penalty does not necessarily deter people from committing certain crimes (obviously they cannot be re-educated by it), so that all that remains is that the community is protected against the repetition of the crime by the particular criminal. But nowadays we have nearly equally effective means of making the community secure, so that even from this viewpoint the death penalty is hard to defend.

In conclusion, it may be said that the breach of law as an attack upon the legal order usually results from the lack of authority of the law and of those who administer it, the officials and judges; this lack of authority also affects the effectiveness of the penalty adversely. If penalties are no longer understood and considered justified, they appear to be arbitrary acts, and even their deterrent effect, if it subsists at all, is greatly limited. Order, which every legal system seeks to realize, ought therefore not to be placed in opposition to justice as if it were a rival value, let alone be placed above it. For justice and order are, as I hope my analysis has shown, dependent upon each other. They cannot be realized in a legal community except jointly.

XXIII. *Constitutional Law as the Basis of the Legal System*

The distinction and differentiation of public and private law, so significant for the jurisprudence of Europe, has been called a decisive achievement of modern thought. Derived from the Roman law of imperial times, it dominated the jurisprudence of European absolutism and of its inheritors. It is intimately linked with the growth of the modern state, and hence also with its problems.[1] This distinction is, however, not really part of the American legal system and thought. In its place we find the distinction between constitutional and other (ordinary) law. The same tendency has appeared in those European countries which have been moving away from the ideas of absolutism—be it monarchical, be it democratic[2]—and have been turning toward genuine constitutionalism. In England even this distinction has never been really accepted; no separation of constitutional and other law is admitted. All law is seen as simply one body for the creation of which the popularly elected parliament is responsible.[3] This does, of course, by no means exclude continual reference, especially in political discussions, to "the" constitution. But such references are not distinctly to a separate body of law.

The idea of a law of the state, that is, of a law to which the several branches of the government are subject and which they

[1] In German, this fact is more readily apparent because of the term *Staatsrecht,* which refers, broadly speaking, to what is called "constitutional law" in English-speaking countries. The contrast is highly symptomatic.

[2] Cf. for this my paper in the special issue of the *Schweizer Monatshefte* on democracy's problems, May, 1957, entitled "Die Europäische und die amerikanische Auffassung der Demokratie," and the references given there. Cf. also the work cited in note 6 below.

[3] Cf. W. I. Jennings, *Parliament* (1940), esp. chap. x and pp. 7, 109–10, 495. There are more and more voices, though, which question the role of parliament; e.g., Ramsay Muir, *How Britain Is Governed* (1930), and G. W. Keeton, *The Passing of Parliament* (1952), who goes so far as to assert that Britain is on the brink of dictatorship.

must obey in the exercise of their "authority," is the bridge between an arbitrary despotic absolutism and a fully developed constitutionalism. In the latter, the "state" in the strict sense disappears. It is dissolved into a multiplicity of authorities united formally by the constitution and in fact by the will of the people as expressed in the programs and activities of the political parties. But in times of emergency the state clearly re-emerges, though in the framework of enabling acts and the like; after the crisis is passed, it disappears again. In light of these facts, which are familiar in the politics of constitutional democracies, the entire law may be seen in terms of a hierarchy of sources of law, the highest of which is the constitution, while the lowest is the measure taken by the police or an emergency authority to deal with a concrete situation. In between, law and ordinance are found. Questions as to the compatibility of a lower with a higher norm are decided by the competent court.

The relative position of a particular norm in the hierarchy of norms in a legal system does not correspond necessarily to the substantive importance of such a norm for the life of the legal community and its members. It may happen that a legal norm in the constitution is relatively unimportant or becomes so in the course of time, while on the other hand an ordinance or measure may be of crucial importance. If this fact is not sufficiently taken into account, serious errors and confusions are the result; they may become so troublesome that they endanger the legal system as a whole. Thus, the so-called security legislation in the United States and elsewhere, and, indeed, often mere police measures adopted for the security of the legal order, may undermine what has properly been termed "constitutional morality" to such an extent that the maintenance of the order itself is endangered. A similar chain of legal steps actually led to the downfall of the Weimar Republic.[4]

In the age of rationalism, from Locke to Kant and Hegel, law was generally looked upon as the decisive mode of political action

[4] See Karl D. Bracher, *Die Auflösung der Weimarer Republik: Eine Studie zum Problem des Machtzerfalls in der Demokratie* (1955).

—law, that is, in the sense of the statutory enactment. Such law was understood to be a norm enunciating a general rule, a thought which Rousseau stressed particularly. Norms generally seemed to these times and their representative thinkers to be the more important and valuable, the more general they were. Thus Locke insisted that the right to formulate such general rules must be divided between king and parliament;[5] not to have this decisive power concentrated in the hands of one authority seemed to him the kernel of an effective separation of powers as he saw it. Montesquieu and Kant, as well as other philosophers of monarchical constitutionalism, were inclined to accept this view, though they likewise stressed the separation of the legislative from the executive and the judicial power.[6] As the idea of government according to law spread in the nineteenth century, there developed the position that all general rules must be put into the form of law, that is, into a statutory enactment. It was also demanded that all ordinances and similar acts of administration concerned with the execution of the law be made only "within the framework of the law," that is to say, be based upon legislative authorization. The strength of this liberal tradition became apparent when totalitarian fascism took over the government and yet retained many of these forms of the government according to law. At the same time, it became apparent that such a legislative basis for administrative acts was not so important as had been asserted by the older theory. For, on the one hand, it became clear that everything depends upon who makes the laws and, on the other, that there must be beyond and above the legislative decision another decision of more general significance, namely, the political decision. We speak in all fields of public activity today of *policy* as the crucial core of political and legislative decisions, and if one were to ask any person involved in the political process what he believed the most important part of it, he would undoubtedly

[5] See John Locke, *Of Civil Government,* Part II, pars. 132, 134 ff. Cf. also his *Essays on the Law of Nature,* ed. W. von Leyden (1954), at the beginning and pp. 108 ff.

[6] Cf. for all this my *Constitutional Government and Democracy* (3d ed., 1950), esp. chaps. xvi–xix.

answer that it was policy.[7] In some of the more recent constitutions, notably in the Basic Law of the German Federal Republic, we find provisions such as that the chancellor determines the basic lines of policy. Policy is the center of the modern legal system. The changed situation as far as law is concerned is vividly shown in the fact that everyone wants to participate in policy decisions, whereas the formulation of these decisions and their transformation into statutory enactments everyone is quite prepared to leave to lawyer-technicians. Every lawyer will recognize that this outlook is somewhat superficial because the formulation itself involves policy decisions, frequently of the most crucial sort. Still, there is a shift in general emphasis that is highly significant.

Totalitarianism may be considered an exaggerated expression of this general tendency toward the emphasis on policy. For in totalitarianism the leaders claim for themselves the right to decide policy matters without any regard to legal forms. The ground alleged for this claim is that certain decisions of social, economic, and international import are so vital and so dependent upon the "logic" of a pseudo-scientific general ideology that all formal considerations of law must be looked upon as insignificant.[8] But where such policy decisions are not involved, there even totalitarian dictatorship can and does maintain the formalities of a government of law, which recommend themselves within the context of a highly technical civilization.[9] As a result of this dualism, the legal situation under totalitarian dictatorship, especially in such less extreme forms as Italian Fascism, is often misjudged both inside the country and out. The average citizen, finding himself in many situations confronted by the same sort of legal formalism he knew from the past, tends to see the key actions of the dictatorship merely as deviations, that is, as unlawful inter-

[7] Cf. my article "Public Policy and the Nature of Administrative Responsibility," *Public Policy*, I (1940), 1 ff.

[8] Cf. my *Totalitarian Dictatorship and Autocracy* (with Z. Brzezinski, 1956), esp. pp. 146 ff. Cf. also Harold Berman, *Justice in Russia* (1950).

[9] It has even been suggested, in view of this extraordinary aspect of totalitarian dictatorship, that it contains two "states," the legal state and the prerogative state; see Ernst Fränkel, *The Dual State* (1941).

ference with the law which he believes still to be in force. In reality, the role of law in the totalitarian society is completely changed. Law here becomes a mere tool in the hands of the political leadership because justice as an autonomous value has disappeared. In its place, social values such as the realization of the economic and industrial goals of Sovietism or of the folk and race notions of Hitler become decisive. In the particular sense, in which law is related to and oriented toward what all members of the legal community believe to be right and justice, one cannot speak of law in these totalitarian systems. This conclusion will, of course, be hotly denied by the totalitarians themselves and their sympathizers; for if one entertains the idea that the Communists are the voice of the proletariat and that the proletariat and the people are identical, then it suffices that the Communist leadership resolves upon a certain line of policy in order to make that policy and all it implies right and just. An analogous argument applies to Hitler and his followers, who claimed that they represented the German people. But as the Soviet system approaches general consensus, the possibility of speaking of its "law" is developing. But does this not mean that the system is ceasing to be totalitarian?

The genuine totalitarian arguments overlook the fact that the participation of the people in line with the conception of true law from Cicero to modern times has called for arrangements whereby this participation is assured within the framework of a constitution resolved upon by the people themselves. This norm of norms, this highest norm,[10] which was clearly recognized by Locke, Montesquieu, and Kant, is the determining consideration. It rests

[10] Kelsen's doctrine about the "basic norm" is a significant attempt to take account of this basic fact of law, but its soundness in the form Kelsen gave it may be doubted. See *General Theory of Law and State* (1945), pp. 110 ff. Kelsen defines a basic norm as "a norm the validity of which cannot be derived from a superior norm" (p. 111). How far Kelsen is prepared to carry his argument can be seen from his application of this idea to international law. Here the basic norm might be formulated as follows: "The States ought to behave as they have customarily behaved" (p. 369). In a review of this treatise I pointed out some years ago that this argument leads one to the battleground at Runnymede and beyond in search of the basic norm for the American legal order (cf. above, chap. xviii, p. 173).

upon fixed judgments as to what is necessary for the realization of justice by law. What then is the essence of law, or rather of the constitution? In what sense is it *basic law,* that is, the framework for all policy? The constitution is an attempt to give definite institutional forms to the political will of a people, of the members of a legal community.[11] This "political will" must be understood as the will to live together in a political community; it corresponds in many ways to what traditional natural law calls the will and the right to self-preservation, admittedly the first right of nature. It is the right to remain or to become an organized people, a nation, structured in many free associations and groups. This idea or norm is basic. The notion that a people could be willing to sacrifice its own existence as a people to some kind of social, economic, or power-political goal contradicts all the facts we know and must be rejected as erroneous. These "facts" upon which the argument rests are clearly made available by what scientific research in the social sciences and in history has shown. We are no longer obliged to derive these propositions, as did the older natural law theory, from a metaphysically grounded view of human nature. Rather, the findings of history, psychology, sociology, and political science enable us to demonstrate the propositions with a high degree of probability.

Thus, the constitution is to be understood as the process by which political action is limited and at the same time given form. The constitution has a definite function in the body politic. The guaranty of basic rights and the separation of powers, whether functional or spatial (federalism), have served as such limits. The basic rights define a sphere, in terms of general norms, which the governmental authorities, including the legislative, may not enter at all, or only under very special conditions. The separation of powers prevents anyone or any group in such a constitutional order from concentrating all power or even a large part of it in his own hands. This thought can be put another way by saying

[11] Cf. my paper "Le probléme du pouvoir dans la theorie constitutionaliste," in *Le Pouvoir: Annales de philosophie politique,* I, No. 1 (1956).

that the separation of powers is meant to prevent anyone or any group from becoming sovereign (see above, chap. viii)—a fact which has been obscured by the doctrine of "popular" sovereignty. What this expression is supposed to mean is that the constitutional legislator, namely, the people, is sovereign. It is of course possible to give sovereignty so vague and general a meaning that this statement would be correct, but that was not the original and significant meaning of the concept of sovereignty. The notion of sovereignty was developed to designate in a particular political community him who has "the last word" on whatever questions he wished to decide himself. The constitutional legislator, on the other hand, has only the one function of amending the constitution, in accordance with procedures contained in the constitution. That is the only, and therefore a very limited, competence of the constitutional legislator. He (or they) can neither make laws and ordinances nor take measures, but is limited to his one function.[12] A constitution is based, therefore, upon a self-limiting decision of the people when they adopt it.

Contemporary constitutions are still largely focused upon legislation as the central task; hence the legislative power is surrounded by careful limitations. The legislative power is generally treated first even now. The French constitution of 1946 and the Italian one of 1947, as well as that of the German Federal Republic, treat it as the foremost power; so does the draft constitution for Europe. It would be more realistic to lay emphasis upon the process of policy decision-making. For this is the decisive power, and only effective restraints upon the exercise of this power will render a government constitutional. It is in keeping with this political reality that elections are increasingly acknowledged to be of great significance and therefore recognized in constitutional law; electoral laws have become genuine "organic" laws, that is, constitutional laws. This is natural enough, for elec-

[12] The more detailed elaboration of these views is to be found in my book cited above, note 6, particularly chaps. vii–xii.

toral laws determine the kind of participation by the citizen in the process of lawmaking and policy decisions.

In conclusion, it may be repeated that the citizen becomes a participant in the creation of the law by reason of his share in making the constitution, as much as by his voting in elections. He maintains the law and he develops it largely by his support of the basic values upon which the constitution rests, for they are, in the words of Rousseau, "the real constitution" which is "graven upon the hearts of men."[13]

[13] Rousseau, *Contrat social,* Bk. II, chap. xii.

XXIV. *Peace and the World Community of Law*

The philosophical view of law I have here developed encounters considerable difficulty in describing the relation of several legal communities as a problem of law. For if law is conceived as not only containing norms but being itself a dynamically normative concept, if law is seen as propelled by its own inner dialectic, as becoming more nearly true law the more nearly it is a creation of the citizen-members of the legal community themselves, then the absence of a world citizenship would preclude the existence of a world law.[1] One way out of this difficulty is to deny the quality of law to international law, and this has frequently been done, not only because of such theoretical doubts, but also because of distaste for the practical aspects of the matter. Certainly, international law does not rest upon a constitution created by a world citizenship. Inversely, one might argue that only the creation of a constitutional order for the whole world could assure that in the relations between peoples, that is, legal communities, law would take the place of arbitrary power and violence. But however desirable it might be to pursue this latter thought,[2] it seems nonetheless possible to attribute to international law, even before the establishment of such a constitutional order for the world, the quality of genuine law, on one condition. The condition

[1] Kant was much concerned with a world citizenship, but in keeping with the cosmopolitanism of the Enlightenment he was preoccupied with what he called "hospitality," that is to say, the ability of people to go anywhere and be treated in a civilized manner. He did not envisage the world citizenship as a basis of a genuine lawmaking function. See "Eternal Peace" in my *The Philosophy of Kant* (1949), where the "third definitive article of the eternal peace" is stated as: "The Cosmopolitan or World Law shall be limited to conditions of universal hospitality," and then elaborated (pp. 446–48). See for contrast Carl Schmitt, *Nomos der Erde* (1950), where order is related to space, so that *Landnahme, Ortung* and *Hegung* become central.

[2] Cf. further *The Philosophy of Kant, passim,* and my *Inevitable Peace* (1948), where the antecedents and concomitants of the notion of a reign of lasting peace under law are explored, with special attention to Kant; cf. also the literature given there.

is that a sufficiently large number of peoples who participate in the creation of this law live themselves in constitutionally organized legal communities. We reject, as Kant did, the notion that the relations between states at his time possessed genuine legal character; we agree with Kant when he called Grotius and others "miserable comforters" because they "justify an aggressive war."[3] International law would likewise cease to be genuine or true law if most peoples lived in totalitarian states. Even today, international law is threatened by the growth of totalitarianism in the world.[4]

But why can international law be called genuine law if it regulates the relations between nations who are constitutionally organized? The reason is the same as that which applies to a very small community of individuals. If we are dealing with a community of, say, fifty persons, genuine law can come into being even without a constitution because the participation of each individual in the process of creating the law can be assured without difficulty. A world community of free constitutional states is in an analogous position. The constitutions of such states usually provide that general international law (or, less satisfactorily, that the generally recognized international law) takes precedence over municipal law, constitutional law included.[5] This general international law

[3] Kant, *op. cit.*, pp. 442–43.

[4] See C. J. Friedrich and Z. Brzezinski, *Totalitarian Dictatorship* (1956), chap. x.

[5] See D. R. Deener, "International Law Provisions in Post-World War II Constitutions," *Cornell Law Quarterly*, XXXVI, 503–33; L. Preuss, "Relation of International Law to Internal Law in the French Constitution," *American Journal of International Law*, XLIV, 641–69. The extended controversy between dualists, like Oppenheim, Triepel, and Anzilotti, who place international and municipal law as two distinct systems of law on a co-ordinate plane, and the monists, who either recognize only national municipal law, or who, like Scelle, Kelsen, and Verdross, place international law above municipal law, cannot be reviewed here. Cf., for key writings, H. B. Oppenheim, *International Law*, I, 20; H. Triepel, *Völkerrecht und Landesrecht* (1899), *passim;* D. Anzilotti, *Cours de droit international,* trans. Gidel (1929), I, 29–38; Hans Kelsen, *Das Problem der Souveränität und die Theorie des Völkerrechts* (1920), pp. 102–241; the same author's *General Theory of Law and State* (1945), pp. 363–80; A. Verdross, *Völkerrecht* (3d ed., 1955), pp. 60–66; Georges Scelle, *Précis de droit des gens* (1932–34), I, 27–42.

rests upon treaties and treaty-like agreements concluded by the several nations who participate in the international legal order. This treaty law becomes more nearly enforcible by means of such constitutional provisions; its breach can in various situations be tried in the courts. As long as there is no world court, or even as long as such a court possesses only limited jurisdiction (the most important limitation of such bodies up to now is the fact that private persons cannot become parties in suits before them),[6] the constitutional courts, like the Supreme Court of the United States, will be competent to deal with cases arising under such treaties. The fact that there exist cases which cannot be brought before such a court is not a peculiarity of international law; such instances occur also in other fields of law when the situation is such that "you may have a right, but you have no remedy." An international legal order becomes problematical when the leaders of a nation which is not constitutionally organized take the position that the breach of treaty law is right and justified. This may happen, as it did quite often among the autocratic states of the past, on the basis of "reason of state,"[7] when it was claimed that the survival of the state was in jeopardy. It happens nowadays when totalitarian states on the basis of their ideological goals, such as the destruction of capitalism, treat international obligations as mere tactical moves in their fight for the "execution of historical necessity." At this point, international law ceases to be real law. In fact, there is the danger that even the constitutionally ordered political communities may consider themselves forced to adopt a policy of disregarding treaties and other international obligations as a means of defending themselves against the violations of international law by others. Such a policy is much more dangerous for these constitutionally organized communities, because it is apt

[6] An interesting exception to this general rule is developing under the Council of Europe; here a judicial body, the European Commission on Human Rights, can deal with complaints raised by individuals under the European Convention for the Protection of Human Rights.

[7] Cf. my *Constitutional Reason of State* (1957) and the literature cited there, especially Friedrich Meinecke, *Die Idee der Staaträson in der neueren Geschichte* (1924), and my review of it, reprinted as an Appendix to the above.

to undermine their own constitutional order. This danger may take shape in political movements and parties who believe that they are justified in breaking all restrictions of the constitutional order, whether they be guaranties of basic rights or organizational limitations like the separation of powers—the argument being that in the face of a totalitarian enemy there are no holds barred, that *inter arma leges silent* ("in an armed struggle the laws are silent"), as a Roman adage had it. As a result, the view may develop that the constitutionally authorized supremacy of international law should be abolished, that is to say, that the particular constitutional order should maintain its law uncontaminated by any international legal thinking.[8]

To escape these uncertainties, the creation of a world constitutional order continues to be advocated. Such a world constitutional law would fix the most important general rules of law on the basis of a participant decision of all the nations, in a constitution of universal scope. Such a project would for realization depend again, however, as Kant showed so impressively, upon whether the nations participating in such a universal constitution were themselves constitutionally organized. Since at least two of the five most powerful nations today are not so organized, there remains only the possibility of restricting the world by legal fiction to those states which are constitutionally organized. The realization of such a world constitutional law then would encounter the resistance of those constitutional states which see in such a "union," which would in effect be a "bloc," an even greater danger than in the present incomplete state of international law. For the conventions and other treaty-like agreements maintained by the totalitarians in their own interest, although they provide no certainty of a perpetual or even of a durable peace, do offer a frame-

[8] The Bricker Amendment in its various editions sought to restrict the superior position of treaties under the American Constitution, which places them above state constitutions and laws but on a par with federal law. We must neglect here the important distinction between self-executing and non-self-executing treaties. Cf. Georges Scelle, "De la prétendue inconstitutionalité interne des traités . . . ," *Revue du droit public et de la science politique en France et à l'étranger,* LVIII (1952), 1012–28.

work for continuous efforts in the pursuit of peace, such as have been made by traditional diplomacy since time immemorial with at least partial success. For even the totalitarian state which recognizes law only as an instrument for the maintenance of rule has an interest, indeed a vital interest, in the maintenance of peace as long as war does not offer the prospect of even greater gains in the long run. International law has been and will continue to be a focal point of philosophical arguments in the field of law precisely because in its sphere the values of order and justice which constitute the dialectic of law, as we have seen, are so sharply confronted. Here, in the international sphere, order clearly represents a predominant interest of the community of participating nations, so that, even when under the circumstances justice and hence true law are only very imperfectly realized, such an order still has meaning and value. It is at bottom a matter of philosophical speculation whether one wishes to attribute to such an order the character of a community of law, as I have shown. Frequently it is considered "realistic" to do so, precisely because order is still a value, even though a lesser one than justice. This view is, however, in a deeper sense—such as is to be derived, for example, from the thought of Thomas Aquinas—less "realistic" because it recognizes only part of the reality that should be realized in an order; it overlooks the fact that an order to be durable must also be just.

Hegel and others, especially the Fascists, were not willing to accept this line of thought, but asserted instead that basic values can be realized only through struggle and war. Apart from the metaphysical adornment which would interpret this struggle as a process of the unfolding of the world spirit, which in the course of this process is said to achieve self-consciousness, I say quite apart from this metaphysics, the facts will not bear out the general proposition that the realization of values presupposes struggle and war. The values which man has been able to realize in the long course of his development have been brought into being not in the course of struggles but in the course of creative processes.

Men have found themselves confronted by tasks and problems which they have solved, if they possessed the capacity at all, by creative work. One of the great creations of mankind is law, just as much as art and science. That the "struggle over law"[9] has played a role, even a significant role, in these creative processes it would be foolish to deny. But all such struggle was an attendant phenomenon which could be regulated to suit the actual requirements of the situation. To legalize the struggle over law, that is, to channel it into legal procedure, is the historical achievement of Western constitutionalism (and its Greco-Roman antecedents). If the world is ever successfully united through a world constitutional law into a great commonwealth, the result will not be a disappearance of the "struggle over law" but an ordering of this struggle which will open up some of its hidden creative possibilities.

For only within the framework of such a world constitutional law would it be possible to integrate the different conceptions of law and justice of the many nations who would participate in such an order, in a slow but steady development. Such a development would not be without a precedent. What has taken place in Germany and other European nations since their national unification, namely, the creation of a national law, is a kind of precedent. What is at present beginning to take place in connection with the efforts toward the unification of Europe points in the same direction.[10] Here too—for example, in the treaty regarding the Coal and Steel Community—supranational law is being created and is crystallizing in a continuing struggle among men thinking in terms of French and German, Italian and Dutch and Belgian law. The common search for what in this particular sphere

[9] This term was coined, as we have seen above, chap. xvii, by Ihering in his *Der Zweck im Recht* (3d ed., 1892).

[10] Cf. more particularly the development in the Coal and Steel Community, as presented by D. G. Valentine, *The Court of Justice of the European Coal and Steel Community* (1955), and Rudolf L. Bindschedler, *Rechtsfragen der europäischen Einigung* (1954), who specifically discusses for each of the units involved the *Rechtserzeugungsverfahren* or procedure for the creation of law.

would be right and just, and hence would be sound law for this emergent community, raises the issue of a common constitutional order, of a European political community constitutionally organized.[11] An eventual world law within the framework of a world constitution seems therefore to be quite in line with the progressive realization of the task which law as the realization of justice presents to mankind. The common concerns of humanity which are growing steadily more numerous as men are brought together can only thus be handled appropriately and justly. The task is an infinitely comprehensive one and will challenge the ingenuity of man for generations to come. But it is quite meaningful if it is seen in the perspective of the kind of philosophy of law which we have sketched here. For according to it, just law is a system of reasonable rules which are grounded in the common experience of man, which seek to realize justice, which are created with the participation of all the members of the legal community on the basis of a constitution, and which rest upon the continuous common effort of these members.

[11] Cf. Arthur MacMahon (ed.), *Federalism Mature and Emergent* (1955), esp. Part IV, and pp. 3–28, 510–34.

Appendixes

Appendix I

*Law and History**

Law is frozen history. In an elementary sense, everything we study when we study law is the report of an event in history, and all history consists of such records or reports. It therefore cannot be my task to develop a sermon on the importance of historical records for the understanding of the law; the tie is too intimate and too obvious to need laboring.

"The work of Professor Maine on 'Ancient Law,'" wrote Professor T. W. Dwight in his Introduction to that book in the sixties of the last century, "is almost the only one in the English language in which general jurisprudence is regarded from the historical point of view."[1] This is an astonishing statement, considering the strikingly historical pattern of the common law. It is possibly correct, if taken *very precisely.* But was not the work of Blackstone or the work of Coke general jurisprudence from the historical point of view? Was it not their preoccupation with history, with the past, which aroused Jeremy Bentham against the jurisprudence of Blackstone and his predecessors? Law cannot of course be identified with "general jurisprudence" in any case; but leaving that issue aside, English and American law appear in fact to be "frozen history"; the institutions by which they are constituted are the outgrowth of that process which in Burke's memorable phrase links the dead of the past with the generations yet unborn.

But what of history? Is history conceivable without law? Certainly not the history of our Western world, though there are civilizations, such as the Chinese during most of its existence, which have not placed law into such a central position. It is patent that

* From the *Vanderbilt Law Review,* XIV (October, 1961), 1027–48.

[1] Introduction by T. W. Dwight to H. J. S. Maine's *Ancient Law* (3d American ed.; 1864), p. ix.

neither medieval nor modern history can be written or understood without careful attention to legal institutions. From feudalism to capitalism, from Magna Carta to the constitutions of contemporary Europe, the historian encounters law at every turn as a decisive factor.

It would seem, then, that any reconsideration of "law and history" is apt to be a string of commonplaces or the beating of a dead horse. Names such as Maine and Savigny, Maitland and Gierke, McIlwain and Olivier-Martin—not to mention Holmes, as the last in a succession of historically minded judges—clearly seem to settle the question of history's importance for law; it would not be difficult to match them with others signalizing the importance of law for history.

Such encounter between history and law is especially frequent in the history of political thought. One has only to open one of the books on the subject in order to discover that such a history is at least half a history of jurisprudence. From the Sophists and Plato to Hegel and Marx, the philosophy of law in historical perspective is inseparably intertwined with the history of political ideas. "The prevalent moral and political theories" were fully recognized by Oliver Wendell Holmes to be the key to the understanding of the law. It is equally true that the living law is one of the focal points of all political theory; in it is crystallized what men in their time consider just, and there can be no understanding of the political order without a grasp of the common coin of such values, interests, and beliefs as the idea of justice embodies at various stages of historical development. Political thought and legal thought are two sides of the same common coin.

The history of political thought and theory is itself not free from formidable difficulties, however. Unless we are to assume that words mean the same at all times or at least over long periods, virtually all the positions which it deals with are highly controversial. Plato and Aristotle, Cicero and St. Augustine, St. Thomas Aquinas and Machiavelli, Hobbes and Locke, Montesquieu, Rousseau and Kant—each and all have been the subject of extended learned controversy over what they *really* said. It may be true, and probably is, that "to know someone else's activity of thinking is possible only on the assumption that this same activity can be re-enacted in one's own mind."[2] But it cannot be "proven" that this condition can be fulfilled, that such re-enactment is possible. Similarly, it may well be that the task of "discovering 'what Plato thought' without inquiring 'whether it is true' " is "self-contradictory,"[3] but it is equally likely that the question whether what Plato thought be true is meaningless unless we first know what it was that he thought. This implies that "an act of thought, in addition to actually happening, is capable of sustaining itself and being revived and repeated without loss of its identity."[4] Such an implication is surely a self-evident proposition. If every thought, like all other acts, happens in context, is "an organic part of the thinker's life," then as the context changes the thought will necessarily also change. If then there is to be any continuity of thought it must be possible to relate degree of stability in context to degree of self-identity in thought. Hence the more abstract the thought, in the sense of being abstracted from specific detail in the context within and to which it applies, the more stable it presumably will be.[5] Here is the key dilemma of all historical effort at dealing with products of the mind which constitute creative responses to concrete problematic situations. Legal history shares it, as does political theory. By referring one to the other, we are possibly inviting the blind to lead the blind.

[2] R. G. Collingwood, *The Idea of History* (1946), Part V, para. 4. I do not share Collingwood's "idealist" premises, but I do find many of his formulations on history good. Cf. M. T. Swabey, *The Judgment of History* (1954), for a sounder position.

[3] Collingwood, *op. cit.*, p. 300.

[4] *Ibid.*

[5] Collingwood observes in this connection that "the mere fact that someone has expressed his thoughts in writing, and that we possess his works, does not enable us to understand his thoughts. In order that we may do so, we must come to the reading of them prepared with an *experience* sufficiently like his own to make those thoughts organic to it." Is it really probable that any man today will be able to share the experience of a fifth-century Athenian sufficiently to think Plato's thoughts on politics? I should say that, as best, only the most general features of such thought may be comprehended.

Neither a reference to the presupposed identity of experience, nor to the constancy in the environment so experienced resolves it.

In our age of doubt and scepticism, the problem cannot be so easily disposed of. "The life of the law" may not be "logic, but experience," as Holmes is ever again quoted as saying (though this view has a hoary ancestory). The wonderful passage which follows that famous generalization provides in a sense the theme for any discussion of law and history which is undertaken in light of the common law.

> The felt necessities of the time, the prevalent moral and political theories, intuitions of public policy, avowed or unconscious, even the prejudices which judges share with their fellowmen, have had a good deal more to do than the syllogism in determining the rules by which men should be governed. The law embodies the story of a nation's development through many centuries, and it cannot be dealt with as if it contained only the axioms and corollaries of a book of mathematics. In order to know what it is, we must know what it has been, and what it tends to become.[6]

The experience, then, is historical experience. This means that without history there cannot be, ther would not be, any law or jurisprudence. History is here conceived simply as the record of human experience. Yet, both "What is law?" and "What is history?" are questions which have not ceased to trouble the reflective student of both fields. It is not my intention to enter upon the task of seeking definitive answers to either of these never ending queries, though I will deal with both again later; rather, I intend to point out that neither question can be answered except within the context of a philosophical appraisal of law or history. And that means inescapably that he would discourse upon "law and history" would have to state first of all the philosophical context within which he is prepared to discuss either "in general." Such an undertaking might be of some interest, especially if the philosophy were novel. For if we stayed with established philosophical positions, such as those of Hegel or Dewey or Jaspers, all we would need to do would be to report what these eminent

[6] Oliver Wendell Holmes, *The Common Law* (1881), p. 1.

thinkers have had to say about our two fields and to match their positions as best we can. Thus Hegel concludes his remarkable but much misunderstood and misquoted *Philosophy of Right and Law* with a brief summary of his philosophy of history. This summary states with admirable succinctness his view of their relationship: Law is the embodiment of the ethical idea emanating from the state; as such it is embedded in history which consists in the unfolding of the world spirit's idea of freedom by way of the states which progressively realize it.[7] And if it were objected that such a view is hardly relevant today, we might reply that its Marxian variant in *Diamat* is still very much with us and indeed perhaps our major plague. But I am not a Hegelian and hence am merely giving his notions as an illustration of a thinker who clearly and explicitly argued the philosophical relation of law and history *in his terms*.[8]

The philosophy of history has moved a long way from Hegel. But it is very much alive. In our day, the skeptical view of Becker for whom every man was his own historian, the biological view of Spengler for whom history was embodied in cultural or civilizational wholes each of which was a law unto itself, its variant in Toynbee who believes in an ascent[9]—these and many lesser (though not less interesting) conceptions testify to the fascination which a view of the whole of man's existence on this globe exerts at present. Indeed, the extension of this view beyond the confines

[7] Georg Wilhelm Friedrich Hegel, *Grundlinien der Philosophie des Rechts* ("The Philosophy of Right," ed. J. Hoffmeister (1955), secs. 341–60. This most recent critical edition omits the additions (*Zusaetze*) which Hegel's editors had inserted on the basis of lecture notes, as well as the subtitle *Naturrecht und Staatswissenschaft* ("Natural Right and Political Science in Outline"). The latter omision is regrettable, since the subtitle better describes the content of the book.

[8] For a brief sketch of Hegel's philosophy of law, see chap. xv above. See the more detailed discusion in Huntington Cairns, *Legal Philosophy from Plato to Hegel* (1949), chap. xiv.

[9] Oswald Spengler, *The Decline of the West* (1926); Arnold Toynbee, *A Study of History* (1934–54). Among the many critical evaluations I especially found myself in accord with H. Stuart Hughes, *Oswald Spengler—A Critical Estimate* (1952), and Pieter Geyl, *Debates with Historians* (1955), chap. viii ("Toynbee the Prophet").

of written records to prehistory and the "endless journey"[10] which precedes it has added both poignancy and a certain weariness to the task, as ever more "cultures" have knocked at the gate to be admitted to "history" as well as to the United Nations. All such endeavors are somehow bound up with the convictions that history is something more than "making sense out of nonsense."[11] To the unsophisticated, history is "of course" that which happened, the concrete actions and events in all their specificity and effervescence. Indeed, many historians continue their arduous labors with something of this sort in mind. They are "looking" for history as it really happened—"*wie es wirklich gewesen.*" This memorable and simple phrase belongs of course to the great Ranke, himself a striking illustration of how far the great historian's achievement is from merely recounting how it really happened.[12] But the perplexing paradox of all historical work is that what actually happened can never be recaptured, although historical research would lose its point without a belief that more of it can be recaptured than is presently known. It is certainly true that each generation rewrites history in terms of its own values, interests, and beliefs, up to a point at least; it is also certainly true that discoveries of new material may from time to time alter important images of past events and personalities. But the quest is never complete, except in regard to such elementary data as the names and dates of particular tidbits. The happenings of history as contrasted with the reports about these happenings, the

[10] Loren Eisely, *The Immense Journey* (1946). Cf. Pierre Teilhard de Chardin, *The Phenomenon of Man* (1959); W. E. Le Gros Clarke, *The Antecedents of Man* (1959).

[11] T. Lessing, *Geschichte als Sinngebung des Sinnlosen* (1915); Carl Becker, *Every Man His Own Historian* (1935), which contains the essay by that name. For contrast, see Reinhold Niebuhr, *Faith and History* (1949).

[12] Fritz Wagner, *Geschichtswissenschaft* (1951), chap. ii, which gives many pertinent citations. The entire work is a most useful compendium of the "theories" of history from the beginning to Max Weber; it is, of course, written from the German perspective. The implicit idealism of Ranke which contradicts his oft- and above-quoted saying can be seen in such statements as "Alles Leben traegt sein Ideal in sich: der innerste Trieb des geistigen Lebens ist die Bewegung nach der Idee, nach einer groosseren Vortreffichkeit . . ." (quoted in Wagner, *op. cit.*. p. 194).

Geschehen in contrast to the *Geschichte*,[13] are devoured by time as soon as they happen. As we go through our days, they vanish into oblivion.

If, then, all history is a gloss upon the happenings, in the form of reports and interpretations of reports—such interpretations relating them to other reports and to thoughts upon them—the intellectual standing of such a gloss becomes a problem. And here the real issue of the relation of law to history is joined. As I see it, the reports of cases which occurred and are made part of the body of the law are related to other such reports in terms of the particular legal concept or rule which they demonstrate as an occurrence in time. Anyone opening a case book in any of the fields of law can see this clearly enough. And a good case book of the older type sought to illuminate the evolution of a concept and the rules it gave rise to by a succession of such cases. Well-known case books, such as Bigelow's or Wigmore's on torts or Williston's on contracts, are essentially histories of the particular legal institution with which they deal. Open any of them and an instance of the proposition just stated suggests itself. Thus in Scott and Simpson's *Judicial Remedies*[14] the first case is Slade's.[15] It is a case from the Court of Queen's Bench, and the report begins as follows:

> Be it remembered that heretofore, that is to say, in the term of St. Michael last past, before the lady the Queen at Westminster, came John Slade, by Nich. Weare his attorney, and brought here into the Court of the said lady the Queen, then there, his certain bill against Humphrey Morley, in custody of the Marshal, etc. of a plea of trespass upon the case. . . .

It then proceeds to tell how Morley defrauded John Slade by not paying him for some wheat that he had harvested and promised to pay for, the wheat growing on land which belonged to John Slade.

[13] The nicety of the contrast is not quite caught by the English words "happenings" and "history"; *Geschehen* carries the connotation of "bygones"—what *has* happened and is now accomplished fact. "Occurrences" suffers from the same defect.

[14] Austin W. Scott and Sidney P. Simpson, *Cases on Judicial Remedies* (1938), p. 23.

[15] 4 Co. Rep. 91a, 76 Eng. Rep. 1072 (K.B. 1602).

But what matters to the writers of this text is the form of pleadings in appellate review in an instance of actions at law. Alongside is placed a case from the Court of Appeals of the State of New York.[16] The vast differences between the England of Queen Elizabeth I and twentieth century America are of no significance to the point at issue which is stated by the text writers as follows: "After final judgment is rendered, the losing party can ordinarily carry the case to a higher court."[17] This statement presents a general principle of the law, deeply involved in the tradition of the "rule of law," a concept which has characterized adjudication over the centuries which have elapsed between the reign of Elizabeth and our time. The stress is on what is and has remained the same rather than on what has changed and evolved. The view is dogmatic rather than historical.

This instance illustrates, as would thousands of others, that the jurist is not concerned with the same dimension of interpretation as is the historian. For to the historian, the key question about the case would be: What does it tell us about the time of Queen Elizabeth? Is there anything here which sheds new light on Elizabeth or on the economic or social relations or any other of a number of possible individual historical features including the law *of her time?* And since the case as reported does not seem to do anything of the sort, it might well be considered irrelevant and trifling to the historian of Queen Elizabeth I's reign. Needless to say, the books on her reign and on the economic and social history of her reign do not make mention of this case. Nor do the legal histories, in fact. If we look up some of the leading texts on English legal history, such as Holdsworth or Pound, we do not find this case;[18] instead we find the rise of the Court of Chancery, from

[16] *Palsgraf* v. *Long Island R.R.*, 248 N.Y. 339, 162 N.E. 99 (1928).

[17] Interesting further points could be made regarding the fact that a "record" of a particular kind, defined at law, goes to the appeals court, embodying a report of what happened which excludes many events. In the days of Queen Elizabeth the record usually contained only the pleadings, the verdict, and the judgment; nowadays it also contains some of the proceedings at the trial.

[18] The case is actually cited by Holdsworth several times but in connection with another matter.

which this case is *not* taken, to be the key feature of the history of English law in this period. By the way, the rise of this court and of its equity jurisdiction has been described by a great legal historian as "an exceedingly curious episode." He added that "the whole nation seems to enter into one large conspiracy to evade its own laws, to evade laws which it has not the courage to reform."[19] The rise of this equity jurisdiction, in modification of the common law, was a matter of "stumbling into a scheme for the reconciliation of permanence with progress." Such a statement suggests that there is no effort made here to relate a decisive development in the history of the law of England with any of the other changing elements in the pattern of English life and politics. I am not going to indicate here what might be some of the correlations that suggest themselves but will merely remark that a deeper probing of the historical setting might well reveal connections which a strictly doctrinal approach tends to overlook.

But I wish to go a step further now and to advance the argument that the specific task of the student of law, of the jurist, is antithetical to that of the historian. By the very nature of his enterprise he is drawn into an ahistorical position.

In a challenging inaugural lecture, Frederic W. Maitland in 1888 discussed the question why the history of English law is not written.[20] He asserted at the outset that "English legal memory" went back to the year 1189 and no further, indeed to September 3, 1189.

> Glanvill had just finished the first text-book that would become a permanent classic for English lawyers; some clerk was just going to write the earliest plea-roll that would come to our hands; in a superb series of such rolls law was beginning to have a continuous written memory, a memory that we can still take in our hands and handle.[21]

Soon these records were to swell to a mighty chorus and "the practical limit set to our knowledge is not set by any lack of evidence,

[19] Frederic W. Maitland and Francis C. Montague, *A Sketch of English Legal History* (1915), p. 123.

[20] Frederic W. Maitland, *Collected Papers* (1911), ed. H. A. L. Fisher, pp. 480–97.

[21] *Ibid.*, p. 481.

it is the limit of our leisure, our strength, our studiousness, our curiosity."[22] It was obvious to Maitland that no one man could possibly hope to read the records even of one such reign as that of Edward I; how could the history of English law ever be written? "Seven hundred years of judicial records, six hundred years of law reports; think how long a time seven centuries would be in the history of Roman Law."[23] Centralization and the good fortune of England's insular position gave her "a series of records which for continuity, catholicity, minute detail and authoritative value has . . . no equal, no rival, in the world."[24] But it is the very fullness of this record which has been a major obstacle to legal history. Yet there are others, the most important being the isolation of English law and the conceit common to the guild that English law is something unique. "History," Maitland observed, "involves comparison and the English lawyer who knew nothing and cared nothing for any system but his own hardly came in sight of legal history."[25] And again: "[A]n isolated system cannot explain itself, still less explain its history."[26] Blackstone could write his remarkable volumes because he had an image of the feudal system, full of holes, in our modern perspective, but still an image that enabled him "to paint his great picture . . . the first picture ever painted"[27] of the history of English land law. So much for Maitland. There can be little doubt that the pursuit of legal history on the Continent was greatly stimulated by the confrontation of the local with the Roman law. The conflict between the two had profound political importance in the bargain; while the Roman law served ecclesiastical authorities at first, the "discovery" of its "true meaning" was a powerful weapon in the hands of the partisans of emperor and king. And eventually both were buried by the ivory tower learning of the great humanist jurists who insisted upon the historical record—Cujas, Doneau, and the rest. The work of these remarkable scholars serves at the same time to bring to light another aspect of the conflict between law and history, namely, that historical learning can kill the value of the

[22] *Ibid.*

[23] *Ibid.*

[24] *Ibid.*, p. 482.

[25] *Ibid.*, p. 488.

[26] *Ibid.*, p. 489.

[27] *Ibid.*

legal doctrine because it removes it from its contemporary application back to its original setting and thereby deprives it of authority and validity. The Roman law, which had been a live source of legal thought in the hands of the great glossators and postglossators who used it for solving the problems of their changing society, was in danger of becoming dead and lifeless once the humanists had fully established its meaning in terms of a society long gone, the pagan world of ancient Rome.[28] However, the much argued "reception" of the Roman law into the German law in the course of the sixteenth and seventeenth centuries, though much lamented by romantics and "Germanists" such as Eichhorn and Gierke, gave it a new lease on life; it also continued in considerable vigor in the south of France until the great codification (see below). This can be vividly seen in Savigny's famous study on possession which makes a startling companion to Holmes's chapter in his *Common Law.* After reviewing the positions of Hegel and Kant which he thinks are related to the positions of the Roman law, Holmes remarks that Savigny did not follow them and quotes him as thinking that "every act of violence is unlawful" and as considering "protection of possession a branch of protection to the person."[29] He puts the matter as if this were a similarly philosophical opinion of Savigny's. But a reading of the adduced paragraph 6 shows that Savigny was arguing from the Roman law itself, was therefore insisting that the right of possession was part of the law of obligations rather than of the law of "things" (*Sachenrecht*). He sees the reason in the *historical* fact that the Romans classified according to the procedural considerations, exploring the distinction between *jus in rem* and *jus ad rem.* He noted that *possessio* had always been a thorn in the side of systematic jurists. All attempts to interpret possession not as a distinct right but as "provisional ownership" are in error. Savigny thinks; he adduces for authority a general principle of the Roman code: "*Nihil commune habet proprietas cum possessione.*" Having thus pointed

[28] Myron P. Gilmore, *Argument from Roman Law in Political Thought, 1200–1600* (1941).

[29] Holmes, *op. cit.*, p. 207.

out the basic *historical* position, Savigny proceeds to explore the linguistic usage of the Roman jurists to fortify his position, distinguishing between *possessio civilis* and *possessio naturalis.*[30] But I have already lingered too long over this fascinating issue. Suffice it to add that Savigny was well aware of the fact that the pristine Roman notions had undergone a basic development in the course of history. The modifications which occurred are clearly seen as the result of *historical* forces.

By the constitution of the Christian Church and of the European states rights have been created and have been linked to the possession and usufruct of the *soil* which the Romans partly did not know, and partly were far from recognizing as rights belonging to an individual. Thus the exercise of episcopal power depends upon the possession (*Besitz*) of the church and its possessions. . . .[31]

But a close examination leads Savigny to the conclusion that the notion of possession in Roman law has "not been changed, but has been very consistently developed." Roman law, then, can be seen here as alive and still providing answers to concrete problems of the "living law," albeit at times rather formal ones. Holmes, in commenting upon Savigny's historically argued position (in terms of authority and precedent), allows himself to be too much influenced by the philosophical generalizations of Kant and his followers. It was not these generalizations but the dead hand of the past that persuaded Savigny to take the position which Holmes criticizes in terms of the common law's view of possession. But I am not sure that he states Savigny's position correctly. I do not read him the way Holmes does;[32] it is clear in any case that he does not enter upon the *historical* argument but treats the discussion dogmatically.

[30] Friedrich Karl von Savigny, *Das Recht des Besitzes* (1st ed., 1803). The paragraphs relevant here and referred to by Holmes are 6 and 7. To these should be added para. 48, in which the concept is discussed.

[31] *Ibid.*, p. 481.

[32] Holmes, *op. cit.*, p. 236. I find nothing in Savigny's careful historical analysis to support the sentence that Savigny "thinks that there must be always the same *animus* as at the moment of acquisition, and a constant power to reproduce at will the original physical relations to the object." See also *ibid.*, p. 238.

Maitland was fully aware of this conflict, but when considering the history of English law, he put it down as hindering the writing of English legal history because of the dogmatic preoccupation of the English lawyer. English lawyers were dealing with medieval law materials as lawyers, not as historians. "What is really required of the practising lawyer is not, save in the rarest cases, a knowledge of medieval law as it was in the middle ages, but rather a knowledge of medieval law as interpreted by modern courts to suit modern facts."[33] Thus a case is the more valuable the more recent it is; "what the lawyer wants is authority and the newer the better; what the historian wants is evidence and the older the better."[34] This point is of crucial importance for the right perspective on our problem. For the lawyer, Coke is better authority than Bracton, but for the historian seeking to interpret the law in the reign of Henry III "Bracton's lightest word is infinitely more valuable than all the tomes of Coke,"[35] not to mention more recent commentary. There is a basic conflict here which bedevils the task of legal history. We cannot say that Maitland has fully escaped it; for he proceeds to expound the notion that "any one who aspires to study legal history should begin by studying modern law."[36] Is it not like saying that anyone aspiring to study the history of philosophy or of art had better first study the contemporary practice of these subjects? No one will deny that such knowledge might be helpful, but is it essential? What then of the study of legal history where it extends to systems of law which no longer are alive? Can they not be studied at all? Indeed, such practical contemporary knowledge might be harmful, if not very carefully controlled, because it might cause the kind of "anachronism" which is so typically ahistorical in the work of, say, Sir Edward Coke. He knew the words and what use they could be made of in seventeenth-century England; he often did not know the meaning these words possessed at the time they were uttered. A medieval historian, fully alert to the conditions of the particular period and region in which

[33] Maitland, *Collected Papers,* I, 490.

[34] *Ibid.,* p. 491. [35] *Ibid.* [36] *Ibid.,* p. 494.

he had become an expert, would presumably be able to interpret more adequately the tenor of the phrases of the period; for law is not something separate and apart throughout the ages. It is part and parcel of the culture which it helps to organize and to define.

Thus legal history is seen as part of cultural history. Yet the term law does not even turn up in the index to Toynbee's magistral tomes—a scandal of sorts, if one remembers that Toynbee is an Englishman. How can culture, or at least Western culture, be imagined without laws? All of man's everyday activities, his government, and his economy are regularized and given form by law. In innumerable ways the history of certain cultures, and more especially Greco-Roman and Western cultures, is the history of the laws governing the communities which compose them. We need not go as far as Sir Henry Maine, who in one extraordinary passage attributed the difference between Roman (Western?) and Indian civilizations to the fact that the Romans had their Twelve Tables. These he saw as "merely an enunciation in words of the existing customs of the Roman people."[37] But he also saw a law that "usage which is reasonable generates usage which is unreasonable."[38] Stressing the common Indo-Germanic ancestry, which the ethnology of his time thought it could show, and acknowledging a "substratum of forethought and sound judgment"[39] in the Hindu jurisprudence, he yet imagined that the lack of an early code had thwarted the development of Hindu society; their law had been drawn up "after the mischief had been done."[40] The civilization of these unfortunate Hindus he saw as "feeble and perverted," while the Romans "*with* their code . . . were exempt from . . . so unhappy a destiny."[41] The foolishness of these comments, in our perspective of comparative cultural history, ought not to be allowed to hide the greater truth dimly perceived by the great Henry Maine, namely that a culture may be shaped, and often has been shaped, by its law.

There is an extraordinary passage in a later chapter (iv) of his work which I now wish to quote *in extenso,* because it pushes this

[37] Maine, *op. cit.*, p. 17.

[38] *Ibid.*, p. 18.

[39] *Ibid.*, p. 19.

[40] *Ibid.*

[41] *Ibid.*

issue further in a direction which seems to me crucial.[42] It ties in directly to what has just been discussed. And it raises a number of issues vital to our main theme. Among these the most crucial is that of the interaction between law and other aspects or components of culture. There are, Maine wrote,

> two special dangers to which law and society which is *held together by law,* appear to be liable in their infancy. One of them is that law may be too rapidly developed. This occurred with the codes of the more progressive Greek communities, which disembarrassed themselves with astonishing facility from cumbrous forms of procedure and needless terms of art. . . . The Greek intellect, with all its nobility and elasticity, was quite unable to confine itself within the straight waistcoat of a legal formula; . . . the Greek tribunals exhibited the strongest tendency to confound law and fact. . . . No durable system of jurisprudence could be produced in this way. . . . Such jurisprudence would contain no framework to which the more advanced conceptions of subsequent ages could be fitted.[43]

If I understand him correctly, Maine wishes here to say that a society which fails to develop a suitably firm skeleton of law is in danger of falling to pieces because there is nothing to hold it together. He did not think that this danger threatened many peoples. Actually one wonders whether the proposition can be maintained in this generality. Certainly the Chinese civilization was built upon a similar confounding of "law and fact"; but the li of the Confucian bureaucracy provided as firm a framework for that society as did law for the West. The legal solution to the problem of political and social order was explicitly rejected in the struggle over the so-called legists.[44] But let us look for the other "danger," especially as Maine thought that "few national societies have had their jurisprudence menaced by this peculiar

[42] This passage was especially drawn to my attention in a discussion by Lon Fuller.

[43] Maine, *op. cit.*, pp. 72–73 (italics added).

[44] See William T. De Bary, Jr., "Chinese Despotism and the Confucian Ideal: A Seventeenth-Century View," in *Chinese Thought and Institutions* (1957), ed. John K. Fairbanks, pp. 163–203, for a recent reappraisal. The "totalitarian" interpretation of Chinese despotism in Karl A. Wittfogel, *Oriental Despotism* (1957), does not convince me.

danger of precocious maturity and untimely disintegration."[45] For the other danger is much more common and it has "prevented or arrested the progress of far the greater part of mankind."[46] It is the danger that "the rigidity of primitive law, arising chiefly from its early association and identification with religion, has chained down the mass of the human race to those views of life and conduct which they entertained at the time when their usages were first consolidated into a systematic form."[47] And "over the larger part of the world, the perfection of law has always been considered as consisting in adherence to the ground plan supposed to have been marked out by the original legislator."[48] What allowed the Romans to escape from this other danger was their theory of natural law. Now in point of fact, modern scholarship has greatly reduced the importance of natural law in the development of Roman jurisprudence[49] and has correspondingly emphasized the traditional, especially the religious, elements—in other words, precisely those elements which Maine saw as the second "danger." But leaving aside the Romans and Maine's questionable interpretation of their theory of natural law as a parallel to Bentham's doctrine,[50] I wish to stress here that Maine insisted that law can seriously affect cultural development, either by giving it too much or too little of a skeleton, framework, stability, rigidity, and so forth. This is, it seems to me, a major insight, and it is grounded in the paradox, the dialectic of the relation of

[45] Maine, *op. cit.*, p. 73.

[46] *Ibid.*, p. 74.

[47] *Ibid.*

[48] *Ibid.*, pp. 74–75.

[49] F. Schultz, *History of Roman Legal Science* (1946); E. F. Bruck, *Ueber roemisches Recht im Rahmen der Kulturgeschichte* (1954). In the latter, the natural law is not treated at all, and Cicero's position is correspondingly reduced to the point where Professor Bruck even says: "Jurist war er schwerlich."

[50] Maine is, of course, aware of the fact that philosophically the two doctrines are far apart; natural law is not "an anticipation of Bentham's principles." Still he considers it "not an altogether fanciful comparison if we call the assumptions [of natural law] the ancient counterpart of Benthamism." The reason is that they both gave the nation and the profession "a distinct object to aim at in the pursuit of improvement." Bentham gave England a "clear rule of reform." In short "law of nature" and "the general good of the community" fulfilled the same *function* in the reshaping of the law. For a sketch of the natural law doctrine, see chap. iv above.

jurisprudence and historical understanding. To put it hortatively: the dogmatic and conceptual foundation of the law needs the softening impact of an inquiry into the past in order to free itself for the future. But such historical "softening" must not be carried too far, or the legal fabric is dissolved and with it the society which it sustains. This twofold danger is by no means restricted to the infancy of human society; it persists to the very present.

In order to illuminate this aspect of the relation of law and history further, the mooted question of codification deserves treatment here. For the issue of codification has helped to precipitate the argument about jurisprudence and history, the argument over whether history and more especially the history of law matters to jurisprudence at all. Savigny's famous essay on behalf of the historical school of jurisprudence[51] was written in response to the proposal made at the time, and in a spirit of patriotism, that the Germans codify their law. Savigny cited Bacon for the opinion that the age in which a code is brought into being must excel the preceding ages in legal understanding, and he drew the inference that, therefore, some ages which might be highly cultured in other respects do not possess the requisite "calling" for making a code.[52] He insisted that Germany was in that position. He built his argument upon a general proposition in line with our analysis here that "a two-fold understanding is indispensable to a jurist: the historical, in order that he may grasp the peculiar [nature]

[51] Friedrich Karl von Savigny, *Vom Beruf unserer Zeit fucr Gesetzgebung und Rechtswissenschaft* (1814). I used the third edition, which contains two appendixes concerned with the matter. Savigny's views have been restudied in the past generation; there is the detailed scholarly biography of Adolf Stoll, *Friedrich Karl von Savigny* (1927), in three volumes; the brilliant essay of Erik Wolf, *Grosse Rechtsdenker der deutschen Geistesgeschichte* (1939), chap. xii; and the penetrating analytic essay by Franz Zwilgmeyer, *Der Rechtslehre Savignys* (1929). All three agree that behind Savigny's historicism there is to be found a dogmatic judgment in favor of the Roman law as the standard of what constitutes high achievement. This non-relative aspect of Savigny is crucial for an understanding of his position on the question of codification.

[52] Bacon's well-known proposals were made to King James and are entitled "A Proposition to His Majesty . . . Touching the Compiling and Amendment of the Laws of England" and "An Offer to King James of a Digest To Be Made of the Laws of England." They are found in Francis Bacon, *Works* (Philadelphia, 1852), II, 229–36.

of each age and of each legal form, and the systematic one, in order that he perceive each concept and each rule [principle] in living connection and interaction with the whole [of the law]. . . ."[53] Savigny felt that the German jurists of the eighteenth century did not possess this equipment, that they were shallow rationalists, and that the new beginning which had been made had not yet progressed far enough, though there was hope. To fix the law at such a point, he felt, was not only useless; it was dangerous, because it clothed with authority an unsatisfactory state of the law, and he reminded his readers of the Code of Theodoric in this connection. He also urged that the German language had not yet developed an adequate legal vocabulary. He then proceeded to analyze the codes that had come into being, more especially the Code Civil or Code Napoléon.[54] His very sharp criticism is primarily directed at the ignorance of the four men who drafted the code, since the *Conseil d'Etat* contained so many (in his view) juristically incompetent persons. How relatively irrelevant this sort of criticism was, has been pointed out.[55] For Savigny was inclined to gainsay the true historical functions of the Code Civil which lay in the cementing of national unity and to belittle the great principles underlying it, namely (1) freedom of the person and of contract, as well as equal right to engage in professions and to possess property; (2) suppression of all the old privileges, equality of all Frenchmen regardless of status, sex, or social condition; and (3) freedom of civil society from all ecclesiastical control. These were of course at the heart of the French Revolution, and for this revolution Savigny had little use.

[53] Savigny, *op. cit.*

[54] For this and what follows, see *The Code Napoléon and the Common Law World* (1956), ed. Bernard Schwartz, especially my essay, "The Ideological and Philosophical Background" (pp. 1–18), and A. P. Sereni's essay, "The Code and Case Law" (pp. 55–79). In a number of other essays, S. D. Elliott, A. von Mehren, Max Rheinstein, and others show how the code has been transformed by legislative and judicial interpretation.

[55] Thus, the renowned René Cassin remarked that "on the technical level, proponents of the historical school could criticize the codification for having ossified the rules of civil law and prevented certain necessary development" ("Codification and National Unity," in Schwartz, *op. cit.*, p. 49).

For him, as for so many other historicist thinkers, the rationalist ingredient of the revolutionary credo was anathema. Yet, the Code contained many notions deeply embedded in the old customary law, or *coutumes,* and it is truly surprising to note to how large an extent Savigny could overlook this element. "The Germanic, conservative and popular content [of the Code] Savigny did not recognize."[56] The "errors" which Savigny charged the drafters with were mistakes about the Roman law which he knew so well; that their great achievement lay in the skilful use of Pothier by Pourtalis he did not acknowledge.

It has been rightly said that "the promulgation of the Civil Code in the year 1804 is, historically, the legislative response to a desire expressed during many centuries by the French people."[57] The Code was not the hiatus in French legal development which Savigny's criticism implied. In the perspective of a century and a half, it is quite plain to see that the Code was a culmination and a starting point. If we approach the Code as historians, the codification can be seen as part of that ebb and flow of ideas by which the law is molded as it evolves. The seamless web of history appears then as not torn apart by a Code but as merely reinforced by such a "digest." Actually, the Code had become an inescapable necessity through the very work of the revolution which *threatened* to disrupt the legal continuity. This threat was averted and the continuity preserved with the help of the code which, in terms of Hegel's dialectic phrase, suspended, superseded, and preserved the old law. At this point, a distinction needs to be drawn between the different kinds of codes.

The idea of a code and a codification appears in at least three distinguishable forms. The Justinian Code represents a first type; one might call it the digest type. It tries to bring together and "digest" a body of existing law, clarifying it, eliminating possible contradictions, but not intending to alter it in any significant way. The work of the American Law Institute has been essentially of this character. Bacon, in the above cited memoranda, spoke as if

[56] Wolf, *op. cit.,* p. 476.

[57] A. Tunc, "The Grand Outlines of the Code," in Schwartz, *op. cit.,* p. 19.

such a digest were what he had in mind. "The work which I propound, tendeth to the pruning and grafting the law, and not to the ploughing up and planting it again; for such a remove I hold indeed for a perilous innovation. . . ."[58] But he actually aimed at the second type. This sort of code seeks to codify the law in terms of natural law or other general principles which would provide a pattern for systematization. These general principles are philosophical and political in nature and serve as a yardstick for the evaluation of existing law; that is to say, such a code seeks the clarification and reformation of the law in whole or in part. General philosophical reason is here assigned a distinctive role. Such were the codes the enlightened despots favored and enacted, the Prussian Common Code and the Austrian Civil Law Code, as well as the more limited codes made under Louis XIV with the help of Colbert. Such a code was in the mind of Bacon, who flattered the king about his knowledge of "justice and judicature" which enabled him to be a "lawgiver"; he proclaimed that "as the common law is more worthy than the statute law, so the law of nature is more worthy than them both."[59] Such codes were in line with the thinking of enlightened despotism. The *philosophes* were the authors of the general principles; the jurists, of the detailed application.

But there was implicit in this kind of thinking a yet more radical position enunciated by the greatest of the *philosophes*, Voltaire, when he exclaimed: "Do you want good laws? Burn yours and make new ones!" Voltaire's dramatic demand symbolizes the revolutionary attitude that underlay the insistent demand for a code of laws during the revolution. The original French revolutionary codes were of this type of "rationality." The draft code of 1793 was revolutionary in both intent and content. It was meant to change everything at once; it was "the fruit of liberty." The drafters told the assembly that "the nation will receive it as the guarantee of its happiness, and it will offer it one day to all the peoples. . . ." There was only one truth, and that was the revolutionary

[58] Bacon, *op. cit.*, II, 231.

[59] *Ibid.*, p. 169. Roscoe Pound, *The Development of Constitutional Guarantees of Liberty* (1957), p. 43, stresses Bacon's favoring absolute monarchy.

ideology which they had embodied in their draft code. A still more radical code was presented the following year; it was, in the words of one eminent French legal scholar, "much more a manual of practical morals than a code of civil law." Neither was adopted. The codifications of the USSR (and subsequently of the Communist states) are really the best examples of this type of code.[60] Thus the problem of codification shows dramatically the range of continuity and change that law in its historical dimension can exhibit.

It is clear that the two-fold danger of which Maine had warned is at the heart of the argument over the problem of codification; that is, does it make the law too rigid, or does it help to give it that tensile strength which it requires for fulfilling its societal functions? As has been often remarked, law in a certain sense is an organon, an organic whole extending over centuries. Being embedded in the history of nations, it must be seen in the perspective of their over-all significance. We may have come a long way from the romantic notions of a Gierke, who would interpret all history in terms of the struggle of the Romanist principle of *Herrschaft* with the Germanic principle of *Genossenschaft;* we may have left far behind the equally romantic notion of a Savigny, who would interpret the Roman law in terms of the folk spirit of the Roman people; we may have outdistanced Maine's utilitarian enthusiasm for the progress from status to contrast as the key to all legal development. But we cannot escape from the need of identifying our own philosophy of history, if we are to see the historical phenomena of law-in-the-making in the perspective of truth claims, whether scientific or humanist.[61]

[60] See H. J. Berman, *Justice in Russia* (1950); Boris A. Konstantinovsky, *Soviet Law in Action* (1953), ed. H. J. Berman, concerned with the codification problem; cf. also Andrei Vyshinsky, *The Law of the Soviet State* (1948), for an ex cathedra exposition.

[61] Besides Collingwood and the writers cited in the next few footnotes, the following deserve mention as significant contributions to the recent discussion: Raymond Aron, *Introduction à la Philosophie de l'Histoire* (1948); Isaiah Berlin, *Historical Inevitability* (1954); Marjorie L. Burke, *Origin of History as Metaphysic* (1950); Theodor Litt, *Wege und Irrwege geschichtlichen Denkens* (1947); Henri Marrou, *De la Connaissance Historique* (1954); U. A. Padovani, *Filosofia e Teologia della Storia* (1953).

Any attempt to answer the question, What is history? involves a philosophy of history in the sense of "general thoughts upon history." We have postponed this question until now, but we can avoid it no longer. Our time has produced a rich variety of answers and rejoinders to answers. Lord Acton, one of the great minds working in that field in the recent past, thought it "the office of historical science to maintain morality as the sole impartial criterion of men and things." Others, from St. Augustine to Hegel, have seen history as the theodicy in which God and the march of spirit were revealed in the world of man.[62] "Historicism," if not of the Augustinian, then certainly of the Hegelian and Marxian, variety, has been flailed again and again from different viewpoints. In a perspective somewhat akin to that of Lord Acton, one contemporary philosopher has juxtaposed a doctrine of natural right with all such historicism, which he has called "self-contradictory or absurd."[63] Another, noting the "poverty of historicism," argues on the contrary that historicism, "an antique and tottering philosophy," proclaims

> social science is nothing but history, not however history in the traditional sense of a mere chronicle of historical facts . . . but . . . of the laws of social development. . . . [I]t could be described as historical theory or as theoretical history, since the only universally valid social laws have been identified as historical laws.[64]

[62] For these, see Karl Loewith, *Meaning in History* (1949), who examines a baker's dozen writers from Burckhardt to Orosius.

[63] Leo Strauss, *Natural Right and History* (1953), p. 25. See *ibid.*, chap. i. Strauss states the position of "radical historicism" as follows: "All understanding, all knowledge, however limited and 'scientific,' presupposes a frame of reference; it presupposes a horizon, a comprehensive view within which understanding and knowing take place. Only such a comprehensive vision makes possible any seeing, any observation, any orientation. The comprehensive view of the whole cannot be validated by reasoning, since it is the basis of all reasoning. Accordingly, there is a variety of such comprehensive views, each as legitimate as any other: we have to choose such a view without any rational guidance" (*ibid.*, pp. 26–27).

[64] Karl Popper, *The Poverty of Historicism* (1957), p. 45. Popper, the philosopher of science, is impressed with the passive, contemplative aspect of historicism, its "quietism"; he notes that "the historical can only *interpret* social development and aid it in various ways; . . . *nobody can change it*" (*ibid.*, p. 52).

In writing thus, he emphasizes the exact opposite of the preceding critic, namely the doctrinaire, dogmatic aspect of historicism as contrasted with its relativist notions. Crucially conclusive against such a view is, in this critic's opinion, the fact that "we cannot predict, by rational or scientific methods, the future growth of our scientific knowledge," and "if there is such a thing as growing human knowledge, then we cannot anticipate to-day what we shall know only to-morrow."[65] The trouble with historicism (and with certain kinds of sociology derived from it) is that it believes it can predict confidently. But neither can you so predict on the basis of some kind of unchanging "human nature," as the other critic with his faith in natural right believed.

The contradiction in the two ways of seeing "historicism" is embedded in the phenomenon itself, as well as in the outlook of the critics. Of these the first hopes to return to an "unchanging world," such as was believed in before the historicists took over; the second wants to transcend the "fear of change" which has driven the historicist into believing in an "unchanging law" which governs the changing world.[66] To both it might be objected that the particular view of history which they reject is the only view worthy of respect as "philosophy of history."[67] For only when history is seen as a whole, is seen as world history with a meaning, can we in this perspective speak of a "philosophy of history." Now it has been asserted that if seen thus, philosophy of history is "entirely dependent upon theology," that is to say, upon the "theological interpretation of history as salvation."[68] Whether this be true or not, it is certainly a fact that such philosophies of history have been a peculiar and distinctive feature of the West, with definite roots in

[65] Popper, *op. cit.*, p. x. The last quoted passage is given by Popper in italics.

[66] Popper, *op. cit.*, p. 161.

[67] This appears to be the tendency of Loewith, who in his discriminating study, cited in n. 62, would not credit "every opinion about history" as a philosophy of history, but only "the systematic interpretation of world history on the basis of a principle" (Loewith, *op. cit.*, p. 11).

[68] *Ibid.* Loewith speaks of *Heilsgeschehen*, that is to say, literally, "the happening of salvation," and the title of the German edition of his book has therefore been changed into *Weltgeschichte als Heilsgeschehen* (1953).

the Bible, more especially the Old Testament. The theological roots may have something to do with the political function which such philosophies have had.

The great syntheses of these philosophies of history are closely related to the unique importance of historical thought for the West. For through them the *self* achieves the relatedness which he seeks as a cultural being. It provides the frame within which it becomes possible to say what needs to be said about the meaning and destiny of this particular human being, as well of man.[69] At the same time, such a projection of the self of man and his culture *expresses* and gives verisimilitude to a sense of superiority—cultural, spiritual, religious. Philosophies of history are, in this perspective, expressions of an intellectual or spiritual imperialism such as has characterized the West until recently and is now being transformed and reincarnated in the Soviet Union. This equality is inherent in such syntheses because they presuppose a universal goal or end of history which can only be asserted on the basis of faith. Thus philosophies of history are expressions of a will to power, a will to conquest even. They correspond to other forms of ideological aggression and the will (or at any rate the desire) to subjugate mankind in terms of its own good. Such destiny is apt to be described as manifest and well calculated to heal the ills of the world, in one form or another. It is evident that all such philosophies are variants upon the theme of the "chosen people."[70] Legal history, though rarely involved in the broad universalism of such philosophies, has tended to partake of the valuational aggressiveness. The well-known conceit of the common law lawyers is readily matched by the "Germanism" of a Gierke or the "Romanism" of a Savigny. That is to say, legal history is frequently infused by a preconceived notion of what constitutes valid law.

As against such extravagances, a more sober view of history, a more skeptical philosophy, might provide a possible antidote. The

[69] Reinhold Niebuhr, *The Nature and Destiny of Man* (1949), II, 299–321 ("Human Destiny"), esp. 299 ff.

[70] For further detail, see my article, "Die Philosophie der Geschichte als Form der Ueberlagerung," in *Wirtschaft und Kultursystem* (1955), ed. Gottfried Eisermann, p. 199, and the literature there cited.

great Burckhardt, in his *Reflections on World History,* clearly indicated his lack of interest in broad constructions. History, he thought, was not a science of objective, "neutral" facts, but a "report about such facts as one age finds remarkable in another." Only by thus selecting and interpreting the reports about past events can we determine which facts are noteworthy, important, of real significance. He noted that "Thucydides may mention a fact the importance of which will only be recognized in a hundred years." Such a view of history is eminently suited to the pursuit of legal history in the best sense. For is it not typical of the work of jurists that they reassess the law of past decisions—judicial, legislative, administrative—in the light of present concerns and preoccupations? But is it enough? Do we not need some kind of notion of an inner development, of an unfolding of the potentialities of the body that is law? In the work of the greatest historians of the law, some such idea seems to have been alive and a major motivating force of their work. Before considering this notion of "intrinsic" development in the Aristotelian sense of a *telos* that is embedded in the seed, let us consider yet another approach.

One of the best-known students of these problems believed that the idea of history could be circumscribed in four basic propositions, to wit, that "history should be (a) a science, or an answering of questions; (b) concerned with human actions in the past; (c) pursued by interpretation of evidence; and (d) for the sake of human self-knowledge."[71] In light of such a characterization, which the author believed to be generally held among historians, he asked the question: Of what can there be historical knowledge? And he answered: of that which can be re-enacted in the historian's mind. Such an answer is obviously favorable to the historical exploration of past events that belong to the realm of the mind, and law is certainly one of these. It reinforces the notion, considered by us earlier, that one should have a knowledge of the law to be a legal historian; it would certainly facilitate the "re-enacting." But is there not a fatal difficulty present also, the difficulty of

[71] Collingwood, *op. cit.*, Introduction. See n. 2 above and accompanying text.

re-enacting anything? Heraclitus' famous proposition that you cannot step into the same river twice, that all is in flux, applies to the subtle matters of the spirit more poignantly than to the "simple" passions felt by all men—love, hatred, ambition, and the rest of which so much ordinary human history is compounded. But can we ever again recapture the way men reasoned about justice in the days of Bracton or even of Coke? It seems most improbable. And when we read the detailed essays of renowned scholars in the field of legal history, it is usually clear enough what has been their concern. Think of the debunking of Magna Carta[72] and the corresponding work on the Declaration of Independence.[73] These two venerable documents of legal history can now be said to represent striking instances of myth-making and myth-destroying. As scholars have succeeded in "re-enacting," they have also succeeded in depriving of genuine legal value these and other records of the past. Is it too much to say that the more fully a particular historical event is understood, the more remote it becomes from present concerns? J. B. Ames recounts a rather touching anecdote of the young Langdell in his memorial article on that great scholar. It takes us back to the days when Langdell was studying and assisting at the Harvard Law School. When a fellow student, the later Judge Charles E. Phelps, surprised him among his books in the alcoves of Dane Hall, studying a black letter folio, Langdell exclaimed, "in a tone of mingled exhilaration and regret, and with an emphatic gesture: 'Oh, if only I could have lived in the time of the Plantagenets!' " To have lived at the time of the Plantagenets—this is indeed the problem, and the more nearly you succeed, the less you have to offer to the twentieth century.[74]

It is then clear (or at any rate suggested) that the continuity of legal thought processes is to a very considerable extent a fiction.

[72] See William S. McKechnie, *Magna Carta* (2d ed.; 1913).

[73] See Carl Becker, *The Declaration of Independence* (1922).

[74] Cf. James Barr Ames, *Lectures on Legal History* (1913), p. 471. It might be remarked in passing that Ames states the subject of his lectures to be "the origin and development of the ideas of crime, tort, contract, property and equity." The next sentence claims that "the common law is essentially of Teutonic origin." It is not fashionable to put it that way today.

No matter how history is conceived philosophically, the cases that are cited over and over produce in line with *stare decisis* a façade of historical support which any close inspection would reveal as largely untenable. At the same time it must be admitted that this fiction is of the greatest legal, that is, dogmatic, importance.

In this country [England] and in the whole common-law world, the place of the systematic fiction is taken to a considerable extent by the fiction of historical continuity. Every decision appears in the cloak of a mere application or adaptation of pre-existing "principles" laid down in earlier judicial pronouncements. Where historical continuity and systematic consistency are in conflict, it is the former which prevails. . . .[75]

In the light of what can properly be called scientific history in the sense previously defined, this continuity is a fact only through its being a fiction; for if the historical appreciation were truly scientific, that is, if it were actually based upon the search and discovery of historical truth, it would forthwith cease to be operative as a fiction; for the cases in the past would cease to have any application to the problems of today.

This is my conclusion, then, but it is less skeptical than it sounds. History in the sense of past happenings is not the "meaningless" to which meaning is arbitrarily assigned. When these happenings are products of the mind, such as legal decisions, statutes, and opinions of jurists, they presumably had a meaning to those who brought them into being. In searching for this meaning, this historian will be sitting in judgment upon the rational content, both in terms of means and ends. Thus "the judicial role appears to fit the historian's activity better than that of the scientist checking hypotheses, the politician promoting his party's cause, or the artist fashioning a work of art."[76] This "judgment" which the historian is called upon to render provides the intellectual bridge between him and the jurist. It is not an arbitrary judgment, such as is often assumed to have been implied in Hegel's famous quote from Schiller's *Die Resignation,* but rather the resigned judgment of the

[75] O. Kahn-Freund, Introduction to Karl Renner's *The Institutions of Private Law and Their Social Functions* (1949), pp. 9–10.

[76] Swabey, *op. cit.,* p. 238.

truth-seeker who knows that he will never know all of it. Why should a past decision provide authority for a present one? Because there is a fair chance that the solution it offered related sound reasoning in terms of justice to that feature of a problematic situation which is persisting in the one now confronting the jurist. It may be fiction, and the farther removed in time, the more likely this is. But "life is but a dream," and even fictions have their place in the economy of the mind, especially the legal mind. The potential antagonism between the historian who may destroy a cherished illusion and the jurist who is called upon to provide reasoned solutions to the problems of injustice that are facing us here and now may be resolved time and again by the re-enforcement of a sharpened critical insight into the true "precedents" which a history of the law can provide.

Appendix II

*Remarks on Llewellyn's View of Law, Official Behavior, and Political Science**

Karl Llewellyn's realistic jurisprudence started out by refusing to define law.[1] A definition both excludes and includes. It marks out a field. Some matters fall inside the field, some outside. Instead of defining law, then, Llewellyn preferred to characterize it. He devoted his attention to the *focus* of matters legal. What he first tried to do was to discuss a point of reference. "A focus, a core, a center —with bearings and boundaries outward unlimited." This sounds bad, but it is good sense; it is no different with biology, which cannot and will not define life, with sociology, which cannot and will not define social life (if it has sense). Even so "scientific" a word as "probability" cannot be "defined." It is of a purely intuitive nature; all we can define is a method of measuring it.[2] Now, obviously, law cannot even be subject to a definition of measurement. Can we then not say anything about it? That may be safest: just let everybody think what he will and trust that the intuitions of men speaking the same language are roughly identical. But Karl Llewellyn is a daring fellow, and therefore, he is willing to discuss what he cannot define, hoping, I take it, that intelligent discussion may enable us to appreciate more fully what we mean by "law." Such a discussion starts from the center or core, because it is obviously more sensible to focus attention on that which is in-

* From *Political Science Quarterly,* L (September, 1935), 419–30. Llewellyn's view is taken from his *Präjudizienrecht und Rechtsprechung in Amerika: Eine Spruchauswahl mit Besprechung* (Leipzig, 1933; 2 vols.). Page citations in the text refer to this work.

[1] See "A Realistic Jurisprudence—The Next Step," 30 *Columbia Law Review,* XXX (1930), 431, and *The Bramble Bush—Some Lectures on Law and Its Study* (1930).

[2] C. Fry Thornton, *Probability and Its Engineering Uses* (1928), p. 3.

contestably law than to go to the periphery of matters legal (if there be such). Now, according to Llewellyn, "the focus of study, the point of reference of all things legal" is "the area of contact, of interaction, between official regulatory behavior and the behavior of those affecting official regulatory behavior or affected by it." From this it follows that "the rules and precepts and principles which have hitherto kept the limelight should be displaced, and treated with severe reference to their bearing upon that area of contact—in order that paper rules may be revealed for what they are, and rules with real behavior correspondences come into due importance." The value as well as the limitations of this approach seem to me to have become apparent through two more recent contributions of Llewellyn to a discussion into which I shall presently enter; but before I do, I should like to call attention to a point which occurs to the political scientist, when he reflects upon the scheme of reference within which Llewellyn explores his regularities of behavior.

In a pioneering venture into the law of sales[3] in the course of which Llewellyn explored the regularities of behavior of sellers, buyers, and what not, his point of reference remained a legal concept: sales. What is more, as a legal concept, it was essentially an American legal concept, and that was his ultimate point of reference. Undoubtedly it was a sound one; but would it be the point of reference of a sociologist, an economist, or a political scientist? To ask the question is to deny it. This query reveals, from the viewpoint of a social scientist, that Llewellyn's scheme of references for the ordering of his regularities is determined for him by the officials who make the law. No matter how disinclined he may be to focus on *words*, his ultimate scheme of intuitions, or "hunches" as he likes to call them, is "defined" for him. No matter how violently he may writhe under it, he has to accept "authority." Compare with his the position of the scientist interested in generalizations. The latter does not ask, What do others consider *important* (whether they be officials of some sort or another,

[3] Llewellyn, *Cases and Materials on the Law of Sales* (1930).

judges, administrators, traders, or what not), but what is *true* (as far as our present knowledge goes).

The realization of this difference between rules and actions seems to me to underlie the ablest critiques of Llewellyn's views,[4] from the standpoint of jurists. It can be summarized in the sentence "The subject matter with which the lawyer deals is not words but their meanings."[5] But the logical counterpart, from the standpoint of one interested in social life as it normally works, not only in America and at present but in all times and places, is the recognition of a different set of verbal reference points, not determined by the verbal preferences of a particular set of officials at a particular time, but evolved out of the materials themselves in terms of striking variations. To put it another way, Llewellyn would investigate actual conduct in terms of existing words, precepts, and rules in order to determine whether these words, precepts, and rules correspond to the actual behavior of officials (more particularly judges) in given and territorially defined jurisdictions; a student interested in one of the generalizing social sciences, like economics and political science, would investigate existing generalizations, "hunches," hypotheses, or whatever you like to call them in order to determine whether they are true or not. To be sure, all sciences, law, history, and economics, as much as the natural sciences, are haunted by the paradox of an insatiable interest in truth, coupled with an equally profound doubt as to its attainment. But while a student of the law wants to know whether a certain proposition is true here and now, in the sense of its carrying a certain meaning for those whose action is going to be guided by that proposition (e.g., the judicial officials), a student of one of the generalizing social sciences wants to know whether a given proposition is true in itself, irrespective of whether it be understood and used by anybody.

Thus the lawyer studying the activities of the Tariff Commis-

[4] See Roscoe Pound, "The Call for a Realistic Jurisprudence," *Harvard Law Review*, XLIV (1931), 697; Morris Cohen, *Law and the Social Order* (1933), pp. 198 *et seq.* and 357 *et seq.;* and Hermann Kantorowicz, "Some Rationalism about Realism," *Yale Law Journal* (1934), p. 1240.

[5] Kantorowicz, *op. cit.*, p. 1245.

sion and from it deriving American tariff law will be inclined to accept the cost-of-production standard, no matter how intrinsically wrong it may be, as constituting an important element of the thought pattern of the commissioners. For obviously, if he were to argue a case before the commission for an increase in a certain tariff schedule, he would have "the law on his side." And if perchance he should wish to argue against it, he will seek to press the argument that in giving the President the power to revise tariffs upward Congress delegated power contrary to the Constitution. The matter was so argued in the Hampton case.[6] But he will be wary to argue with whatever officials he is "contacting" on the merits of the cost-of-production standard alone; for although no court is obliged to enforce that which is impossible, the hypothetical reasoning of generalizing sciences, such as economics, makes it very difficult to prove something to be impossible, no matter how difficult or improbable, not to mention the all-important fact that the judicial official's comprehension of what an economist might say is likely to be limited. In other words, what is after all one of the most important behavior patterns of judicial officials is that they are trained in the law. This law teaches them that the legislature is, within broadly defined limits, omnipotent, i.e., it can order what it pleases. That a rule to the effect that all Americans should walk on their heads would be invalidated in spite of the most magnificent efforts of all Americans is not very likely to occur to lawyers when they consider the cost-of-production standard for tariff rates because their training has not accustomed them to ask: Can this be done? Is this true? But rather must they ask: Should this be done? Has it been ordered?

The fact that the law and the science which deals with it are so much concerned with one national set of rules, and their meaning within the context of national boundaries, gives particular significance to Llewellyn's effort to set forth the nature of the American judicial process to German lawyers.[7] For here he is entering the

[6] *J. W. Hampton, Jr., & Co.*, v. *United States* (T. D. 41478), 49 Treas. Dec. 626, and 276 U.S. 394.

[7] See his *Präjudizienrecht und Rechtsprechung in Amerika*, esp. Part I.

historical, if not the sociological, field by attempting to expound what is of general significance. Karl Llewellyn's intimate familiarity with the German language enabled him to create a whole set of truly suggestive words which if absorbed into German legal thought will add new life to an ancient pursuit. One's only regret must be a seeming lack of familiarity with older German writings on cognate topics; the work of men like Gneist and Redlich would have deserved his more careful attention. But historical perspective is not Llewellyn's forte. In the light of what we have already said this seems rather curious; his insistence upon testing rules and precepts of law by studying actual regularities of behavior of officials administering the law as set forth above would lead one to believe that historical materials would greatly interest him, but they do not seem to do so. Take the case of *Abbott of Lewis* v. *Bishop of Ely* (1304), from which he gives an extract.[8] This case presumably established a certain rule of procedure, i.e., it associated certain words with certain behavior patterns and thereby gave them meaning. In putting before German readers this tradition of Anglo-Saxon law it is of course illuminating to suggest the meaning of a significant rule by telling the story of how it arose (the case), but this very circumstance should have suggested to Llewellyn the extent to which words have always been tested by reference to behavior (the older word was "facts"). If something is wrong with the rule now—if it does not correspond to actual behavior, as Llewellyn would say—this could as well be shown by studying the historical context and thus revealing that the behavior to which the rule once referred has no counterpart under modern conditions. But he prefers the "facts" which the social scientist can lay his hands on in the contemporary context, and there is much to be said for so doing whenever it is possible. After all, he is a lawyer, and a teacher of lawyers, who wants to know what is going on now.

As one would expect, from the book alone, one of Llewellyn's primary concerns had to be with the rule of *stare decisis*. Once more he thereby proves our contention that as a lawyer he has to

[8] *Ibid.*, II, 3.

start from the rule. To begin with, he points out that the technique of deciding cases by precedent (*Präjudizienwesen*) is hardly systematized at all. It is therefore an art rather than a science (which remark suggests that "science" for Llewellyn does not mean generalizing science but "systematized body of knowledge"). "What has been written about case law," he says, "gives no systematic treatment. It consists of unsystematic, scattered fragments each of which was written for the case in hand" (p. 2). The inherent contradictions of these scattered pronouncements would lead one, from a scholarly point of view, to construct several "ideal types" (Max Weber) of case law technique. Different judges will base their reasoning upon different ideal conceptions. With these statements we are carried right into the center of Llewellyn's approach to legal problems, his insistence upon looking for the actual behavior of judges and trying to ascertain what they are doing, rather than starting from a preconceived notion such as the idea that there *must* be *one* case law technique because . . . and then forcing the available materials into the bed of Procrustes provided by such preconceived notions. Whatever may be the objections to such a procedure from a legal point of view (and certainly jurists like Kelsen with their insistence upon the unity of the legal order and upon a watertight separation of norms and facts will object), it seems a very desirable kind of inquiry from the standpoint of a social scientist.

The one aspect which wants clarification most is best stated in the form of the following question: What is the difference between legal science as conceived by Llewellyn and the several generalizing social sciences? The writer has no objection to a healthy amount of overlapping; he agrees with Llewellyn that "the social sciences are not staked out like real estate." To continue the analogy: a farmer and an artist may both be interested in a bit of meadow; yet their "viewpoint" is not only different, but this difference can be made plain. Similarly, what is the difference in outlook, in viewpoint, between Llewellyn's legal science and other social sciences? The problem which is posited by this question has been obscured by the fact that Llewellyn, when speaking generally, has concentrated his attention upon the behavior of judges. In studying case law technique in many fields, this emphasis would be entirely appropriate. Yet he realizes, and his text on sales shows it, that there are many other behavior patterns involved in shaping the law. He once stated it thus:

> Close around it [the behavior of judges] lies the behavior of other government officials. On the other hand, the sets of accepted formulae which judges recite, seek light from, try to follow. Distinguishing here the formulae with close behavior-correspondences from others; those of frequent application from those of infrequent. Close around these again, lie various persons' ideas of what the law is; and especially their views of what it or some part of it ought to accomplish. At first hand contact with officials' behavior, from another angle, lies the social set-up which resists or further reflects the impingement of his acts. Farther from the center lies legal and social philosophy. . . .[9]

Nobody who reflects upon this quotation will question Llewellyn's assertion that "included in the field of law under such an approach is everything currently included, and a vast deal more." For if we now proceed to make an inventory of the various fields of law and outline in programmatic fashion what the lawyer-scientist should study, according to Llewellyn, we come very near to absorbing most of the materials of all the social sciences, in so far as these materials deal with the contemporary American context; and if the European lawyers followed Llewelyn's example, that would take care of European materials, and so for other nations. This was strikingly illustrated by Llewellyn's attempt to explore the applicability of his methods to the field of constitutional law. "Our working constitution," he said in "The Constitution as an Institution,"[10] "embraces the interlocking ways and attitudes of different groups and classes in the community." The specialists, the public, and the interested groups all play their role in shaping the "actual constitution." In differentiating this constitutional field from what he calls "the governmental machine at large" or "the mere working government," he would have us consider it as "the *basic* ways of government." Leaving aside the difficulty of determining what is basic (though this is a serious matter), we venture the guess that if Llewellyn should now turn his attention from constitutional to

[9] "A Realistic Jurisprudence," p. 465.

[10] *Columbia Law Review*, XXXIV (1934), 1, 18.

administrative law, he would demand that we study the actual conduct of officials, in other words, "the mere working government."

The problem which bothers me is whether such a description of the actual behavior of officials can be undertaken without a conceptual scheme of some sort—no metaphysical scheme of "eternal truths," but a hypothetical scheme of scientific concepts with which to order the social materials in terms of similar materials elsewhere. According to Pound, the father of the sociological approach to jurisprudence in this country, the function of the jurist or legal scholar is this (if I interpret him correctly): the jurist employs the conceptual scheme offered him by the mass of legal rules or norms ("standards of oughtness of behavior"—Llewellyn). He interprets these rules by determining their meaning as they were framed and with respect to their intended scope. This task would, of course, involve a study of the uniformities (or rather regularities) of behavior required by the rules from the viewpoint of the rulers and of those ruled. But it would *also* involve a study of the logical relationships of various rules to each other with a view to elaborating them into a conceptual scheme. To be sure, the scheme may be and perhaps always will be imperfect, but logic remains one of the standards by which to evaluate a normative rule. On the other hand, the generalizing social sciences are concerned with discovering recurrences and regularities of behavior in terms of conceptual schemes evolved out of these behavior patterns themselves and therefore transcending national boundaries. Obviously, this kind of effort (whatever its value) is something different from what Llewellyn has in mind, though it may at times be of great value to him in directing his attention in certain directions. Perhaps it would be best to illustrate the difference in terms of a specific example.

In the Myers case[11] the Supreme Court held, roughly speaking,

[11] 272 U.S. 52. See also "The Power of the President To Remove Federal Officers," Senate Document No. 174, 69th Cong., 2d sess., for the briefs and oral arguments. James Hart, *Tenure of Office under the Constitution* (1930), and Edward S. Corwin, *The President's Removal Power* (1927), are the most elaborate criticisms, not limited to the legal aspect. But neither of them urges the view suggested in the text.

that Congress cannot limit the President's power to remove the members of the quasi-judicial administrative tribunals. The elaborate argument of the majority of the Court, written by Taft, held, among other things, that the President's removal power must be maintained because otherwise the President would be unable to assure the faithful execution of the laws as the Constitution demands.

Made responsible under the Constitution [Taft wrote] for the effective enforcement of the law, the President needs as an indispensable aid to meet it the disciplinary influence upon those who act under him of a reserve power of removal. . . . There are . . . strong reasons why the President should have a like power to remove his appointees charged with other duties than those above described [the political]. The ordinary duties of officers prescribed by statute come under the general administrative control of the President by virtue of the general grant to him of the executive power, and he may properly supervise and guide their construction of the statutes under which they act in order to secure that unitary and uniform execution of the laws which Article II of the Constitution evidently contemplated in vesting general executive power in the President alone. Laws are often passed with specific provision for the adoption of regulations by a department or bureau head to make the law workable and effective. The ability and judgment manifested by the official thus empowered, as well as his energy and stimulation of his subordinates, are subjects which the President must consider and supervise in his administrative control. Finding such officers to be negligent and inefficient, the President should have the power to remove them. . . . Otherwise he does not discharge his own constitutional duty of seeing that the laws be faithfully executed.

Now all the legal arguments I have read on this decision have been concerned with ascertaining just what the meaning of these words might be. The conclusions reached by commentators are, of course, profoundly affected by their views as to the rule of *stare decisis.* Even with the greatest scepticism regarding mere word patterns,[12] the interest of the student of law remains focused on the word patterns as the most significant element of judicial and legal behavior. But the question which no student of the law asks is this: Is it true that the power of removal is essential in order to

[12] See H. Oliphant, "A Return to *Stare Decisis,*" in *American Law School Review,* VI, 215.

secure the uniform execution of the laws? It so happens that the severest doubt must be entertained regarding the truth of this assertion.[13] The experience of many governments has shown that there are very different ways of insuring administrative responsibility.

Now there is no question that American courts are, under the influence of men like Brandeis, becoming increasingly sensitive to "scientific" opinion outside the lawyers' briefs, but this does not invalidate our view that we are dealing here with a fundamentally different outlook. At any rate, the extent to which this is no longer true depends upon the extent to which judges (and other lawyers) are social scientists besides being lawyers. The desirability of such a state of affairs does in no wise prove, however, that it would be desirable for judges not to be lawyers at all, nor does it argue that the best occupant for the Supreme Court would be a man who had never read the Constitution.

It goes without saying that Llewelyn is far from such radical views. In fact, he seems to be extremely proud of his legal craft. A good part of that attitude is due, no doubt, to what one writer has called Llewellyn's professional prejudice in speaking of the law as mainly the behavior of judges, in spite of the admitted qualifications we have already examined. This is nowhere shown so strongly as in his book on *Präjudizienrecht*. What he wished to drive home to his German readers is just this fact of the importance of judicial behavior as an all-important concern of the American jurist who would ascertain the meaning of his norms. There is much in his discussion that no American lawyer or political scientist will find occasion to quarrel with, but there is reason to quarrel just a little with this overemphasis upon the controversial aspects of the law and the consequent tendency to identify law with legal controversy. The United States would be a desperate community to live in if it were true. But most of us ascertain the "meaning" of the law, much of it in statutes and administrative regulations, and

[13] See C. J. Friedrich and Taylor Cole, *Responsible Bureaucracy—A Study of the Swiss Civil Service* (1932), and C. J. Friedrich, "Responsible Government Service under the American Constitution," in *Publications of the Commission of Inquiry into Public Service Personnel* (1935), chap. iii.

then act accordingly. The student of social and political problems is much more interested in this regular behavior than in the narrow area of controversial conduct, though he would certainly not exclude the latter. This can, I believe, be brought out in a concluding illustration, relevant to the rule of *stare decisis.* It is a very controversial subject among legal scholars, and the present author enters upon it with some fear and trembling.

American jurists who have studied the actual practice of *stare decisis* readily discovered that there were, besides mere neglect of it, at least two generally accepted ways of behaving according to it. You may call them the broad and the narrow interpretation,[14] or you may call them the strict and the loose view,[15] but they are both practiced and applied under different circumstances by lawyer and court. The strict view, according to Llewelyn, is employed in dealing with unwelcome precedents and "is the recognized, legitimate, honorable technique for whittling precedents away. It is a surgeon's knife." The loose view, on the other hand, "is a device for capitalizing welcome precedents. . . . This doctrine is like the other, recognized, legitimate, honorable." The doctrine of precedent, therefore, "is two-headed. . . . It is not one doctrine, but two, . . . and two which *applied at the same time to the same precedent, are contradictory of each other.*" This observation of Llewellyn's is central to the core of his problems, for, as he says, "until you see the double aspect of the doctrine-in-action, . . . you [do not] appreciate how little, in detail, you can predict *out of the rules alone;* how much you must turn for purposes of prediction, to the reactions of the judges to the facts and to the life around them."

This is probably very sound practical advice, but what strikes the political scientist as typically legal is that Llewellyn stops there. He has found what works; that is all he cares about, or rather seems to at this point. Now let me show the significance of this. In his *Präjudizienwesen,* his realistic view of the nature of precedent leads him, by inference, to challenge a long-accepted

[14] See Oliphant, *loc. cit.*

[15] See Llewellyn, *Bramble Bush,* pp. 63 *et seq.*

view concerning the difference between Anglo-American case law and Continental European statute law. His general view may be challengingly overstated thus: there is in actual practice very little difference between the American and the German way of deciding cases. Speaking of the tendency of courts to reverse themselves, Llewellyn says: ". . . opposite views may succeed each other rapidly in the same court and in the same field of law, a tendency which does not seem unfamiliar in German courts" (p. 3). And again: "We say the judge *must* follow precedent; in Germany such following comes about in practice (whether one likes it or not). In both countries precedents are often and unexpectedly not followed—we experience that, even if we do not recognize it consciously" (p. 9). It would be wearisome to quote a goodly number of similar statements running through Llewelyn's discussions. I am inclined to agree with his opinion, but I am dissatisfied with his just stating it and dropping it then and there. As a social scientist, I am immediately and almost subconsciously pushed on to the question: Why does the same actual behavior presuppose such very different verbal behavior? Or, to express it more simply: What conditions explain the need of the rule of precedent?

We are here confronted with one of the typical occasions where the student concerned with one of the generalizing social sciences can make a significant contribution, irrespective of its practical significance (though that may be great). What condition makes the German judge follow precedent, even though there is no rule to make him believe in it? Briefly, it is the fact that he is the member of a bureaucratic hierarchy. His promotion depends upon his standing with the officials in the Ministry of Justice. It is they who determine which *Amtsgrichtsrat* shall become a *Landgerichtsrat.* Now these officials, as all administrators do, like the fellow who conforms. So the judge also wishes to conform. But this desire to conform is also present where the rule of precedent prevails. As Llewellyn himself has pointed out, "Precedent is the official analogue of what, in the individual, we know as habit."[16] The significant difference is that the rule of precedent *must* point to some-

[16] Llewellyn, *Bramble Bush,* p. 61.

thing beyond mere inertia. To be sure, "it takes time and effort to solve problems. Once you have solved one, it seems foolish to reopen it." But dissent arises from the conviction that the problem has *not* been solved. This suggests that Llewellyn's "explanation" is not sufficient. Inertia works anyway; no need for a rule of precedent, then. At this point, the mere inspection of the facts gets you no further; you are stuck.

The problem can only be resolved in terms of a general knowledge about the politics of bureaucracy, on the one hand, and of a free association, on the other. For, to put it succinctly, the American judge is first and foremost the member of an ancient craft guild. In such free associations, make-believe is very essential for maintaining social coherence. While a bureaucratic hierarchy can count upon the individual official's desire to avoid arousing the displeasure of his superiors, within a free association convincing rationalization is essential and the rule of precedent is a mighty factor in making the rationalization convincing. This illustration will, I hope, show further what seems to me the distinguishing feature of the generalizing social sciences; for this discovery has no immediate practical significance for the American lawyer unless it be this. Inasmuch as the rule of *stare decisis* is the most vigorous living expression of the background of the American judicial process, efforts to weaken the belief in it may be the result of the weakening of that guild background. Those who are engaged in forwarding this development may be assumed to be foes of such guild traditions. They are likely to be men who are convinced (without perhaps knowing it themselves) that other make-believes than Coke's "artificial reason of the law" must be created, if the "decisions" of the judges are to be acceptable to their brethren of the bar and to the community at large. "Realism" like "objectivity" may be merely a particularly virulent form of partisanship.

Be that as it may, the comments which a legal scholar may draw from kindred social scientists will afford him the strictly theoretical pleasure of possibly understanding better why something which he knows to be so is as it is. . . .

Bibliography

Bibliography

In view of the large amount of literature on legal philosophy, it seemed best to organize the material in relation to the chapters.

GENERAL LITERATURE FOR CHAPTERS I AND XVII TO XXIV

Of works published since 1900 the following historical and systematic ones might be mentioned:

ALLEN, C. K. *Law in the Making*. 1927, 1958.
BAUMGARTEN, ARTHUR. *Rechtsphilosophie*. 1929, 1947.
BINDER, JULIUS. *Philosphie des Rechts*. 1925.
BINDING, K. *Die Normen und ihre Übertretung*. 4 vols. 1872–1920.
BODENHEIMER, EDGAR. *Jurisprudence*. 1940.
BRUNNER, EMIL. *Gerechtigkeit*. 1943.
CAHN, EDMOND N. *The Sense of Injustice*. 1949.
CAIRNS, HUNTINGTON. *Legal Philosophy from Plato to Hegel*. 1949.
CARDOZO, BENJAMIN N. *The Nature of the Judicial Process*. 1923.
———. *The Growth of the Law*. 1924.
CATHREIN, VICTOR VON. *Recht, Naturrecht und positives Recht*. 2d ed. 1909.
COHEN, MORRIS R. *Law and the Social Order: Essays in Legal Philosophy*. 1933.
COING, HELMUT. *Die obersten Grundsätze des Rechts*. 1947.
———. *Grundzüge der Rechtsphilosophie*. 1951.
DUGUIT, LÉON. *L'état, le droit objectif et la loi positive*. 1901.
———. *Traité de droit constitutionel*. 1911. 2d ed.; 1921–25.
EHRLICH, EUGEN. *Grundlegung der Soziologie des Rechts*. 1913.
EMGE, C. A. *Geschichte der Rechtsphilosophie*. 1931.
ENTRÈVES, A. PASSERIN D'. *Natural Law: An Introduction to Legal Philosophy*. 1951.
FECHNER, ERICH. *Rechtsphilosophie: Soziologie und Metaphysik des Rechts*. 1956.
FRANK, JEROME. *Law and the Modern Mind*. 1930.
FRIEDMAN, W. *Legal Theory*. 1944.
FRIEDRICH, CARL J. *Man and His Government*. 1963.
———. *Transcendent Justice: The Religious Dimension of Constitutionalism*. 1964.
FULLER, LON L. *The Law in Quest of Itself*. 1940.
———. *The Morality of the Law*. 1964.

GENY, FRANÇOIS. *Science et technique en droit privé positif*. 1913 and later.
GOODHART, A. L. *Essays in Jurisprudence and the Common Law*. 1931.
GRAY, J. C. *The Nature and Sources of Law*. 1909.
HALL, JEROME. *Studies in Jurisprudence*. 1958.
———. *Comparative Law and Social Theory*. 1963.
HART, H. L. A. *The Concept of Law*. 1961.
HOHFELD, WESLEY N. *Fundamental Legal Conceptions*. 1923.
HOLLAND, T. E. *Elements of Jurisprudence*. 13th ed. 1925.
HOLMES, OLIVER WENDELL. *The Common Law*. 1938.
KAUFMANN, ERICH. *Kritik der neukantischen Rechtsphilosophie*. 1921.
KAUFMANN, FELIX. *Logik und Rechtswissenschaft*. 1922.
———. *Reine Rechtslehre*. 1923.
KELSEN, H. *Allgemeine Staatslehre*. 1925. English ed.; 1945.
———. *Reine Rechtslehre*. 1934.
———. *What Is Justice?* 1957.
KOHLER, JOSEPH. *Lehrbuch der Rechtsphilosophie*. 1909. 3d ed.; 1923.
KRABBE, H. *The Modern Idea of the State*. 1922. Dutch original, 1915.
LASK, EMIL. *Rechtsphilosophie*. 1905.
LEIBHOLZ, GERHARD. *Politics and Law*. 1965.
LEVI-ULLMAN. *Eléments d'introduction générale à l'étude des sciences juridiques*. 2 vols. 1917–28.
LLEWELLYN, KARL. *The Bramble Bush*. 1930, 1961.
———. *The Common Law Tradition*. 1960.
———. *Jurisprudence: Realism in Theory and Practice*. 1962.
MAYER, MAX E. *Rechtsphilosophie*. 1922.
PASCHUKANIS, E. *Allgemeine Rechtslehre und Marxismus*. 1927.
POUND, ROSCOE. *An Introduction to the Philosophy of Law*. 1922.
RADBRUCH, GUSTAV. *Rechtsphilosophie*. 1914. 3d ed.; 1932. 4th ed.; 1950. English ed.; 1950 (with an Introduction by E. W. PATTERSON).
RECASÉNS SICHES, LUIS. *Direcciones contemporaneos del pensiamento juridico*. 1929.
ROMMEN, HEINRICH A. *Die ewige Wiederkehr des Naturrechts*. 1947.
———. *The State in Catholic Thought*. 1945.
SALMOND, J. W. *Jurisprudence*. 1891.
SALOMON, MAX. *Grundlegung der Rechtsphilosophie*. 2d ed. 1925.
SAUER, W. *Lehrbuch der Rechts- und Sozialphilosophie*. 1929.
SAUTER, J. *Die philosophischen Grundlagen des Naturrechts*. 1932.
SCHREIER, FRITZ. *Grundbegriffe und Grundformen des Rechts*. 1924.
SHKLAR, JUDITH N. *Legalism*. 1964.
SHUMAN, SAMUEL L. *Legal Positivism: Its Scope and Limitations*. 1963.
SOMLO, FELIX. *Juristische Grundlehre*. 1917.
SPIEGELBERG, HERBERT. *Gesetz und Sittengesetz*. 1935.

STAMMLER, RUDOLF. *Lehrbuch der Rechtsphilosophie.* 3d ed. 1928.

——. *Die Lehre vom richtigen Rechte.* 1902. 2d ed.; 1926. English ed.; 1925.

STONE, J. *The Province and Function of Law.* 1946.

VECCHIO, G. DEL. *The Formal Bases of the Law.* 1914. Contains the three basic works of Del Vecchio: *I presupposti folosofici della nozione del diritto,* 1905; *Il concetto del diritto,* 1906; *Il concetto della natura e il principio del diritto,* 1908.

VERDROSS, A. *Abendländische Rechtsphilosophie.* 1958.

WEBER, MAX. *Wirtschaft und Gesellschaft,* Part II, chap. vi. English ed.; 1954 (ed. MAX RHEINSTEIN, trans. EDWARD SHILS).

WELZEL, HANS. *Naturrecht und materiale Gerechtigkeit.* 1951.

WOLF, ERIK. *Grosse Rechtsdenker der deutschen Geistesgeschichte.* 2d ed. 1944.

CHAPTER II

FINKELSTEIN, L. *The Pharisees.* 2 vols. 1938.

GRESSMANN, H. (ed.). *Altorientalische Texte und Bilder zum Alten Testament.* 1926.

KITTEL, R. *Geschichte des Volkes Israel.* 7th ed. 1932.

MEYER, EDUARD. *Die Israeliten und ihre Nachbarstämme.* 1906.

SMITH, J. M. P. *The Origin and History of Hebrew Law.* 1931.

WEBER, MAX. *Religionssoziologie,* Vol. III. 1921. English ed.; 1930 (ed. TALCOTT PARSONS).

CHAPTER III

Besides the general works on the history of philosophy and more particularly on Greek philosophy, such as those by Zeller, Windelband, Gomperz, and the classic treatments of the philosophy of Plato and Aristotle, such as those by Wilamowitz-Moellendorf, C. Ritter, A. E. Taylor, W. D. Ross, and W. Jaeger, the following may be consulted:

BARKER, ERNEST. *The Political Thought of Plato and Aristotle.* 1906.

FRIEDRICH, C. J. "Two Philosophical Interpretations of Natural Law," *Diogenes,* No. 10 (1955).

HEINIMANN, FELIX. *Nomos und Physis.* 1946.

LATTE, KURT. *Heiliges Recht.* 1920.

MORROW, GLENN R. "Plato and the Law of Nature," *Essays in Political Theory,* ed. MILTON R. KONVITZ and ARTHUR E. MURPHY. 1948.

MÜLLER, GERHART. *Studien zu den Platonischen Nomoi.* 1951.

STRAUSS, LEO. *Natural Right and History.* 1953, chap. iv.

WILAMOWITZ-MOELLENDORF, U. *Staat und Gesellschaft der Griechen.* 1910.

WILD, JOHN. *Plato's Modern Enemies and the Theory of Natural Law.* 1953.

——. *Plato's Theory of Man.* 1946.

WORMUTH, F. D. "Aristotle on Law," *Essays in Political Theory*, ed. MILTON R. KONVITZ and ARTHUR E. MURPHY. 1948.

CHAPTER IV

Besides general treatises on Roman law, I would mention particularly:

CAUER, FRIEDRICH. *Ciceros politisches Denken*. 1903.

KROLL, WILHELM. *Die Kultur der Ciceronischen Zeit*. 1933.

PLASBERG, OTTO. *Cicero in seinen Werken und Briefen*. 1926.

PÖSCHL, VIKTOR. *Römischer Staat und griechisches Staatsdenken bei Cicero: Untersuchungen zu Ciceros Schrift "De re publica."* 1936.

POHLENZ, MAX. *Antikes Führertum: Ciceros "De officiis" und das Lebensideal des Panaitios*. 1934.

SABINE, G. H., and SMITH, S. B. *Cicero on the Commonwealth*. 1929, especially the Introduction.

SCHULTZ, FRITZ. *History of Roman Legal Science*. 1946.

CHAPTER V

ARENDT, HANNAH. *Der Liebesbegriff bei Augustin*. 1929.

ARQUILLIÈRE, H. X. *L'Augustinisme politique*. 1934.

BARKER, ERNEST. Introduction to *City of God*, in Everyman's Library (no date).

CARLYLE, R. W., and CARLYLE, A. J. *A History of Medieval Political Theory in the West*, Vol. I. 1903.

FIGGIS, J. N. *The Political Aspects of St. Augustine's City of God*. 1921.

GIERKE, OTTO VON. *Die Staats- und Korporationslehre des Altertums und des Mittelalters*. (*Das Deutsche Genossenschaftsrecht*, Vol. III.) 1881.

GILSON, ÉTIENNE. *Introduction à l'étude de St. Augustin*. 1931.

HORN, CARL VICTOR VON. *Beiträge zur Staatslehre St. Augustins nach "De civitate Dei" I*. 1934.

SCHILLING, OTTO. *Die Staats- und Soziallehre des hl. Augustinus*. 1910.

TROELTSCH, ERNST. "Augustin, die christliche Antike und das Mittelalter," *Historische Bibliothek*, Vol. XXXVI (1915).

CHAPTER VI

CARLYLE, R. W., and CARLYLE, A. J. *A History of Medieval Political Theory in the West*. 6 vols. 1903–6 (for this chapter see especially Vol. V, Part I, chaps. iv–vi).

DEMPF, ALOIS. *Sacrum imperium*. 1929.

ENTRÈVES, A. PASSERIN D'. *The Medieval Contribution to Political Thought*. 1939.

Gilson, Étienne. *Le thomisme*. 1927 (English translation by L. K. Shook of the 4th ed. was published in 1956 under the title, *The Christian Philosophy of St. Thomas Aquinas*).
Jenks, Edward. *Law and Politics in the Middle Ages*. 1919.
McIlwain, C. H. *The Growth of Political Thought in the West*. 1932.
Previté-Orton, C. W. *The "Defensor pacis" of Marsilius of Padua*. 1928.
Vinogradoff, Paul. *Roman Law in Medieval Europe*. 1909.

CHAPTER VII

Allen, J. W. *Political Thought in the Sixteenth Century*. 1928.
Gilmore, Myron. *Argument from Roman Law in Political Thought, 1200–1600*. 1941.
Mesnard, Pierre. *L'essor de la philosophie politique du XVIe siècle*. 1935, 1952.
Savigny, F. K. von. *Geschichte des römischen Rechts im Mittelalter*. 1815–31.
Stintzing, R. *Ulrich Zasius*. 1857.

CHAPTER VIII

For Althusius and Grotius, compare also the extensive literature cited by Wolf.

Baudrillart, Henry. *Bodin et son temps*. 1853.
Chauviré, Roger. *Jean Bodin, auteur de "La république."* 1914.
Friedrich, C. J. *"Politica methodice digesta" of Johannes Althusius (Althaus)*. 1932.
Gierke, Otto von. *Johannes Althusius und die Entwicklung der naturrechtlichen Staatstheorien*. 1880.
Hancke, E. Bodin. *Eine Studie über den Begriff der Souverainetät*. 1894.
Huizinga, J. *Hugo de Groot*. 1925.
Mesnard, Pierre. *L'essor de la philosophie politique du seizième siècle*. 1936.
Tooley, M. I. *Introduction to Bodin: Six Books of the Commonwealth*. 1955.

CHAPTER IX

Alston, L. Introduction to *"De republica Anglorum" of Sir Thomas Smith*. 1906.
Church, R. W. Introduction to his edition of Book I of *Ecclesiatical Polity*. 1868.

ENTRÈVES, A. PASSERIN D'. *Medieval Contribution to Political Thought.* 1939.

———. *Riccardo Hooker.* 1932.

JASZI, OSCAR, and LEWIS, JOHN D. *Against the Tyrant: The Tradition of Tyrannicide.* 1957.

MCILWAIN, C. H. *The High Court of Parliament and Its Supremacy.* 1910.

MAITLAND, F. W. *Constitutional History of England.* 1908.

PAGET, F. *An Introduction to the Fifth Book of Hooker's Treatise of the Laws of Ecclesiastical Polity.* 1899.

CHAPTER X

BROAD, C. D. *The Philosophy of Francis Bacon.* 1926.

CHURCH, R. W. *Francis Bacon.* 1884.

HOLDSWORTH, W. S. *A History of English Law.* 3d ed. 1922.

MCILWAIN, C. H. *The Political Works of James I.* 1918.

POLLOCK, FREDERICK, and MAITLAND, F. W. *History of English Law.* 2d ed. 1899.

WOODHOUSE, A. S. P. *Puritanism and Liberty.* 1938.

WORMUTH, F. D. *The Origins of Modern Constitutionalism.* 1949.

CHAPTER XI

LAIRD, JOHN. *Hobbes.* 1934.

PLAMENATZ, JOHN. *The English Utilitarians.* 1949.

ROBERTSON, GEORGE C. *Hobbes.* 1886.

STEPHEN, LESLIE. *Thomas Hobbes.* 1904.

STRAUSS, LEO. *The Political Philosophy of Thomas Hobbes.* 1936.

TÖNNIES, FERDINAND. *Hobbes Leben und Lehre.* 1896.

WARRENDER, HOWARD. *The Political Philosophy of Hobbes: His Theory of Obligation.* 1957.

WORMUTH, F. D. *The Royal Prerogative: 1603–1649.* 1939.

CHAPTER XII

BARCKHAUSEN, HENRY. *Montesquieu.* 1907.

BLITZER, CHARLES. *The Political Thought of James Harrington.* 1954.

DEDIEU, J. *Montesquieu.* 1913.

FRIEDRICH, C. J. *Constitutional Government and Democracy.* 1937, 1950 (especially chap. i and the literature given there).

GOUGH, J. W. *Locke's Political Philosophy.* 1950.

GROETHUYSEN, B. *Die Entstehung der bürgerlichen Welt- und Lebensanschauung in Frankreich.* 2 vols. 1927–30.

KENDALL, WILLMORE. *John Locke and the Doctrine of Majority Rule.* 1941.
KLEMPERER, VIKTOR. *Montesquieu.* 2 vols. 1914–15.
LASLETT, PETER (ed.). *"Patriarcha, or, the Natural Powers of the Kings of England Asserted" and Other Political Works of Sir Robert Filmer.* 1949.
LILJEGREN, S. B. *James Harrington's "Oceana."* 1924.
MCILWAIN, C. H. *Constitutionalism, Ancient and Modern.* 1940.
MIRKINE-GUETZÉVITCH, BORIS, and PUGET, HENRY (eds.). *Montesquieu: Sa pensée politique et constitutionelle, 1748–1948 bicentennaire de "L'esprit des lois."* 1948.
SMITH, H. F. *Harrington and His "Oceana."* 1914.
SOREL, A. *Montesquieu.* 1887.

CHAPTER XIII

DUFF, R. A. *Spinoza's Political and Ethical Philosophy.* 1903.
FREUDENTHAL, JAKOB. *Spinoza, Leben und Lehre.* 2d ed. 1927.
MEYER, RUDOLF W. *Leibniz und die europäische Ordnungskrise.* 1948.
RUCK, ERWIN. *Die Leibnizsche Staatsidee.* 1909.
SCHMALENBACH, HERRMANN. *Leibniz.* 1921.
STAMMLER, GERHARD. *Leibniz.* 1930.
THIEME, S. *Das Naturrecht und die europäische Privatrechtsgeschichte.* 1947.
WELZEL, HANS. *Naturrecht und materiale Gerechtigkeit.* 1951.
WIEACKER, FRANZ. *Privatrechtsgeschichte der Neuzeit.* 1952.
WOLF, ERIK. *Grosse Rechtsdenker der deutschen Geistesgeschichte.* 2d ed. 1944, chaps. viii-x.
WOLFSON, H. A. *The Philosophy of Spinoza.* 1934.

CHAPTER XIV

CASSIRER, E. *Kants Leben und Lehre.* 1923.
———. *Die Philosophie der Aufklärung.* 1932.
———. *Rousseau, Kant, Goethe.* 1945.
COBBAN, ALFRED. *Rousseau and the Modern State.* 1934.
DERATHÉ, ROBERT. *Jean-Jacques Rousseau et la science politique de son temps.* 1950.
FRIEDRICH, C. J. *Inevitable Peace.* 1948.
GROETHUYSEN, B. *Origines de l'esprit bourgeois en France.* Vol. I. 1927.
HARTMANN, N. *Die Philosophie des deutschen Idealismus.* Vol. I. 1923.
HENDEL, CHARLES W. *Jean-Jacques Rousseau, Moralist.* 1934.
LINDSAY, A. D. *Kant.* 1934.
MORNET, D. *Les origines intellectuelles de la révolution française.* 1947.
PATON, H. J. *The Categorical Imperative.* 1947.

VAUGHAN, C. E. *The Political Writings of Jean-Jacques Rousseau.* 1915.

CHAPTER XV

BINDER, JULIUS. *Philosophie des Rechts.* 1925.
DULCKEIT, GERHARD. *Philosophie der Rechtsgeschichte.* 1950.
HARTMANN, N. *Die Philosophie des deutschen Idealismus.* Vol. II. 1929.
HIPPOLYTE, JEAN. *Genèse et structure de la phénoménologie de l'esprit.* 1946.
HOOK, SIDNEY. *From Hegel to Marx.* 1936.
KRONER, RICHARD. *Von Kant bis Hegel.* 1921–24.
LÖWENSTEIN, JULIUS. *Hegels Staatsidee.* 1927.
LÖWITH, KARL. *Von Hegel zu Nietzsche.* 1941.
LUKACS, GEORG. *Der junge Hegel.* 1948.
MARCUSE, HERBERT. *Hegels Ontologie und die Grundlagen einer Theorie der Geschichtlichtkeit.* 1931. English edition; 1941.
MOOG, WILLY. *Hegel und die Hegelsche Schule.* 1931.
ROSENZWEIG, FRANZ. *Hegel und der Staat.* 1920.
SCHWARZ, JUSTUS. *Hegels philosophische Entwicklung.* 1938.
STEINBUECHEL, THEODOR. *Das Grundproblem der Hegelschen Philosophie.* 2 vols. 1933.
STOLL, ADOLF. *Friedrich Karl von Savigny.* 1927–29.
WOLF, ERIK. *Grosse Rechtsdenker der deutschen Geistesgeschichte.* 2d ed. 1944, chap. xii.
ZWILGMEYER, FRANZ. *Die Rechtslehre Savignys.* 1929.

CHAPTER XVI

ADLER, MAX. *Kant und der Marxismus.* 1925.
BERMAN, HAROLD. *Justice in Russia: An Interpretation of Soviet Law.* 1950.
HOOK, SIDNEY. *Reason, Social Myths and Democracy.* 1940.
———. *Towards an Understanding of Karl Marx.* 1933.
LEDERER, EMIL. *The State of the Masses.* 1940.
PASCHUKANIS, E. *Allgemeine Rechtslehre und Marxismus.* 1927.
POPPER, KARL. *The Open Society and Its Enemies.* Vol. II. 1945.
RENNER, KARL. *Die Rechtsinstitute des Privatrechts und ihre soziale Funktion.* 1929. English ed.; 1949 (ed. O. KAHN-FREUND, trans. AGNES SCHWARZSCHILD).
VISHINSKY, ANDRÉ. *The Law of the Soviet State.* Translated by H. W. BABB. 1948.

Indexes

Author Index

Subject Index

[I did not include in this index certain very general terms, such as "philosophy," "norm," "society," "government," "community," and the like, because they occur too frequently. Likewise, I included only the more important references to the terms included in the Index. Nor does this topical index cover the footnotes. Names have been put into a separate index. References to myself have been omitted.—AUTHOR.]

Index